The Beauty of Craft

Photograph by Stephen Hulyer.

The Beauty of Craft

A Resurgence Anthology

Edited by Sandy Brown and Maya Kumar Mitchell

Designed by David Baker

Green Books

Candlestick by James Kendrew.

First published in 2004 by Green Books Ltd,
Foxhole, Dartington Totnes, Devon TQ9 6EB
www.greenbooks.co.uk

In association with *Resurgence* magazine,
Ford House, Hartland, Bideford, Devon EX39 6EE
www.resurgence.org

Distributed in the USA & Canada by Chelsea Green Publishing Company
www.chelseagreen.com

Printed in England by Butler & Tanner Ltd, Frome, Somerset
on Revive Special Silk, which is made of 30% post-consumer waste,
10% pre-consumer waste and 60% virgin wood fibre.

ISBN 1 903998 42 5

17th-century Japanese Shino-type stoneware plate.

Editors' Note

This anthology has been divided into chapters to show the different faces of craft. The craftspeople themselves and their work, however, are by no means limited to these chapter headings. All the creative people featured here make work that is imaginative, playful, profound, honest and far-reaching. They cannot be described by any categories.

The crafts tradition is long and rich, and we have not attempted a historical overview. We have focused on living craftspeople, most of them still producing. Even so, this could not begin to be a comprehensive representation of the many wonderful craftspeople working today. The inspiration for the book was those articles already printed in *Resurgence*, and we supplemented these in order expand the breadth of crafts covered. There are many whom we would have liked to include, but did not have appropriate material or space. We apologize for these absences.

Thanks go to June Mitchell for valuable editorial advice and assistance. Thanks go to Karen Holmes for administrating and co-ordinating the work. Thanks go to the Crafts Council for sponsoring the book by providing financial support.

Special thanks go to the many photographers who have so generously given us use of their work.

Finally, thanks go to all the contributors, writers and craftspeople who have kindly permitted us to use their artwork and articles in this anthology, free of charge.

CONTENTS

5 **EDITORS' NOTE**
MAYA KUMAR MITCHELL

8 **FOREWORD**
SANDY BROWN

11 **INTRODUCTION**
MAYA KUMAR MITCHELL

WORLD OF CRAFT

16 **CREATIVE MOMENTS**
GLASSBLOWING
PHILIP BALDWIN

22 **ART ELEVATED,
CRAFT DEGENERATED**
FRAGMENTATION
JOHN LANE

26 **WONDER OF WORK**
OVERVIEW
JOHN SEYMOUR

30 **INUIT SOLUTIONS**
DESIGN
VICTOR PAPANEK

34 **THE NEW ALCHEMISTS**
RECYCLING
ANNA CHAMPENEY

36 **KINGDOM OF BEAUTY**
POTTERY
BREON O'CASEY

40 **CONTEMPORARY
CONCERNS**
CRAFT TODAY
TANYA HARROD

WAYS OF LIVING

46 **SHOJI HAMADA**
POTTERY
EDWARD HUGHES

48 **CLIVE BOWEN**
POTTERY
GERALDINE NORMAN

52 **RICHARD BATTERHAM**
POTTERY
DAVID WHITING

55 **MAKING IN THE CITY**
POTTERY
EDMUND DE WAAL

58 **JOHN MAKEPEACE**
FURNITURE MAKING
SARAH HUDSTON

62 **DAVID DREW**
BASKET MAKING
RICHARD BOSTON

64 **KAZUO HIROSHIMA**
BASKET MAKING
LOUISE ALLISON CORT

CULTURE OF COMMUNITY

70 **AMISH THREAD**
QUILTING
ROBERT HUGHES

72 **A TALE OF TAPESTRY**
WEAVING
CLIO MITCHELL

76 **LIVING TRADITIONS**
TRIBAL ART
SATISH KUMAR interviews
HAKU SHAH

82 **ALL HANDS TO WORK**
LOCAL ECONOMY
SATISH KUMAR

86 **MADE TO MEASURE**
LEATHER WORK
ROGER DEAKIN

90 **WILLOW WORKERS**
BASKET MAKING
OLIVER LOWENSTEIN

92 **WAY OF THE COOK**
COOKING
JULIA PONSONBY

CONTENTS

CARING FOR NATURE

ENDURING SKILLS

SEEKERS OF MEANING

98 **TREADING LIGHTLY**
ENVIRONMENT
ALEXANDER MURDIN

100 **GUY MARTIN**
FURNITURE
SANDY BROWN

102 **LIVING STRUCTURES**
WILLOW WORK
JON WARNES

104 **GROWING WITH GRATITUDE**
GARDENING
BRIGITTE NORLAND

108 **BUILDING LIKE GARDENING**
ARCHITECTURE
BRIAN RICHARDSON

112 **EARTH SCULPTORS**
COB
LORNA HOWARTH

115 **MADE OF MUD**
COB
IANTO EVANS

118 **SAVING THE SWILL**
BASKET MAKING
MARY BARRATT

120 **TINO RAWNSLEY**
BODGING
PETER BUNYARD

122 **BUILDINGS LIKE TREES**
ARCHITECTURE
WILLIAM MCDONOUGH
interviews TIM STEAD

128 **POETRY OF PRACTICE**
WRITING
JOHN MOAT

131 **ROMAN LETTERS**
LITHOGRAPHY
KEN SPRAGUE

132 **LIFE OF BOOKS**
BOOK BINDING
MAUREEN DUKE

135 **BILL PHIPPS**
SILVERSMITHING
MARGOT COATTS

138 **GWEN HEENEY**
CERAMICS
SANDY BROWN

141 **BREON O'CASEY**
HANDSKILLS
KITTY CORRIGAN

144 **MARTA DONAGHEY**
JEWELLERY
SANDY BROWN

145 **THE HARMONY IN HAND TOOLS**
WOODWORK
JOHN BROWN

148 **WITH THE GRAIN**
WOODWORK
BARRIE THOMPSON

150 **ON THE MEND**
REPAIRING
ROGER SCRUTON

154 **CONTINUAL RENEWAL**
CRAFT TRADITIONS
KAMALADEVI CHATTOPADHYAY

160 **KEITH CRITCHLOW**
ARCHITECTURE
SATISH KUMAR interview

164 **BOBBIE COX**
WEAVING
SATISH KUMAR interview

168 **KAFFE FASSET**
KNITTING
SUE LAWLEY interview

172 **SPONTANEOUS POTTING**
CERAMICS
SANDY BROWN

177 **SPIRIT IN THE WOOD**
CABINET MAKING
DAVID CHARLESWORTH

180 **TOBIAS KAYE**
WOODWORK
SATISH KUMAR interview

184 **LET THE INGREDIENTS SING**
COOKING
ED BROWN

186 **WABI SABI**
AESTHETICS
LEONARD KOREN

188 **DETAILS OF CRAFTSPEOPLE AND CONTRIBUTORS**

190 **ACKNOWLEDGEMENTS**

Love of everyday things

When the plate we eat from, the bowl we drink from,
and the spoon we hold in our hand are works of art,
then our lives are enriched every day.

BY SANDY BROWN

TANYA HARROD, in her magnum opus *Crafts in the 20th Century*, says that crafts-people are those who gather inordinate joy in labour. This is true: the pleasure obtained in making, in expressing oneself through handling the materials, through experiencing the sense of touch and developing a fulfilling visual vocabulary is certainly something that drives the makers in this book. They have an intimate affinity with their chosen materials, just as a loving mother has an intimate affinity with her baby. In fact, this affinity with the chosen materials is the love-affair which characterizes craftspeople. And it shows in the work. Whatever the maker is feeling during the making is captured in the work. When that feeling is love, joy in labour, it is there in the materials, in the very fibre of the piece. There for us all to receive. And just as a loving parent can facilitate a child rich in the sense of her- or himself, so a loving craftsperson who is an artist can facilitate a work of art rich in its sense of being. The best craftspeople are artists.

The craftspeople featured in this book are those whose work has a spiritual dimension. This comes from working intuitively; from developing a medi-tative sense of the here and now. Working intuitive-ly means that often what the idea is, if there is one, is not apparent until after the work has been pro-duced. Working intuitively means playing, starting with an empty mind not knowing where one is going. It means working on the periphery of one's consciousness; being open to accidents.

The work of most craftspeople has its roots in the function of objects, even if from those roots many makers are increasingly branching into making work which is sculptural and abstract, concerned with form, colour and the expression of a visual lan-guage. I do so myself, and enjoy the freedom it offers as we expand into new territories. This enlarges our sense of what is possible. And it further fuzzes the boundaries between art and craft.

But it helps enormously in the appreciation of crafts to know the nature and context of the histor-ical roots, just as it does in any art form. Each per-son who starts working in clay, metal, wood, or textiles, as he or she develops the love for their materials, inevitably wants to know everything about their chosen material, what has been made in it during the previous several thousand years, and whose work they admire most. All of this knowl-edge of the history and culture of their chosen material will feed their creativity and inform their current contemporary work. This cultural history of contemporary crafts deserves to be more widely known.

As the mainstream Art world moves more and more away from things, and into concepts, video, ideas and intangibles, the Crafts become increasingly important. Crafts are therefore expanding and being seen in our culture to occupy the whole spectrum of actual hand-made pieces; of things which exist in real three-dimensional space and which you can touch.

William Morris and Soetsu Yanagi (author of *The Unknown Craftsman*) would be astonished to see the Crafts in such a healthy state in our high-tech post-industrial age. In some ways it is thanks to their

18th-century iron kettle by unknown Japanese craftsman.
Photograph by Yutaka Seki.

enthusiastic advocacy of, as they saw it, humble crafts-people, that we today have so many people engaged in making things. Yet they were wrong to criticize the artist-craftsperson, as they are the source of the energetic dynamism today. It is clear that more and more people love making things, love the connectedness with their materials, can express themselves through that relationship, and love the satisfaction that comes from seeing the fruits of their effort.

An important change to be welcomed is that the 21st century is becoming increasingly feminized, to balance the go-getting masculine competitiveness of the last two or three thousand years. Women who once sacrificed their own values to gain access to the male dominated world of work are now regaining respect for their own creativity. This period will later be seen by historians as a time of huge social and cultural change in which, at last, women can be respected and adored for being themselves. This is closely intertwined with the increasing awareness, which *Resurgence* is helping to develop, concerning the vulnerability of and need for respect for the Earth.

One consequence of this feminization is that ritual is becoming increasingly important. When we use craft objects, made by the best practitioners who are artists, the most important aspects of our lives can be touched by art. By this I mean the every day aspects, the ordinary life in our homes, where we can have the most intimate relationship with art. Art is not something which lives solely in a gallery, or just on our walls, but can actually be what we live with and use every day. Once, when I was running

a workshop for children I needed some pots to contain their coloured glazes and was offered some hand-made pots to use, which had been made by beginners. I was touched and I must admit surprised by the way the children responded to being allowed to use these pots with pleasure and delight.

The table we eat from and put our elbows on, the bowl we drink tea from, the knife and fork we hold, the textiles we touch and see and wear; the sculptural object of contemplation we see everyday in our bedroom; the organic form in the garden; when these objects are works of art our lives are immeasurably enriched, each day and every day. Art is then central to our lives.

I see people who live with artist-made objects unconsciously creating rituals when they use them. A meal becomes a meditative contemplation. An offering of a piece of cake, for example, when the plate is a work of art, can inspire the host to acquire a painted or handwoven napkin, and then to acquire a hand-made fork, so that the way it is then offered is charged with the ceremony of ritual. I see this development of ritual as being central to the future of crafts, and a tremendous opportunity to bring a non-religious spirituality into our culture.

In the machine-age, crafts in our culture are actually much stronger than they were thirty years ago. The traditions are being revitalized, transformed. There are many more makers, many more galleries showing them, many more people seeking them out, which makes it much simpler now. We can live with the crafts, worship them, just because we love them.

MAKER AND MATTER

Our Relationship with Things

BY MAYA KUMAR MITCHELL

OUR ENVIRONMENTAL crisis could be described as a crisis in our relationship with matter. We condemn our society for being materialist, for being passionate about things, and we see that the desire for material fulfilment has led to a destructive relationship with our physical world. Rather than delighting in the enchantment of the bodily, 'western' society treats abominably the material world with which it is so fixated. We are obsessed with stuff, with having things, yet we do not respect and honour those things, nor the natural world from which they are created. We seem to be living a strange contradiction: in the face of our utter, unquestionable dependence on the Earth, we have allowed a dangerous greed to overtake and dominate what could be a healthy appreciation. Appreciating things, we are motivated to value, to respect, to enjoy, and to care for all that is matter.

In contrast, the replacement of well made, durable and loved objects by industrial 'products', clumsily put together and quick to fall apart, made of deadened materials with neither voice nor wholeness, has been disastrous for both the natural world, which becomes merely a resource for these products, and for our homes where we, the so-called wealthiest, live with an excess of impoverished material things. This process has also impoverished the working lives of many people across the earth.

Craftspeople and artists are working in this context to maintain their relationship with their materials. And by so doing they offer us all an opportunity to regain a relationship with things. By listening to the 'raw' material, a craftsperson shapes and works it in such a way that in the end the character of the stuff itself, whether red Devon clay, the heart of an oak, or the gleaming depth of silver, shines through and speaks to us of itself.

Every aspect of our daily lives involves objects which could be either mass produced or hand-made. But some of these are much more apparent than others. Many people, for example, may have a strong contact with pottery, and delight in using ceramic plates and dishes. But how often mass produced cutlery and glassware are laid alongside! Of course price, and therefore sheer availability, has

much to do with this. But it is important to observe where crafted items are less and more present in our daily lives. Woodwork and pottery are probably the most widely used crafts, while hand-made clothes and shoes are a luxury reserved for the very rich.

So in part these essays draw attention to the less remembered objects which we use daily, but from whose origins and makers we are often distanced and can even forget they exist. Crafts remind us of maker and material, they bring to our mind both the natural origins and the cultural traditions from which a thing has been created. Much more than merely fulfilling a function, they enrich our lives.

WHAT IS CRAFT?

The word craft has long resisted definition, being creatively unpredictable, something this anthology revels in. From their different starting points these essays explore and elucidate what makes up the worlds of craft, of art, and the closeness and difference between them. This has enabled us to include creative work not always associated with craft, such as cooking, writing and gardening. We do not want craft to be a closed concept; it can be opened up so that the interface between 'art' and 'craft' is a fluid and indeterminate one – perhaps the river of creativity flows between these two banks.

Craft often gets described in negative comparison with art, craft being 'a bit like art only useful and not so amazing', which immediately reveals that to be useful is of lower status, that we want to be amazed, and increasingly by sensationalism rather than skill. But no one defines art in relation to craft. Art stands alone. For centuries now, art – often with a capital A – has come first. Yet 'fine art' was once part of the broader world of craft.

The Greek *techne*, speaking above all of skill and technique, offers another way of understanding what art means, and embraces the presence of skill in any sphere of life. Thus we speak of the art of cooking, teaching, loving, even living. From here, working with specific materials is obviously a way to develop and hone one's skilfulness, with those materials but also beyond them. The practice of an art or

19th-century Shodai stoneware plate by an unknown Japanese potter. Photograph by Yutaka Seki.

An artist is a maker of things,
and not of pictures of things.

ERIC GILL

a craft seems, from many of these articles, to be akin to a spiritual practice, and yields other fruit besides that of beautiful work.

The people who speak here about the 'art of crafting' are not concerned with the glamour, originality or brilliance often associated with being an artist, but with the daily relationship, both harmonious and confrontational, with materials, intentions, necessities and possibilities. There is a discipline involved in this kind of creativity which its practitioners find demanding and rewarding.

This is very much in contrast with the latest trend in which craft has become 'the new art' whose success is rated, like that of much fine art, by how many thousands of pounds it can be sold for. Here the object, and thereby its maker, are part of a social structure which exists to demonstrate the status and wealth of the patron, rather than being part of a cultural tradition, a part of the society in which such creation takes place. Such a role removes craft from being part of ordinary life, where it is so necessary and so precious.

Craft is a practice, and art or fine art was once one form of this practice. In societies where the gods are fully present and the spiritual life vivid, the role of images and sculptures as an inspiration for worship, or as the very expression of the divine, is as practical as any more 'tangible' aspect of life. In such a context art indeed has a 'function' and does not exist as an 'added extra'. How did beauty become an economic luxury?

Craft is a work of transformation, through which a natural material takes on form and meaning in the human world, but without losing its essence as wool, wood, clay, silver or stone. . . . It continues to speak in the voice of nature and the elements. Mass produced objects, on the other hand, tend to have their original nature destroyed so that a form can be superimposed without any of that original, natural character speaking up, interfering, interrupting. Plastic is ideal for this, because it has no real character, it is malleable and dead. But other materials can also be sufficiently processed to lose their character, and become only the form which is asked of them: they become objects of utility, designed rather than created, and without heart.

To speak of something being well-loved is not merely a turn of phrase, it is a description of the way matter responds to loving hands – hands which feel and hold and take care. How well can you love a plastic container? How well can it age?

These reflections perhaps make it inevitable that a book about crafts will have something of a nostalgic quality. None of the craftspeople featured here, however, concern themselves with that, although some of the commentators do. In our times to work as a craftsperson, or to live with crafted things, is to live outside of society's conventions, but this only makes the importance of such a calling more stark.

CRAFTWORK IS NOBLE WORK

The involvement, at once natural and deeply committed, with which craftspeople work, is impressive and attractive. It enables us to realize that work can be seen as an experience, an expanding, a channel of engagement between oneself and the world, not a chore or a constraint in an otherwise comfortable life. In this way yielding to work enables the self to become part of the active world, as the hands are part of the body.

In the same way that art and craft cease to be divided, so working and living lose their antipathy and one's way of working is part of one's way of living, just as eating, washing, or talking are part of one's life. The possibility of being reconciled and united with what we depend upon – our work – is truly inspiring in a culture where work is resented as a constraint upon freedom, and the ideal life is an idle life.

CRAFT AT THE CENTRE

The essays gathered together here are stimulating and surprising. Craft shows itself to be at the nexus of many elements of human life. The use of tools has an important role in human history, and the development of tools, techniques and skills continues to be an expression of human nature and of specific cultures. Through these essays and their different voices we can see the role of craft in relationship to community, to work, and to economics. Craft brings us into contact with nature and with environmental issues. Craft is a way of developing creativity, consciousness and spirituality. The work of all these craftspeople touches these many different areas. The essays have been put into sections only in order to highlight the themes which are treated more explicitly, and to show both the importance of these themes and the different ways they are approached by different craftspeople.

The connections between the crafts and these many aspects of human life shows in how many ways the world of crafts can offer something of enduring value to our lives, including and beyond the craftwork we may welcome into our homes.

'Craft' refers to both the work of creating and the finished piece. The word unites both the action and the results of the action, both process and product. Craft is for doing and for having, for using and for enjoying. The act of making remains present in the final form, just as the final form is itself present in the making and leads it forward. The word 'craft' reveals the intimacy of these, of maker with thing, and of maker with making. The relationships between us, our creativity, and our material things need to be nurtured and made healthy. The craftspeople for whom making these connections is their primary work are guiding lights and secret treasures.

WORLD OF CRAFT

Have nothing in your house that
you do not know to be useful or
believe to be beautiful.

William Morris

New Sentinels by Philip Baldwin.

CREATIVE MOMENTS

The better the craftswork, the better the art.

BY PHILIP BALDWIN

Witches Blue. Photographs by Dan Kramer.

CRAFT IS ONE OF THOSE words full of shadings, with various meanings and implications. In its most primary sense, we may say that most of us are bad craftspeople at a lot of what we do, but many of us get good at one or a few things we do. These are often referred to as hobbies. Occasionally they are a way of life, a career, a life's work. There is an anecdote which my partner Monica Guggisberg and I often cite at the end of public lectures we give about our work:

"A good friend of ours has recounted the true story of an anthropologist who went to study the behaviour of a particular tribe of aboriginal peoples in New Zealand. One day he went to the chief of the tribe and asked him a question. How much time did the chief think his people invested in work per day? The chief was perplexed by the question and upon reflection said that he would have to consult with the tribal elders in a leisurely fashion and that the man should get back to him in about three weeks' time. When the anthropologist returned, he asked the chief, 'Have you had the opportunity to reflect upon my question?' The chief replied that yes he had, and that after considerable discussion it had been decided that the people of the tribe invested four hours a day in work. The rest of the day was spent making things."

Craft is about making things. That is, it is about the process of making things, not the things themselves, not the results. The results are objects, books, songs, paintings, operas, statues, theatrical productions, movies, meals, airplanes or baseballs, and yes, baskets, those too. We forget that all creators, whether basket weavers or writers, are obliged to be craftspeople in order to make their work. While we're at it, pickpockets are craftspeople too, along with car mechanics and the makers of golf balls.

But wait – something is missing here. What about quality, the quality of what we make, the aesthetic value or beauty or meaning of the thing? How shall we compare, say, the graphics of the 1960s Volkswagen and Guinness ads (two absolute classics of their genre) with the paintings of David Hockney or the music of Elvis? Simply put, where does workmanship end and pure creation take over? The answer, I believe, is that there is no demarcation line. These things take place simultaneously and side by side. One without the other makes a sorry showing. There can be no art without craft, whether it be good or bad. However, there is plenty of craft that has no relationship to art per se. Take for example the manufacture of rubber tyres, in which good craftsmanship is essential for our safety and well being. Or take an example closer to home: a well-crafted blowing iron is enormously helpful for making good glass.

The editors have asked us to grapple with this subject of art and craft, a subject which normally I studiously avoid as I prefer to hope we have outgrown it. The British journal *CRAFT* (probably the best journal of its kind in the world today) has been celebrating and showcasing fine works of art for thirty years. The fault-lines are tradition-based and habituated. Painting is art; sculpture is art – unless of course it is made out of wood, in which case we call it craft! Most of us know this to be ridiculous, but traditions and habits die hard.

A further complicating factor revolves around the issue of functionality, although strictly speaking this is in another domain. A functional object is not considered pure art today. It is decorative art, or applied art, or it is design. Only when the thing becomes abstract can we call it pure art. This too I would suggest is silly. But culture loves codifiers, and good luck getting past their clutches. In this case there are some interesting explanations, which confuse us still today.

A good analogy comes with the technological development of photography, which has been a great influence in moving painting from representation to abstract form. Representational painting today is apt to be referred to as illustration, which many consider a "lesser" art. By the same token, photography took a hundred years of development before it began to claw its way into the realm of fine art. Man Ray today still bears the scars of this battle. Headlines were made in the *New York Times* a few years ago when the dealer Barry Friedman in New York finally fetched over $1 million for a Man Ray work. But behind all this chatter the essential issues remain for the thoughtful viewer: what is moving, what is uplifting, what is inspirational, what is original, what touches our soul?

One more word about functionality. As with the development of photography, functionality has been co-opted by the machine age. The ability to turn out good design by the thousands obviates the need to do these things by hand. Thus the artisan turns from functionality to sculpture, as the painter went from portraiture and landscape to impressionism and abstraction. And yet there are exceptions. We call such artists craftspeople.

People are forever asking, "How long does it take you to make one of those?" The question never fails to irritate me; until I stop to think that it's exactly the sort of goofy question I myself am prone to ask. There are two answers which make sense. The first is "twenty-five years, the amount of time we have been making glass". The second is more confusing. In the course of a month we may actually blow glass for eight to ten days. Then there are about fifteen days for all the rest: marketing, administration, packing, shipping, the telephone,

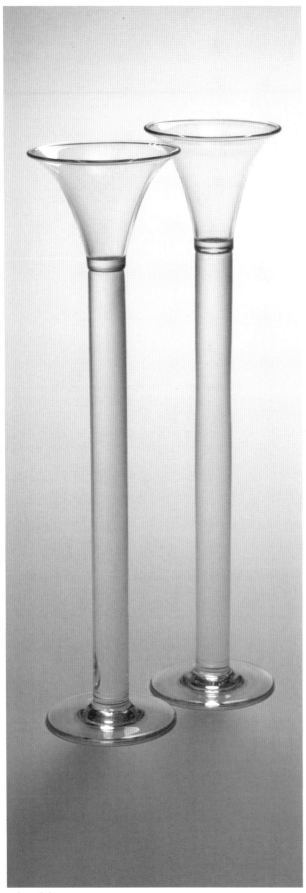

Chandeliers, 1990.

the computer, travel and on and on. And the creative moments that prop up this house of cards? Five minutes? An hour? A day? A lifetime? Most honestly, it's five minutes and a lifetime. And while we're at it, the DNA of our ancestors and the cultural milieu in which we've been working all our lives – especially, in my case, the explosive years of the 1960s. That's because the 60s and early 70s weighed in pretty heavily around issues of body, of mind, and of heart. Robert Pirsig's tome *Zen and The Art of Motorcycle Maintenance* was revelatory to me, expressing things I already knew in my gut, if not in my mind. To weave together into a single "career" the head, the heart, and the mind: this was a worthy challenge.

The reader will notice that I keep saying "our". This is because I work in partnership with Monica Guggisberg, a fellow glassmaker with whom I have collaborated throughout my professional life in glass. Our creations are a synthesis of shared ideas and thoughts, the results of a very long and ongoing conversation. In the beginning we called ourselves glassblowers. Then we said glassmakers, then designers, and finally, about ten years ago, artists. That's the job description that naturally gets put down on those immigration forms. Why? Is it because the work has gradually evolved into abstraction and sculpture? Because we have become pretentious in our outlook? Because the marketplace demands it in order for us to be taken seriously? Or because we finally had the confidence to believe the quality of our creations merited the word? Art implies something creative and moving, at the least beautiful or, alternatively, provocative. And it absolutely embraces craft and craftsmanship, the talented execution of an original idea. The better the craftswork, the better the art. Except for the exceptions.

For many years our work was almost entirely about functional design. We aspired to contemporary design, whether it be hand-made or machine made. We still do, although it is a relatively small part of our oeuvre. And it is here that the notion of craft and craftskill take on their most special meaning for me personally. The discipline of constantly repeating a given piece of work, of constantly remaking the same object was never to my mind a boring, repetitive task. Because it was entirely made by hand, the discipline demanded in getting two to look the same, and then a dozen and then hundreds became a consummate challenge. Customers would say, "Oh, but each one is different, each one is a work of art." And I would invariably take issue and say, "No, exactly not. Each one is an effort to be as close to the other as possible, to follow the form and shape and presence of its colleague as faithfully as it can. That's the art in the thing for me!" And in this respect

Sienna, 1995.

Cortigiane e Guardiani, 1997.

the making of such objects becomes a form of yoga, an endless discipline, a jest, a mantra repeated and repeated, with every now and then a result slightly more exquisite than the last. Out of this practice there come moments of joy. And because the thing is physical, because it is rendered and made from the materials of the earth, it hangs around, it lingers for a moment and attests in its pure physicality to the process of its making, which we call craft. ●

Vases Satinati, 1996.

ART ELEVATED, CRAFT DEGENERATED

All skills should be equally celebrated.

BY JOHN LANE

If we believe that we are living souls, God's dust and God's breath, acting our parts among other creatures all made of the same dust and breath as ourselves; and if we understand that we are free, within the obvious limits of mortal life, to do evil or good to ourselves and to the other creatures – then all our acts have a supreme significance. If it is true that we are living souls and morally free, then all of us are artists. All of us are makers, within mortal terms and limits, of our lives, of one another's lives, of things we know and use.

Wendell Berry

THE GREAT INDIAN PHILOSOPHER of the arts and crafts, Ananda Coomaraswamy, wrote that the artist is not a special kind of person, but that every person who is not a mere idler or parasite is necessarily some special kind of artist. In all the Traditional cultures – the ancient cultures of Islam, the lands of the Buddha and the Christian faith as well as all the world's indigenous peoples – religion permeated life. And the crafts, however utilitarian, acted as a living channel for the transmission of divine power and blessing.

Traditional art was therefore almost always anonymous. The craftspeople, be they carvers, masons or artisans, enjoyed a certain social status but saw themselves more as ritual practitioners than as geniuses. The great cathedrals of northern France and the temples of southern India were created by people whose names have rarely been recorded; the statues of the Buddha at Polonnaruwa in Sri Lanka, the carvings of Old Testament figures in the Royal Portal at Chartres, the exquisite tile-work of the dome of the Masjid-i-Shah in Isfahan, and of course, countless pots and icons and artifacts, were created by unknown craftsmen and women largely on the basis of traditional models. These were not single and solitary births but, as Virginia Woolf observed, "the outcome of many years of thinking in common, of thinking by the body of the people, so that the experience of the mass was behind the solitary voice."

These then were created by men and women who had no yearning for individual innovation or a striving for fame; they did not think of themselves as outsiders fundamentally different from or opposed to society at large, but as its servants, the servants of the faith. And as the faithful transmitters of archetypal and transpersonal realities, mediators of the sacred, their work appealed to aristocrat and scholar, peasant and town-dweller alike. Every English parish church bears testimony to this appreciation.

In the Inuit culture, there is no distinction between utilitarian and decorative objects. The Eskimo simply says, "A man should do all things properly."

The same was true of all the Traditional cultures until the influence of Western attitudes began to overpower time-honoured attitudes. "In pre-European days," says the Maori John Bevan Ford, "my ancestors had no word for art; it was all pervasive." The Sanskrit language also possesses no equivalent for the word 'art' as it is used in modern European languages. In fact the Sanskrit word for art, *shilpa*, embraces a wide range of activities that include not only what Westerners would describe as crafts, but ritual activity and such skills as cooking, perfumery, love-making and engineering. Vatsyayana's classic Indian text, the *Kama Sutra*, lists sixty-four arts considered to be accomplishments. In addition to instrumental and vocal music, drawing and dressing, he includes arboriculture, the care of trees, conjuring, manicure, needlework, bookbinding, woodwork, the game of chess, good manners, massage and the art of cheating!

Ladle and spoon in sycamore by James Davies. Rural History Centre, University of Reading.

But the totality of this approach was not limited to the Indian continent; other cultures did not separate the 'fine arts' from 'craftsmanship', 'craftsmanship' from 'labour', and beauty from everything else. This is certainly the case with a culture such as the Balinese, boasting one of the richest expressive traditions of the human race. Here, too, there is no word to describe those activities for which the peoples of Europe and North America have developed not only an expansive vocabulary, but an impressive tradition of philosophical and critical literature. Among the latter, appreciation of an 'artwork' invariably involves developing an awareness of its place within a tradition of influence and innovation among other 'artworks'. In Bali, learning to practice and appreciate an art involves learning by doing – *participation*: picking up a flute or playing the gamelan. 'Art' is the unselfconscious development of a skill.

I have seen much of this for myself. In Mamallapurim in Tamil Nadu I observed skilled craftsmen carving images of the Hindu gods and goddesses. They sat on the dusty kerbsides of a road more like workmen than 'sculptors'. In Novgorod I saw old women kissing ancient icons, windows on a spiritual world painted by monks centuries before their time. In Kyoto I saw priceless utensils and crockery still being used in the tea ceremony and in the cathedral of Chartres observed

the carved capitals of the columns as perfect as anything by later Western sculptors. In these places 'art' and religion were indivisible.

Yet, if many of the objects made by the craftspeople of the theocentric cultures were directly related to worship – a stained glass window of the redemption in a Christian cathedral; a bronze image of the goddess Durga riding her vehicle, the tiger, in a Hindu temple; a reliquary guardian figure from Gabon in a headman's hut or a fourteenth century Egyptian glass lamp in a Cairo mosque – objects of more everyday usage such as a North American Indian tepee or a haircomb were often no less irradiated with a kind of cosmic authority. These too were also created anonymously and with no thought of 'art for art's sake'. As an old craftsman in the city of Fez told Titus Burckhardt, "This tradition [of comb-making] can be traced back from master to apprentice until one reaches the Lord Seth, the son of Adam."

And so it was everywhere and for century after century. But as the Middle Ages waned and the theocentric civilization was replaced by one in which the human rather than the divine became the centre of the universe, the most progressive minds in Florence began to flex their wings. Some time in the middle of the fifteenth century, painters, sculptors and architects, among them Leonardo da Vinci and

'Wellhead and Mountains', panel of stoneware tiles by Bernard Leach. York City Art Gallery.

Michelangelo, Brunelleschi and Masaccio, began to question their status and demand equality with the poets. They began to disassociate themselves from the workers of the manual crafts. Inspired by the consciousness of their talent, they sought to attain recognition of their professional status and in their discussions on the subject they made it their business to emphasize the most intellectual elements of their work. "I would wish the painter to be as learned as he can in all the Liberal Arts," wrote the architect and theorist, Leon Battista Alberti, in his influential Latin treatise on painting published in 1435. For him, painting consisted first and foremost in the rendering of the external world according to the principles of human reason. Therefore he could no longer acknowledge a theory of the Arts which did not allow any place to naturalism or the scientific study of the natural world.

The idea of the 'Fine Arts' came into existence in this way. In general the principal aim of the Artists was to dissociate themselves from craftsmen and women. At the same time critics begin to have the idea of a work of art as something distinct from an object of practical utility, as something which is justified simply by its beauty. It is here that a complete Humanist doctrine was formulated for the first time.

The ambitions of the Florentine painters and sculptors were, as we know, realized. In due course they were to be accepted as full members of Humanist society, and in the process to establish a hitherto inconceivable concept and realm: the idea of Art as a self-validating, self-referential domain. It was the idea of Art as an autonomous activity existing beyond all ethical and social considerations. It was the concept of an Art which had no other objective than aesthetic delectation. In consequence, this was the turning point that marked the end of the anonymous craft tradition and the beginning of the

24

'Cray', printed chintz by William Morris. William Morris Gallery.

Artist as hero, the Artist with his or her unique vision, the Artist as genius – the Artist with clean hands.

Of course craftsmen and women have continued to make every kind of everyday object – bone combs and candlesticks, farm wagons and jewellery, stone walls and cooking pots, but their work has lost much of its former status and importance. It has been been subtly denigrated. Real Artists are people like Michelangelo and Titian, Rubens and Bernini, men (rarely women) who found favour and employment in the Courts of Europe, men whose Art spoke exclusively to the educated and aristocratic, the wealthy and the idle. The advent of industrialism gravely worsened this position; many skilled artisans drifted into the towns to form the mass of dispossessed and unskilled proletariat.

Today, craftsmen and women such as gardeners and hairdressers, boat builders and cooks, plaster-

ers and restorers, are rarely, if ever, considered alongside their more favoured creative contemporaries. Jamie Oliver is not regarded as the equal of, say, David Hockney, nor as far as I can remember has any creative craftsman or woman – a Richard Batterham or a David Leach – been rewarded with a knighthood. Nonetheless, the solitary craftsperson has a paramount historical significance.

Such a life can be dismissed as inconsequential only by those who refuse to see the overriding contribution that the craftsperson is making today. By poverty of means, by great skill, by love and creative action, they are contributing an example for others to follow. They live frugally and spend their days doing that which they most authentically believe. Future generations without our present resources, with land abused and cities characterized by size and ugliness, may look to them for guidance toward the salvation of their world. ●

WONDER OF WORK

The only happy life possible to a woman or man is a life
in which honest and noble work is the greatest joy.

BY JOHN SEYMOUR

PRACTICALLY EVERY ARTIFACT a person uses today can easily be made from oil-derived plastic, in a large factory, by machine-minders whose chief quality is their ability to survive lives of intense boredom. Even the machine-minders are being replaced rapidly by robots who, we are told, don't get bored at all. Artifacts so produced often do their jobs perfectly well. They are ugly, for beauty in an artifact depends on the texture of some natural material combined with the skill and loving care of an artisan; they are short-lived, so consequently our world is becoming choked with partly degraded, broken-down plastic objects, and their production is causing the pollution of our planet on a scale never before experienced. But, by and large, they work.

If everything we use is to be ugly and boring to make, what is the purpose of living at all? Was there once really something people called the quality of life? A satisfying quality of life, that is? Could there be again? Or are we, as a species, doomed to live out the rest of our destiny doing boring jobs and surrounded by mediocrity and ugliness?

Now it is often said that it is mass production which makes it possible for so many of the members of our grossly distended human population to have as many objects as they do have. This argument begs two questions. The first is, do we need as many objects as we think? I often walk round local shops and look with amazement at the merchandise. I cannot see how the possession of nine-tenths of it could in any way add to a person's happiness or bring him or her nearer to what one could describe as the 'good life' at all. Nine-tenths of it will quickly end up on the rubbish dump and prove that it should not have been made in the first place. The other question is, do people need mass-produced rubbish when a growing proportion of the population is unemployed? The only

possible justification for producing the rubbish is that there are not enough workers to make good high-quality artifacts. But there are enough workers. Or there could be enough workers if young people were trained to do good and interesting jobs.

Are we justified in using articles, no matter how convenient it may be for us to use them, that we know were produced in conditions which bored and even stultified the human beings who had to make them? Surely, it must be possible to produce the things we really need without causing our fellow humans to live and work in such conditions?

THE CHATTI OR THE DEBBIE

Did I say that mass-produced objects can do their jobs perfectly well? If I did, I was contradicting the great Bengali poet Rabindranath Tagore who, comparing a *debbie*, or four-gallon can once used for petrol, with a *chatti*, which is an earthenware pot created by a village potter, described the former object as *mean*. The *debbie*, he wrote, carried water just as well as the *chatti*, but while doing so the *debbie* looked ugly. The *chatti* not only did the job of carrying water just as well as the *debbie* but it did more – it delighted and pleased both the user and the onlooker. He could also have added that the use of the *chatti* helps to give a living to a friend and neighbour in the village: the use of the *debbie* merely compounds the pollution and adds to the degradation of our planet.

The use of artifacts made from natural materials gives a pleasure far in excess of the pleasure that we may derive from simply doing the job. The form, the texture, the subtle feel of such artifacts, together with an awareness of their origins – in trees, a crop growing in a field, part of the hide of an ox, part of the living rock – add greatly to the pleasure of seeing and using them. Wood, iron and

Making a traditional Irish Currach: a simple willow-framed, fabric-covered boat. Photograph by David Baker.

steel (including that excellent material stainless steel), other metals both precious and base, beautiful gems and stones, stone, leather, natural fibres such as wool, hemp, flax, cotton, silk, jute and manilla, clay: these materials, shaped and put together by the hands of skilled human beings, provide all the artifacts that we should legitimately need. If something cannot be made with these natural materials, I simply don't want it.

The very intractability of a natural material imposes a discipline that forces the craftsman and women to produce something beautiful as well as useful. It is the grain of wood with its liability to split along one place and not the others, that forces the carpenter, the wheelwright, the cooper, the turner or the shipwright to fashion it in certain ways, to use the qualities of wood and overcome its disadvantages, that imposes a pattern of beauty on wooden objects. It also forces workers to learn the mystery of their craft and this elevates them high above factory operatives.

It has been the limitations of stone as a building material which have forced the builder, over the centuries, to develop the great beauty of arch and vault, of column and arcade and flying buttress. Concrete, which, when reinforced, can be made to any shape, is rarely made into anything beautiful at all.

REAL COSTS

Hand-crafted goods often cost more than the mass-produced equivalent initially, but do they in the long term? Surely it is more economical to pay money to a friend and neighbour – a local craftsperson – to make something good for you than to pay a little less money for some rubbishy item mass produced far away. The money you pay your neighbour may come back to you. By helping to keep your neighbour in business you are enriching your own locality. Furthermore, you are increasing the total sum of real enjoyment in the world, for your craftsperson almost certainly enjoys making the article for you and you will certainly enjoy owning and using it.

Now people who seek for and demand articles made by craftsmen and women are often described as élitist. This is a good kind of élitism. Come and join us! There is plenty of room in this élite, room for all in fact. Nobody has to put up with mass-produced rubbish. The stuff simply did not exist two hundred years ago and yet human beings got on perfectly well, and lived until they died, as we do today. There are people who can't afford to join our élite, I hear you say. Oh yes they can – all they have to do is make out with fewer unnecessary articles than they have come to believe they need now. The word élitist is used nowadays as if there is something shameful about

being a member of an élite. I would find it shameful not to be a member of this particular one.

And so, slowly and steadily, I am ridding my home, as far as I can, of mass-produced rubbish, and either learning to do without certain things or else replacing them by articles made out of natural materials by people who enjoyed making them and who, by long diligence and training, have qualified themselves to make them superbly. This has brought me into contact with many craftspeople in Ireland where I live, in Wales where I used to live, in England where I was born, in France, Germany, Austria, Italy and Greece, and even the Middle East and in Africa. Some of these people were poor – some were struggling for a living – but poor or not they had one thing in common: they enjoyed their work. They took a great pride in it and, if you showed an intelligent interest, they loved to show what they were doing and how they did it.

REWARDS

Older craftspeople still have that ancient attitude to the reward for work that used to be universal but is, alas, now seldom found. And that is the attitude that there should be a fair reward for good work. Nowadays the predominating attitude is "I charge what the market will bear." I will never forget the time I finally persuaded that great craftsman Mr Harry King, the boatbuilder of Pin Mill in Suffolk, to build me a 14-foot wooden dinghy. This was soon after the Second World War, when it was hard to find craftspeople to make such an item. For a long time he refused, but finally he relented.

"How much will you charge for her?" I asked. Later I learned that you do not ask such people how much they will charge, at least not in Suffolk.

"Three pun' a foot," he snapped.

"But, Mr King, everyone I have been to charges *four* pounds a foot! You must have made a mistake!"

"Three pun' a foot's my price. If you don't like it you can go somewhere else!" he replied. "I don't hev to build ye a dinghy!"

The real craftsperson does not need more than enough. In our times of social mobility, everyone is after more than enough. We no longer ask "What is our product worth?" or "How much do I need?" but "How much can I get?" I have known many young people who have tried a craft and given it up because they found that, although they could make enough, they could not make more than enough. And more than enough is what they feel they require. A planet on which every inhabitant tries to get more than enough is a planet that is in for a hard time. And in the final reckoning I am sure that having more than enough does not make us more happy. You can definitely have too much of a good thing. What makes a person happy is

The problem is imagining the hands as mindless,
as only physical. We moralize work, forgetting that the hands
love to work, and that in the hands is the mind.

James Hillman

doing work that he or she loves doing, being fairly paid for it, and having it properly appreciated.

APPRENTICESHIP

But to become superbly good at one of the crafts is not easy. Many a young person tries it and fails in the attempt. The old-fashioned apprenticeship system was the best system that there has ever been for young people. The young people were subjected to pretty rigorous discipline – maybe in some cases too rigorous – but by this they were taught not only their craft but also the habit of hard work that would later enable them to enjoy life and prosper at their trade. For the master craftsperson is a happy person. They glory in their skill and they work, drink their wine or their beer with zest, look forward to their food and sleep well at night! Boredom they are strangers to. If they look back over their life surely they do not regret the hard apprenticeship that qualified them for being what they are? Surely it is better for a young person to be subjected to some pretty hard discipline and earn low wages for a few years, and then spend the rest of their lives as respected and self-respecting craftspeople, than to tumble straight into a factory, no matter how good the wages are. I include here the 'professions' in my assessment; a good doctor or a good dentist is a master craftsperson too and should be treated as one, no more, no less. And there is nothing higher, on this planet at least, that man or woman can aspire to.

During my researches I was struck by the isolation of many of the craftspeople I met. When I talked to the old people – some of whom were in their eighties and still working – I had the impression that in their young days they were not isolated at all. At that time there seems to have been a great interdependence of craftspeople in the countryside. Each craftsperson was dependent on his brother craftsmen of different trades in order to be able to carry on their own trade. The fisherman, for example, was dependent on the farmer who grew the flax for his nets, the net maker who made them, the basket maker to make traps and pots, the boat builder who built the boat. The boat builder in turn was dependent on the blacksmith who forged the chain plates, spider-bands, anchors, chains, and dozens of other items needed for a fishing boat, the woodsman who felled and carried the timber for

the boat, the sawyer who cut it up, the oil-miller who made the linseed oil needed to preserve it, the flax spinners and weavers who made the canvas for the sails, the sail maker who made them, the rope maker who spun and twisted the hemp for the ropes, the iron founder who cast the pigs of ballast for the bilge – and so it went on and on. All these interdependent craftspeople once knew each other. They could go to their supplier and discuss with them exactly what they wanted. Each saw the beginning and the end of what they had created, and each one of them probably thought of their own contribution as they ate the fish that the fisherman caught.

PROGRESS

The dream of high industrial and technological civilization is fast turning into a nightmare. It may be 'progress' for scientists to devise ever more sophisticated and complicated ways of making what we think we need, but it is hell for the men and women who have to drag themselves to the dreary places where they make these things to watch the dials and press the buttons, and it is hell for the men and women, increasing in numbers all the time, who are told they are 'redundant'. Redundant human beings? Mass industry has, from its inception, had a strong tendency to class its operatives as mere components of the machine. Like the machine the worker becomes just a means to an end. No, man is not a means; he is an end. No, people are not means.

Whether human beings just get fed up with a way of working which is boring and sordid and produces ugly things, or whether the constraints imposed by the dwindling resources of our planet finally halt the Gadarene rush to the cliff's edge, in the end, if human beings are to survive at any kind of level of true civilization, craftspeople must triumph.

The only whole and happy life possible to a woman or man on this planet is a life in which work – honest and noble work – is the greatest joy. Leisure yes, but leisure can only be joy if it is true leisure, which means leisure from work. That good craftsman, Eric Gill, once wrote: "Leisure is secular, work is sacred. The object of leisure is work, the object of work is holiness. Holiness means wholeness." ●

INUIT SOLUTIONS

Design to the Eskimo is an act, not an object; a ritual, not a possession.

BY VICTOR PAPANEK

Eskimo clothing as architecture.

Insulation layer: A pad of dried grass absorbs both perspiration from the skin and external moisture seeping through outer gloves or boots. Pads are replaced daily during winter months.

Outer tunic: Seal skin tunics are worn by men and women in warmer weather, both sexes wear fox skin in colder weather, men wear caribou skin tunics in the dead of winter. All three types are worn with the fur side out. (Animal furs are windproof and may be easily beaten free of blown snow with a flat piece of bone or driftwood.)

Inner tunic: Undershirts made from non-porous bird skins are worn with the feathers next to the body.

Mittens: Seal skin gloves are worn in warmer weather or when dexterity is required. Bear skin or musk ox skin gloves are used in colder weather.

Pants: Bear skins for men; fox skin for women. Both types hang from the hips without belt or suspenders and fit loosely to provide ventilation for the lower body. (Women wear seal skin under-drawers; men wear nothing beneath their pants.)

High boots: The upper part of the boot is made of tanned and bleached seal skin. Seal skin used for the soles is chewed into a tough fibre by Eskimo women to withstand rocks, jagged ice and sub-zero ground temperatures. All seams are sewn watertight.

Low boots: Slippers of bear, caribou or musk ox skin may be worn on the trail. Fur insoles are frequently added to provide more warmth.

Socks: Arctic hare pelts or caribou skin worn with fur side inward.

Evaporation dynamics: Ample air flow is allowed in the fit to prevent the body from becoming soaked in sweat which would quickly freeze in Arctic temperatures. The design of Eskimo clothing applies the basic principle that hot air cannot escape downward. Loose fit permits circulation of body heat which can only escape if outer tunic hood is loosened at the neck.

IF WE DEFINE design as finding working solutions immediately applicable to problems in the real world, Eskimo are some of the best designers. They are forced into excellence by climate, environment and their space concepts. At least equally important is the cultural baggage they carry with them.

Survival is the keyword to the existence of mankind; how survival is achieved will vary with cultures, peoples, climate, environment and resources.

Except for the thermonuclear threat, so-called civilized peoples enjoy so many built-in protections, and are so lost in the routine preoccupations of daily life, that the survival question is shunted off. But to folk living on a more 'primitive' level, survival is close at hand. It has the immediacy of essentials: food, clothing, shelter against the elements, and tools for fishing, hunting, protection or defensive/offensive action against wild beasts and – all too often – other men. To this we can add objects and artefacts with ritualistic meaning, personal adornment, and storage devices.

Eskimo survival is all these things, but under even more restrictive conditions. Unlike people of moderate climate, Eskimo existence rests on continuous accommodation to nature. Eskimo depend on cooperative interaction with the environment, because nature itself is too harsh to overcome.

It is not just climate that delimits. The materials Eskimo historically had available to work are modest and frugal: ivory, bone, driftwood, rawhide, fur pelts and skins, small pieces of wood, and lately, metal.

Designers know that tight limits and tough constraints help force good innovative design into being.

The illustration 'Eskimo Clothing' (Fig.1), shows how in dressing for the hunt in an extremely inhospitable climate, clothing takes on the characteristics of architecture. There are insulation spaces, outer layers that act like vestibules or airlocks, and I draw attention to the exclusive use of natural materials.

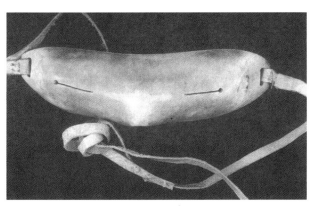
Snow goggles.

Recently Eskimo have experimented with artificial fur, and found the results literally deadly, as only natural skins and fox fur work in snow, ice and extreme cold. The expression *sagluyok nuya* ('hair that tells lies') describes their disillusion.

The face section of the picture shows a pair of snow-goggles. These are carved from fossilized walrus ivory. Note how the fluid carving will produce a sensuous fit to the brow of the wearer. The eye-slits are extremely narrow to prevent snow blindness; however at the back edges these slits become rounded holes to provide for greater peripheral vision. Snow goggles are kept extremely slim, so as to expose the wearer's cheeks fully: this is how even the slightest changes in wind direction and moisture are sensed – important navigational aids to Eskimo.

MANY TIMES AMONG the Eskimo I was amazed by their powers of observation in both detail and precision. Continually they saw things I did not. They would spot a seal on the ice, and even when they pointed to it, I was unable to see it until we were much closer. A sled or a boat would be seen long before I could do so, and when it left again the children would continue to watch it long after it had gone from my visual field.

This is not to suggest that their eyes are better optically than mine, they are not. It is only that such experiences are meaningful to Eskimo, and that they have become excellent observers through years of unconscious practice and training.

Connected to those strong powers of observation is a highly retentive and detailed memory. Even with observation quite brief, details will be absorbed and remembered for extremely long time periods. Kazingnuk, an elderly hunter, could guide a hunting group efficiently through an area he had not seen since his youth, and then only once. When we travelled by sled through unfamiliar country, Kazingnuk would continuously glance backward. Each of these brief looks would familiarize him with how the environment would look on our return. And even years later the route would be firmly established in his mind and instantly retrievable.

UNTIL THE LAST twenty or so years, Western notions of rectangular enclosed space were unknown to most Eskimo. Summer tents of sealskin or caribou-hide are circular and dome-shaped, as are winter igloos. There are no vertical walls, parallel planes, right angles or even straight lines.

More importantly; an Eskimo doesn't mould an igloo from the outside (as Canadian children playing Eskimos do), but from the inside looking outward. He will stand in the centre and build a series of concentric circles that diminish in diameter as they rise upwards. When the final piece at the top has been popped into place, like a hemispherical keystone, structure and builder have become one. Only now will be cut a small crawl-hole, as door, at the base. Among the Igluligarjumiut Eskimo of the Keewatin district, skins are stretched on sinews against the interior snow wall. This creates a cold-air insulation chamber between, and makes it possible to maintain interior temperature at 15° Celsius (59°Fahrenheit), without damaging the structure. Contrary to Hollywood-induced popular notions, every igloo has a number of rooms. Usually an air-lock-like vestibule goes past store rooms for dead seal, then through a 'hall' from which several rooms are accessible, with a seal-oil lamp burning in each room and a snow sleeping platform. The igloo creates an omni-directional space from which Western concepts of linear or hierarchical order, sequence, series, are curiously absent.This results in the igloo becoming a scale-model of the Eskimo world.

In winter the horizon will recede far into the distance and there is no distinguishable difference between Earth and Sky. Without perspective (except when the sun is close to the horizon and briefly sidelights the ground), there is no middle distance, no features except wind-devils, and when snow fills the air, up and down, near and far lose all meaning, and one is blinded by whiteness: *Aputakuyuitok*. The bowl of ground and sky are one with the igloo. In part the Eskimo system of orientation rests equally on this featureless multi-directional home and landscape.

Face protector, caribou-hide and fur with fox trimmings, Greenland.

The walls of homes are usually covered with pictures from magazines or photos. In the snow-house these also reduce dripping. To a newcomer it is startling that little effort has been made to place these images 'right-side up', they seem placed haphazardly. Yet the relationship between viewer and image is so active that the spectator is drawn into the images, moving in and about in a haptic manner, so that considerations of 'up' or 'down', 'left' or 'right' are of no importance. Whenever a magazine arrived for me, my Eskimo friends would gather around me in a circle to look at the illustrations, with the younger ones reading the text. Never was there the slightest jostling for position – it wouldn't occur to Eskimo that reading something upside down or sideways is in any way different. The children would sometimes make fun of my turning and twisting my neck to see pictures 'correctly'.

This radically different orientation system could be the result of Eskimo living in an aural, acoustic, non-linear bubble of space, caused by their living in a society that is pre-literate and has not been moulded by linear thinking. It is a fact that Eskimo, when asked to draw a map of a coastline, will do so with their eyes closed whilst listening to the sound of waves lapping against the shore - frequently such maps drawn 150 years ago are as accurate as modern ones prepared from aerial photos. To me the land seemed monotonous and without details. But this was only indicative of my own insensitivity. To my Eskimo friends, the environment was full of meaningful reference points and extremely varied. When I drive through New York City – a place of total chaos to Eskimo – I assume that a rectangular grid overlays the city's streets, and certain buildings, markers and street signs will delineate my route. Eskimo have natural signifiers, but these are not markers or points but relationships. These relationships may be among wind; salinity of the air; slight contour changes; type, moisture and hardness of snow; moisture content of the air; distance to shore; and ice crack. Returning from the hunt with neither moon nor stars visible, when even the lead dog could only barely be seen, we were unable to find snow usable for building an igloo for the night. We continued, twisting and turning over the sea ice, until we arrived at the (unlit) settlement some five hours later. Had we missed the white igloos on whitish ice by even 100 metres in the dark, we would have perished. The orientation of Eskimo – as miraculous to Westerners as the homing instinct of birds – is a necessity for survival honed to perfection by a lifetime of experience. It has to do with *abstracting essentials* from landscape and climate, which is a strong basis for all art and design, not just among the Eskimo.

ESKIMO HAVE AMAZING abilities to master at once intricate mechanical mechanisms. Marshall McLuhan writes: "Eskimo have proved to be wizard jet mechanics without benefit of any training whatever. These mechanisms they grasp by ear, inclusively, not by eye, analytically." Most Eskimo are top-rate intuitive mechanics. They enjoy taking apart and reassembling watches, jet engines, electric and electronic tools, all machinery. They will correctly repair instruments that Canadian or American mechanics, flown in to fix, have been unable to do. Working frequently with handmade tools, they make replacement parts of metal or ivory. Piluardjuk used the rear axle of a US Army truck and, finding it too large for his jeep, reduced the diameter by nearly half, using handtools only. At a lecture in Toronto, Edmund Carpenter told how he, being asked by a missionary to fix a complex machine that had stopped working, had removed the inspection panel and immediately realized that it was far too intricate to repair or even to understand. An Eskimo who had watched, slipped his hand in, made some quick adjustments and it was fixed.

The explanation of these abilities comes from various parts of the culture. First there is great manual dexterity, learned through the actual making of small objects that must work. Then there is Eskimo time/space orientation. Conceptually space and time are never separated, but any situation, tool, artefact or machine is seen as a dynamic process. Then, as we have seen, Eskimo are keen observers of details with enormous ability of recall; finally their space concept is not one of static enclosure (such as a room with walls and boundaries), but as direction in operation.

As among the Balinese of Indonesia, I found that there is no word for 'art' or 'artists' in Eskimo. There are only people. Where the Balinese say, "We have no art, we just do the best we can," Eskimo say, "A man should do all things properly." There is no distinction made between decorative or utilitarian things. All men are carvers, all Eskimo sing. When a song rises within you, you sing; when you feel a form emerging from ivory, you let it fulfil itself. Similarly the language really has no words that mean the same as our 'create' or 'make', which imply an individualistic, personal act. 'To work on' is the nearest Eskimo term, which signifies that the material itself (driftwood, ivory, etc) has a role equal to that of the carver to develop in the process. Again, like the Balinese, Eskimo are more interested in the activity of creating in partnership with the material, than in the end product.

In the West we think of the end products of Design (or Art) as possessions; to them these are transitory acts, relationships. All authentic Eskimo sculpture is quite small, usually no longer than 10cm

Tupilak in the shape of a drummer, whale tooth ivory, Greenland.

(under 4 inches), and without a base to rest on. Figures are carved in the round, with great detail even to the animal's sex organs, but never with a favoured side for viewing. It is carried in one's clothing, passed from hand to hand for viewing, and then negligently dropped in a toolbox or simply lost. Design to the Eskimo is an act, not an object; a ritual, not a possession. A distinctive sign of traditional art is that ivory sculptures roll about clumsily, since they lack a base. Again: Eskimo view their work dynamically and omni-directionally, they are to be turned this way and that, explored by the hand in a continuation of the way in which the carver originally explored the piece of ivory, asking it, "What do you want to become?"

The truly ephemeral nature of Eskimo Art and Design (another similarity between Eskimo and Balinese) is best shown through the carving and traditional disposal of *Tupilak* by the coast Eskimo of Greenland. *Tupilak*, which means 'harmful ghost' in most Canadian Eskimo languages and creoles, describes small ivory carvings. They are, like all true Eskimo carvings, small and, lacking a base, can't stand properly. Their function was originally to absorb all bad and violent feelings and emotions of the carver. Once completed and beautifully finished, the carver would toss the *Tupilak* in the Ocean or into a brook. This would externalize and get rid of rage and hostilities, and leave the carver and his family cleansed of aggression and hatred.

Without engaging in polemics, it is safe to say that design in the West suffers from too much 'easy living', meaningless comfort and so-called labour-saving devices. This is no plea for Puritan or Calvinist harshness. But the reason why competition sports equipment, camping and rockclimbing gear, gliders, gourmet cooking pots and chefs knives, and – sad to say: weapons for hunting and war – work so well and look so good may lie in the need for optimal performance under marginal conditions. Design for very elderly or severely handicapped people also sets the stage for tools that must work well in situations that are difficult. And many of these designs serve superbly well.

It is only when we look at the mind-blinding displays of everyday consumer goods that we see that we have a great deal still to learn from other peoples. My own notion is that a good place to start are the Eskimo – the best designers in the world? ●

THE NEW ALCHEMISTS

Transforming waste into gold.

BY ANNA CHAMPENEY

Chandelier made from found objects, by Madeleine Boulesteix.

A USED TEABAG, a plastic milk bottle and an empty sardine tin. These may seem strange and unexpected muses for artists, and yet, it is precisely these common, everyday objects which are inspiring a group of designers and makers in Britain today. Hailed in the mid-1990s as the 'New Alchemists', these makers and designers are metaphorically turning rubbish into gold through their imagination, resourcefulness and fresh approach to design and contemporary craft.

These makers are aware of and influenced by worldwide traditions of recycling and are inspired by concepts of designing and making from both outside and within Britain. However, it is still often assumed that using recycled materials is due largely to difficulties experienced in obtaining new materials, with the implication that using recycled materials is a second choice.

There is a common assumption that recycled design is synonymous with ecological design. There can be no doubt that makers are aware of environmental issues and it is indeed true that some designers and makers are passionate advocates of environmental responsibility and place this at the core of their work. As the chandelier-maker Madeleine Boulesteix states, in working with recycled materials she is "definitely rebelling against current outrageous consuming habits". But others have questioned the tendency which exists to impose an environmental meaning on to all objects made using recycled materials. Walter Jack has gone so far as to say, "I think there is a sometimes spurious ecological justification for work using recycled materials."

It is perhaps the frustration at the inability of galleries or the media to see beyond green issues that leads the New Alchemists to stress the other reasons for using recycled materials. What particularly inspires these makers and designers are the unique qualities of the materials themselves as well as the resourcefulness and imagination required to transform these low-status objects into new, desirable articles of beauty and style.

IT WAS Marcel Duchamp's 'readymades' (involving the re-presentation of everyday articles) in the first decades of the twentieth century which led to a radical change in the way many artists felt about using apparently everyday articles in their work. This idea remains central to the way the majority of designers and makers approach using recycled materials in Britain today.

These makers and designers are drawing from such a wide and varied base of ideas and influences in their work. It is not uncommon for makers to move from one craft, art or design area to another, and this flexibility has enabled them to become aware of design, craft and fine art history in a particular way. Indeed, one of the chief hallmarks of contemporary craft in the nineties, across the board, not simply in recycled design, has been variety. There is a confidence in the work of the established designers and makers working with recycled materials; they may be experimenting, but it is an assured form of experimentation. They may be open to the ideas of free association with recycled objects but they are, nevertheless, masterful in their handling of materials.

Whilst the influence of certain key movements in art and design has shaped these makers, they cannot be said to be adhering to a shared aesthetic approach. Perhaps the chief factor which is notable in all designers and makers is their passion for and acute awareness of the potential of their materials. Some, such as Madeleine Boulesteix, express this as "loving objects with character" whilst others refer to the inherent beauty of objects that have gone through their lives.

The idea of breathing new life into what was lifeless, creating permanence in something which was designed as temporary, is a particular challenge these makers relish. Val Hunt speaks of her jewellery as the "reincarnated end results" of working with old beer cans; furniture-makers Vicki Govan and Richard Warner speak of a "symbolic renewal of what was lifeless". In essence, these makers are expressing through their work the age-old concepts of reincarnation and alchemy — of constant renewal and transformation, mirrored in the growing political focus on urban regeneration and the strengthening of community spirit, as much in rural areas as in cities.

IF THE IMPACT of these makers is as considerable as it would seem, then their way of working is already becoming a mainstream option. Both Walter Jack and Madeleine Boulesteix speak of recycled design as an established genre. It is their confident belief, increasingly confirmed by the recognition of the buying public and by official craft and design bodies, that using recycled materials is a valid form of creative activity and a quite legitimate first choice for designers and makers.

There can be no doubt that a whole generation of students has been influenced by the ideas and styles of this group of makers and the future of working with recycled materials ultimately rests with them. The challenge for future makers is not to emulate the styles of current makers, nor to follow their lead in working with particular kinds of recycled material, but to strive to create their own personal style of making based on the realization that the true spirit of freedom in working with recycled materials lies in the relationship between maker and materials, combined with the ability to respond to the particular spirit of the age in order to create designs which are truly objects of our time. ●

KINGDOM OF BEAUTY

Do we want ennoblement of the pot or ennoblement of the potters?
An open letter to Bernard Leach.

BY BREON O'CASEY

DEAR BERNARD

In the first chapter of *A Potter's Book,* you insist on the importance of a standard in pottery, and that standard of the highest. Just as Auden defined the duty of a poet as the protection of the language, so you saw your duty to the craft of pottery as, not the protection of its traditions, since in England there were none, but setting a standard: a rock on which tradition could be built.

You say, "Even more unfortunate is the position of the average potter, who without some standard of fitness and beauty derived from tradition cannot be expected to produce, not necessarily master-pieces, but even intrinsically sound work . . . . He is indeed constrained to look to the best of the earlier periods for inspiration and may, so far as stoneware and porcelain are concerned, accept the Sung stan-dard without hesitation. As it is there are a few English craftsmen potters who do accept it and their work is incomparably the best that is now being turned out."

You quote Soetsu Yanagi, "So long as beauty abides in only a few articles created by a few genius-es, the Kingdom of Beauty is nowhere near realiza-tion." You say, "And to this one can only add that until a life synthesis is reached by humanity the individual potter can only hope to deepen and widen his consciousness in anticipation and contri-bution towards that end." Sad, sad words. And today, if one looks around, the outlook seems the same; and I can't help feeling that if you were writ-ing your book today instead of fifty years ago, the same words would be in the same order.

True, there are many young potters, or cerami-cists rather, who think the Sung standard meaning-less; and whose only standard is that a pot must be original, that is, have no standards. Their great God is originality. This is the age of the individual potter, and how can individual potters show their individuality without being original?

As you say, "There is such an obsession with the individual point of view among English craftspeo-ple, that one often hears them ridicule the very idea of a new communal standard." Since their God is originality, and since you have never made an original pot in your life, every single pot you ever made was a copy of another pot by somebody else, (and yet you cannot touch clay or paper without your own unique and, yes, original spirit shining through), how can you expect them to follow your beckoning finger? Away from originality, away from ego, up and up into the Bahai foothills in search of humility and the Holy Ghost? No thank you. As you say, the vow of poverty is the road to the gate-way to the riches of Heaven. Not on your life.

But suppose I were wrong, and that original pots were the true expression of our age rather than the Sung copycats. What difference would it make? Still, "So long as beauty abides in only a few articles created by a few geniuses, the Kingdom of Beauty is nowhere near realization." Fifty years on, and nothing has changed.

But there is a slight difference. Yesterday it seemed that mass production was here to stay: that one might look wistfully back, to quote you again, "to the age-old traditions of handwork, which enabled humble English artisans to take their part in such truly human activities as the making of medieval tiles and pitchers and culminating in magnificent cooperations like Chartres Cathedral."

Stoneware Vase, by Bernard Leach.
Leicestershire Museums, Arts and Records Service.

But that these were days that would never return; and that at best, the crafts would exist in a sort of uneasy partnership with an indulgent industrial society, using chosen craftspeople as 'designers' of their products, no longer supplying the poor people's home with chattels, but the rich people's homes with ornaments.

But then along comes the economist Mr Schumacher with his book *Small is Beautiful*. He looks at our fixed industrial society with a very sceptical eye, and wonders ". . . whether modernization, as currently practised without regard to religious and spiritual values, is actually producing agreeable results. As far as the masses are concerned, the results appear to be disastrous – a collapse of the rural economy, a rising tide of unemployment in town and country, and the growth of a city proletariat without nourishment for either body or soul." His basic argument is this: The fatal error of our system of economics is the belief that the problem of production has never been solved by the machine. (Good news for the craftsperson.) But this is an illusion due to the fact a) industry is living on irreplaceable capital (fossil fuels) which it treats as income; b) the tolerance margins of nature are being ignored; and c) the human substance (you and I) is being ignored. And to ignore any one of these three is to head for disaster. "And what can we do now," asks Schumacher, "while we are still in the position of never having had it so good? To say the least – which is already very much – we must thoroughly understand the problem and begin to see the possibility of evolving a new life-style, with new methods of production and new patterns of consumption: a lifestyle designed for permanence. In industry, we can interest ourselves in the evolution of small-scale technology, 'technology with a human face', so that people have a chance to enjoy themselves while they are working instead of working solely for their pay packet and hoping, usually forlornly, for enjoyment solely during their leisure time."

That was Schumacher, now here is Bernard, "The necessity for psychological and aesthetic common foundation in any workshop cannot be exaggerated, if the resulting crafts are to have a vitality. That vitality is the expression of the spirit and culture of the workers. In the factories the principal objectives are bound to be sales and dividends and aesthetic considerations must remain secondary. The class of goods maybe high, and the management considerate and even humanitarian, but neither the creative side of the lives of the workers nor the character of their products as human expressions of perfection can be given the same degree of freedom which we rightly expect in hand work".

That was Bernard, now here is Schumacher, "The Buddhist point of view takes the function of work to be at least threefold: to give people a chance to utilize and develop their faculties; to enable them to overcome their egocentredness by joining with other people in a common task; and to bring forth the goods and services needed for a becoming existence. To organize work in such a manner that it becomes meaningless, boring, stultifying, or nerve-racking for the worker would be little short of criminal; it would indicate a greater concern with goods than with people, an evil lack of compassion and a soul-destroying degree of attachment to the most primitive side of this worldly existence. Equally, to strive for leisure as an alternative to work should be considered a complete misunderstanding of one of the basic truths of human existence, namely that work and leisure are complementary parts of the same living process and cannot be separated without destroying the joy of work and the bliss of leisure."

By now, Bernard, I hope that it will not be clear whether you or Schumacher is speaking: your aims seem to be so similar, the only difference I can see is that whereas your main concern is better pots, Schumacher's is better people.

Let us consider the better pots: You quote Soetsu Yanagi as follows, "One may ask, what then is the nature of the beauty which has been discovered by these tea-masters? In the first place it is non-individualistic. As in medieval Europe art meant adherence to tradition, so in the East all works of art or crafts are governed equally by common principles. Some of the most famous tea-bowls were originally the simplest of utensils in popular use in Korea or China; many of them were the rice bowls of Korean peasants. But the amazingly keen eye of the *Cha-no-yu* master has discovered in these odd, neglected pieces a unique beauty; for what most appeals to him are things originally made for everyday use." (The amazingly keen eye of the tea-masters has missed one thing: if a people are living their life in balance with the life around them, if their traditional way of working is sound and sensible, all their pots will be beautiful, just as all the women will be beautiful: they will simply be beautiful in different ways: that is the Kingdom of Beauty).

Let us consider this Korean rice bowl spotted by the amazingly keen eye of the *Cha-no-yu* master. Did the Korean potter who made it know he had made a masterpiece? Did he find it desperately difficult to make? Did he find it difficult at all? Was he a saintly man, a man of great intellectual powers, or was he a run-of-the-mill Korean? Was the Korean who bought it from him aware she was buying a masterpiece, or did she think: 'this one will do'? Did the family of the Korean who bought it handle it with the reverence of the tea-master, or did they handle it with easy prudence, knowing – or thinking they knew that if they broke it, they could get another one just as good? It was made by a potter whose

> A pot in order to be good, should be a genuine expression of life.
> It implies sincerity on the part of the potter
> and truth in the conception and execution of the work.
>
> *Bernard Leach*

father, grandfather, great grandfather, great great grandfather spent their working lives making similar shapes; it was made easily, casually, comfortably, as a woman knits. And how can this be done easily, but well enough to satisfy the eye of the *Cha-no-yu* master without a tradition, and how can a tradition be arrived at without copying, copying, copying?

But copying what? Not Sung. The only potters qualified to copy Sung pots are potters who have broken one, and not been too worried by the fact: Sung potters. It doesn't really matter what the tradition is based on, what matters is that the potters are willing to spend their working life copying. Which brings us back to Schumacher. If he is right, what we will see in the future is the gradual breaking up of the large companies into smaller and smaller units using less and less sophisticated technology: a mirror image of the history of the industrial revolution. And if this happens, what will happen to standards? They will sink through the floor. If one can judge by the products of the existing small potteries now, they have already sunk. We produce the most ill-conceived and worst designed pottery that has ever been seen on this planet. But this will be, must be, the basis for our tradition, not Sung. (Or as well as Sung).

We have considered that small band of potters who have based their work on Sung, and, yes, their work is incomparably the best that is now being turned out, and we have glanced at the work of the art school trained modern ceramicist, who is concerned with experiment and originality; but these two groups, familiar with the Crafts Council grants, with an eye out for a teaching post, interested in exhibitions of their work, hoping to make a name for themselves (*mea culpa!*), are only a small fraction of the whole. The rest, the invisible majority, are out, not to make a name, or get their work into the V&A but to rub along. Interested in selling their work to tourists, small shops, willing to let the public watch them at work, content to copy, even if they only copy themselves, wouldn't know a Sung if they tripped over one, these are the ones: Schumacher's troops, our only hope of finding the Kingdom of Beauty on this planet.

What am I trying to say? I am trying to say that ten bad potters is better than one good potter. That is, an ennobled human being is better than an ennobled pot. You, Bernard, were concerned with trying to ennoble the pot; Schumacher was concerned with trying to ennoble the person and indirectly the pot. If Schumacher is right, and the industrial society we live in is not as permanent or as stable as it seems, a new energy and purpose is given to the role of the craftsperson. Today's unemployment figures make this a vital problem. As we see now only too vividly, what good is a thriving economy (even if it were thriving) or a prosperous country, if three million of its citizens are unemployed, and most of the rest are in dull jobs getting duller. Attempting to ennoble the pot (and hence the potter) had led to a select few potters and a select few buyers, and no impact at all on the economy as a whole. Let us see what attempting to ennoble the potter will do. For a start, standards will have to take care of themselves. Sung must have come from somewhere. When the white Christians forced the black slaves to forsake their heathen Gods to worship Christ and his saints, the black slaves hid their heathen images behind the statues of the saints so that in worshipping one they worshipped the other; and gradually the two blended into one new God and the whole became the new religion of Banta, so Sung will have to face up to Mickey Mouse, and Tang get along with art nouveau, to forge our new tradition, a blending of all these different, diffuse, even contrasting images, into a unified whole. One cannot see any official body, even the amazingly keen eyes of the Crafts Council, wanting to spend good money on this ugly duckling, and it will have to struggle along on its own two feet. Probably just as well.

So, Bernard, there is a glimmer of a hope that the Kingdom of Beauty will come again to England's green and pleasant land, and be equally disregarded, and English potters will throw bowls for drinking tea as beautiful and as common as those Korean bowls your tea-masters so admired, and you will be the man who got us all going, and forced us to think beyond our selfish thoughts of aggrandizement to the humble role we must play to secure, what Soetsu Yanagi called the Kingdom of Beauty, and what Schumacher called a rational lifestyle designed for permanence. ''Tis all one'. ●

CONTEMPORARY CONCERNS

What is the place of craft in a full world?

BY TANYA HARROD

IN 1911 THE YOUNG Charles Edouard Jeanneret set off on what he was to call his Voyage d'Orlent. Years later, when he was a famous architect better known under the pseudonym Le Corbusier, he set about editing his account of that journey – which had taken him from Vienna to Budapest and Belgrade, over to Bucharest, on to Constantinople and then to Athens. The text was largely based on letters he sent to friends in his home town of La Chaux-de-Fonds in French-speaking Switzerland, and reading it now is an extraordinary experience. I suppose I believed that Le Corbusier had little time for the past. Most of us have a vague memory of his drawings of futuristic cities, in which high-rise buildings loom over a landscape of parks and superhighways. He has, indeed, been blamed for many of the ills of postwar urbanism. But Le Corbusier, like many early modern twentieth century figures, was at once Progressive but also distinctly ambivalent about progress.

On his 1911 journey round the Balkans and Eastern Europe he was disgusted by the modern cities which he visited, and correspondingly deeply touched and moved by the vernacular art and craft which he encountered. He became a pottery enthusiast, buying traditional vessels wherever he went. He also studied the local peasant costume and jewellery and made detailed sketches of traditional building techniques. He bought kelim rugs. Yet a sense of impending loss and sadness runs through all his writing at that time. He knew that the skills and the way of life he was witnessing were unlikely to survive untouched. He loved it all – the pottery, the textiles, the folk music and the whitewashed village houses. But by 1925 he had decided that it was dangerous to be sentimental about these increasingly peripheral cultures. Beneath an image of a beautiful

Serbian pot which he had brought back in 1911 he wrote savagely: "Folk culture in its lyric power . . . What about the immortal pose of Ruth at Jacob's well and the really beautiful industry of the potter which seems to have been the companion of civilization since time began? Finished! Replaced by a tin can."

Was Le Corbusier right? In Britain plenty of men and women disagreed, believing that it was possible to extend the vernacular tradition. The simplicity and power of many vernacular forms fitted neatly into the modernist canon of beauty, along with the art and craft of medieval Europe and the Far and Middle East and of Africa, south of the Sahara. Thus the early twentieth century saw potters of the power of Michael Cardew, Bernard Leach and Katherine Pleydell-Bouverie, stone-carvers like Eric Gill and weavers like Ethel Mairet. Earlier, ostensibly purer, making processes were retrieved to create work of integrity. Admittedly the audiences for this work were small and the makers privileged, but no one can deny that craftswomen and craftsmen made a serious contribution to modern art and design throughout the twentieth century.

What about the position of craft in Britain today? The situation is confusing and complex. But one strand of activity is still with us. The crafts have managed to carry on developing the kind of modernist paradigm rooted in abstraction, archaism and pure form that came into being in the first two decades of the twentieth century. The modernist project lives on dynamically in the ceramics of Gordon Baldwin and of Alison Britton. Britton's fine pieces combine the painterly and sculptural concerns that we associate with the early days of heroic modernism in the fine arts. The same might be said of the pure abstraction of the textiles of Stella Benjamin or the pure but disturbing forms of

'Double Pot', by Alison Britton. Hove Museum and Art Gallery. Photograph by David Cripps.

the rather younger ceramicist Nicholas Rena.

But currently craft, in common with contemporary design and fine art, is addressing new problems, ones that will surely be of interest to *Resurgence* readers. To summarize these concerns:

1. Today more of us are consumers than are producers. Thus, design, craft and art seek to comment on this massive paradigm shift in our society from production to consumption.

2. Artists are consumers too. Thus we encounter work where the artist operates as a consumer in order to produce – finding and adapting objects with a narrative charge.

3. Linked to this is a loss of interest in the kind of originality previously central to the idea of an avant-garde. Copying, remaking, reconstituting, replicating now seems central to the visual arts and to other areas like popular music, where the new heroes are not musicians but DJs who mix and collage existing material.

4. This in turn relates to an existential problem – why make art or craft in such a full world? Is it a responsible thing to do? Is there even an aesthetic need, given that existing objects are so rich in semiotic meanings that they cry out to be recycled and re-contextualized?

ONE PECULIARLY BRITISH reason for craft practice was that it stood for the antithesis of soulless mass production. But from the consumer's point of view, mass production has ceased to be mass. We now have unprecedented variety and choice in consumer goods. Soon, we are told, we will be able to customize products individually using computer-aided making processes. And we seem to have largely given up on Arts and Crafts ideas about 'joy in labour' – at least as far as the workers in the Far East who actually make the goods we buy are concerned.

This shift, in which consumption becomes the dominant paradigm, is however being commented on by artists. Instead of making in lonely studios, artists are out and about, scavenging, picking over and adapting objects. This is not a new activity (one only has to think of Marcel Duchamp's bottle rack and urinal), but I would argue that today's interest in what used to be called the 'ready-made' operates in a different spirit. Duchamp was marking the heroic status of the early modern artist (able to call anything art). He was not commenting on the waste and the shame of over-consumption in the same way as artists, craftspeople and designers do today.

Stuff – things – can be used light-heartedly or seriously. The design group JAM, who position themselves on the fringes of the craft world, take existing objects objects from a full world – and transform them, so that washing machine parts become lights and aluminium ladders become chairs and tables. Jamie Auley, Astrid Zola and Matthieu Pollard employ a musical metaphor for the title of their firm. They are jamming with quotidian materials to create new forms. A similar interest in existing objects transmuted is found in the work of Michael Marriott, whose XLI chair was originally made from recycled tea-chests. The chair is now produced in quantity by a manufacturer. But its craft origins and its adapted materials are what gives the chair its distinctive visual presence.

Adapted materials can convey ideas which have a tragic rather than a witty or surreal dimension. Take the recent installation by the British/Nigerian artist Yinka Shonibare. He meditates on Britishness and Africanness by creating the kind of carefully made mannequin in period costume which we would expect to find in a room setting in an old-fashioned museum. Except that the costumes are made of cloth still specifically produced for the West African and Caribbean market. The stuff, the cloth, is powerful and recognizable, and we can read its use here in many ways. I'll hazard one. Shonibare's costume designs refer to eighteenth- and nineteenth-century British elegance and wealth. But the actual material reminds us of the source of that wealth in the plantations in the West Indies and the rather later mad scramble to exploit African territories south of the Sahara.

This kind of politicized re-representation of material is being taken up by first nation artists in North America and Canada. I'm thinking in partic-

ular of the Canadian-Indian Brian Jungen who cuts up Nike Air trainers, using their distinctive markings to fashion simulacra of North West Coast Aboriginal Art. Here the comment runs somewhat in reverse; a global product is rendered poignantly regional and specific.

Another discernible tendency across all visual disciplines is to copy, to replicate images and objects. For instance, the painter Michael Raedecker uses found images. Many appear to come from 1950s North American house and garden type magazines, which he recreates in paint and embroidery in a fashion which suggests the interior design and architecture sketches of the period. The use of stitching, of embroidery, further complicates the status of these images. Embroidered pictures are highly gendered and more likely to seem amateur than professional. We find a similar use of imagery in the work of the potter Richard Slee. In one recent piece, the image of a roof with a loft extension window – something to be found in any home improvement magazine – has been stencilled on to a hexagonal dish. Richard Slee, like Raedecker, takes banal images and by presenting them blandly, makes them mysterious. We find ourselves asking why the artist chose this material. Why so quotidian and everyday? Ordinariness can be shocking. Arm Hunt works rather differently. Once a painter, she now painstakingly embroiders images based on photographs of iconic early modern buildings. The results are unsettling. The medium and the image should logically be in opposition, but the small, intense examples of visual recycling which she presents are unexpectedly integral and satisfying.

THE CONSUMPTION PARADIGM explains why so many artists currently take an interest in fakes and translations and why there is a reliance on what already exists in so much current art and craft. For instance, Tracey Rowledge's goldtooled binding for an early edition of James Joyce's *Ulysses* is taken directly from an intense network of ballpoint scribbles on a random piece of card which Rowledge found in the streets near her studio. Rowledge likes to cherish the most forlorn, casually abandoned scraps of paper. For her they are examples of what she calls "a poignant moment in time", and she transmutes and reprocesses this material with high skill into permanence.

The sculptor Rachael Whiteread is attentive to existing objects in a slightly different way – it is absence, not-there-ness which interests her, and she goes to great lengths to cast negative spaces – the inside of a house, a room, a bath, and most poignantly a whole library in Vienna's judenplatz. It would be hard to think of a better way of using process to convey an iconography of memory and of loss. As you can see, much of this work is very much

'Standing Form', stoneware by Gordon Baldwin. Photograph by David Cripps.

about process, about procedures for making art in difficult times, art in a full world.

To take another example: casting is central to the potter Carol McNicoll's work. She uses found objects of no obvious artistic merit purchased in junk shops, which she then casts in multiples and sets to performing tasks – carrying bowls, and teapots. Her ceramics are made stranger by their surface decoration – covered in decals wrenched out of context - cowboy scenes and vines on ceramic carthorses, vine leaves on a multiplication of a plastic-turbaned figure who once held a box of tea in a shop window – now cast in triplicate and set to holding grapes. This last piece is a haunting object: the figures appear to dance and move; they are covered in a vine-leaf transfer; they hold the grapes and they are the vine. They belong in the domestic interior, but all the familiarities of the bourgeois souvenir are mingled – the vine leaf, the colonial memento, the grapes and the grapedish.

I'll end with this description of art made in an overcrowded world of goods. It seems to encapsulate the consumption paradigm in craft: There is nothing inherently 'green' about craft practice. But craft, and art and design can convey powerful messages about over-consumption. A great many young artists and makers seem to be issuing a warning. Look, they seem to be saying, let us think very carefully about making anything at all. Our world is already very full. ●

WAYS OF LIVING

As I watch the throwing by Hamada,

or one of his men, the realization

is always the same: the skill and fluidity of

movement and the resulting work is the

outcome of an approach which is foreign to us.

Pots are not made, they flow.

There is harmony of living and working,

work is not work, it is life.

Janet Leach

Oblong vase, stoneware. Iron rust glaze with copper green dip, by Shoji Hamada.

45

SHOJI HAMADA

The great Japanese potter Shoji Hamada made pots to use
and also to free himself from ego.

BY EDWARD HUGHES

SHOJI HAMADA liked to be known quite simply as a potter. In 1955, at the age of sixty, the Japanese government made him one of the first National Living Treasures. Consummate craftsman and artist, eloquent in clay and word, Mr. Hamada inspired countless craftsmen and women in both East and West. Without Hamada, whose greatest talent was to make tradition relevant in a changing world, the Folk Craft Movement in Japan would not have seen the continuing success that eluded the Arts and Crafts Movement in Britain.

It was in St. Ives that Hamada found his true vocation, the years in England between 1920 and 1923 proving to be of profound significance. Indeed, "The landing of Bernard Leach and Hamada Shoji on the islands of Britain in 1920 was for craftsmen potters the most significant event of the twentieth century," observed Michael Cardew.

In 1909 when Leach arrived in Japan to teach etching and introduce contemporary Western painting to the Japanese, Hamada was a youth of fourteen who wanted to become a painter. Encouraged by his father, Hamada spent all his spare time sketching, and making regular visits to the studio of a relative who was a painter. The precocious fourteen-year-old was having his sketches and paintings printed in magazines and journals for boys.

Despite his obvious artistic talent, the young Hamada sensed a need to make things for everyday practical use, so when he read Renoir's words, "If half the would-be painters in France were transformed into craftsmen, it would benefit both painting and the crafts," they struck a peculiarly resonant and timely chord.

With single-minded determination and sense of purpose, he mastered not only physics, chemistry and mathematics, but also became proficient in English in order to enter the prestigious Tokyo Institute of Technology, where he studied ceramics. Hamada received a thorough technical training, but he deplored the lack of throwing tuition (indeed most of the students graduated without going near a wheel). It was only after obtaining a position at the Kyoto Ceramic Testing Institute that Hamada was taught to throw.

Hamada first saw the pots of Leach and Tomimoto during his school days, in 1912 at the Mikasa Gallery in Tokyo. Captivated, he took every opportunity to see their work, but it was not until a Tokyo exhibition in 1918 that he met Leach. Hamada's new-found dedication was witnessed in his extensive travels around Japan, visiting the famous pottery kilns during summer vacations. Later, while testing their tens of thousands of ten-moku, celadon and copper-red glazes, both Hamada and his friend Kawai dreamed of becoming artist potters. Working hard and travelling widely, they visited Okinawa, Korea and China, searching out living craft traditions and finding great inspiration.

IN THE SPRING of 1919 Hamada went to Abiko to see Yanagi and Leach. Three days were spent talking, mostly about pots, each being equally impressed by the other. When Bernard Leach was about to return to England in the summer of 1920, Hamada had already received offers of two very good and tempting positions, one in China and the other in Tokyo, yet he chose to help Bernard Leach set up a pottery at St. Ives in the far western corner of England. There Hamada and Leach re-discovered English slipware – crucial not only to Hamada but to all the founding members of the Folk Craft Movement in Japan.

Although the central project was to build a traditional wood-fired, high-temperature-climbing kiln, the first in Europe, they also made raku and slipware. Raku, though familiar to both, did not seem right in England, but an extraordinary enthusiasm overtook them when they made traditional slipware, encouraging them to compete with each other in making larger and better dishes and to rediscover the traditional slip decorating techniques. Often

*Large dish, stoneware. Copper green glaze with black iron
and white glaze decoration.*

Hamada would throw a dish and Leach decorate. A magnificent piece of slipware by Hamada, decorated with a Bull, the constellation of the Plough, and even signed by Hamada in the Toft style, can be seen in the collection of the City Museum Art Gallery, Stoke-on-Trent.

It was Hamada's ability to enter into the life of the community with an open and enquiring mind that made his St. Ives years so educational and made him so beloved of everyone he met. Over tea with local families, Hamada and Leach used slipware that had feather-combed decoration. One night at supper they were served pie baked in an old slipware dish; an experience Hamada never forgot. Such pots were so common that they were not and are still rarely displayed in museums, but the directness and simplicity of this slipware with its freely trailed designs made a deep impression on Hamada, and, later, on Yanagi and his friends in Japan.

Leach and Hamada continued to puzzle how these beautifully simple pots had been made, and the answer is reputed to have come during afternoon tea, when in cutting through the blackberry jam and cream they eventually discovered the technique. Delighted, they rushed into the pottery to try it out. It worked, and both were thrilled that this discovery had come out of everyday life.

At the home of Ethel Mairet in Ditchling, Hamada discovered the simple slipware of E. B. Fishley, the North Devon Fremington potter, whose pots inspired Michael Cardew to become a potter and join Hamada and Leach at St. Ives in 1923. In Ditchling, Hamada had a glimpse of the future. Ethel Mairet, together with Eric Gill and other artists, personified the right way of working for Hamada, dyeing and weaving her own wools, letting the material and process bring out her true creativity and artistic talent.

In St. Ives, life was basic. For three-and-a-half years Hamada lived in a corner of the pottery, sleeping on a bed he built himself from kiln wood, growing his own vegetables, and cooking rice in the evenings, developing a life of self-sufficiency close to the earth. Regularly Hamada took himself off for meditation and solitary walks on the moors and cliff tops, and it was there one day (as he describes in *Hamada Master Shoji Potter*) that a surprise encounter with a cuckoo awakened him to his true self. The ego that oppresses many artists slipped away and he was both ready and eager to take up his destiny in Japan. By the end of 1923 the pottery at St. Ives was established. In 1923, his final year, Hamada produced two memorable exhibitions at William Paterson's Gallery in London, landmarks in the history of English twentieth-century studio pottery.

Hamada's genius was his ability to absorb and digest his experience in England, especially English slipware. He settled in Mashiko and became the catalyst for and embodiment of Yanagi's Folk Craft philosophy. Digging deep into the traditions of the past he found clear spring water that nurtured and regenerated tradition. Hamada's way of life and working was so natural and healthy that he could not help creating work 'born, not made'. ●

POTTERY

CLIVE BOWEN

Well-made pots should be a part of everyone's life.

BY GERALDINE NORMAN

IN AN AGE where many people have lost touch with religion, art has been upgraded to quasi-religious status – with museums playing the role of temples and exhibitions that of religious festivals. In many ways this is an aberration but here and there you come across an artist whose work speaks innately of the absolute, the silent, source of all creation.

Potters and other 'craftsmen' can achieve such artistry as well as painters and sculptors; pottery has always been regarded as an art form in the East, and is nowadays also treated as such in the West. Since the beginning of the twentieth century, in reaction to the uniformity of industrial production, Western 'artist potters' have set up their own kilns, designing, modelling and throwing their pots by hand. One particular potter, Clive Bowen, stands out from the rest. He runs the Shebbear Pottery in north Devon where he makes brown glazed earthenware close to the traditional pottery made in the area for centuries. Clive never signs his pots. He likes to identify with the 'anonymous craftsmen' of the past who produced beautiful objects which gently and unostentatiously enhanced the lives of those who used them – the cooks, the people who ate off them and the washers up. He does not agonize over making the perfect pot that will show off his genius. 'I just make pots', he says. And then, hesitatingly, he explains something that goes deeper about the process. 'There's something called 'losing your tail'. It means not thinking too much about what you're doing, just flowing. In the end it's not you that is making the pot'.

Clive's pots are cheaper than those of most other potters. The Victoria and Albert Museum shop, which put on a one-man show of his work in 1993, complained that he was not charging enough. Clive does not like to deter his clients from putting a pie dish in the oven by charging for it as an 'art work'. In his own home, well made pottery is an ordinary part of daily life – storing the flour, pouring the milk, passing the butter. . . . This integration of his pottery into family life is characteristic of the Shebbear Pottery. Since nothing is signed: you may not recognize that the model horses in the showroom are made by his daughter or that his son is adding to his pocket money by making bowls.

Clive and his second wife Rosie have created a home filled with children – his and hers and theirs – whose relaxed charm draws in friends, neighbours, other potters, and visitors from distant lands. It is no surprise to find a Japanese potter making the apple crumble for dinner while Rosie mucks out the stables. Ducks waddle in the mud between the stables and the field – mud which converts into slipware decoration on Clive's pots.

When you walk into the kitchen, to be enthusiastically greeted by a wagging Jack Russell puppy, to tread on a plastic toy discarded by the six year old, to sip tea out of a wonky mug from the kiln or munch some exquisite pie thrown together by Rosie in one of Clive's slipware pie dishes (her cooking can match the artistic finesse of his pots), you have the pleasing sensation of good human lives being lived in and around the gentle artistry of potting.

THE SHEBBEAR POTTERY is tucked into a fold of hill in the romantically untidy farming country that lies between Dartmoor and the sea in north Devon. Clive, his assistants, visitors and children make their pots in a converted cow byre, equipped with three potter's wheels of different design, a pug for mixing clay, and ranks of deep shelves for drying the pieces before they are fired.

The patch of grass that fills the middle of the old farmyard is edged with shrubs, with herbs, with potted geraniums in season and arum lilies indicating that Rosie is a gardener as well as a cook. On the opposite side to the cow byre is a rambling wooden shed, purpose-built to contain the wood-fired kilns. There are three of them, a small independent kiln, and a massive round kiln, with an eight feet diameter roughly finished in clay, connected underground to a brick chimney kiln whose bulging interior narrows some twenty feet above the ground to carry the flames and smoke through the roof of the shed into the Devon sky. The two combined kilns, which can hold some 1,000 pots, are fired six or eight times a year. It takes thirty-six hours with shifts of stokers working through the night to raise the temperature at controlled time intervals to dry, harden and glaze the pots. The massive quantities of wood required are offcuts from a local sawmill.

Attached to the farmhouse, down another side of the yard, is the showroom where the finished products are displayed, garden pots and useful kitchen wares, including a few spectacular large storage jars and dishes. They have rich brown, yellow, earth-red and green glazes; patterns are scratched in them (sgraffito) or trailed with liquid clay (slip) or the glazes themselves are mixed and mottled. Bowls that open at a satisfying angle, almost a straight line, combine brown and gold with a wavy intersection dictated by the pull of gravity on the liquid slip – a pattern more satisfying than any precisely designed by the human brain. One of the joys of the wood-fired kiln is the role of controlled accident in dictating forms, texture and colour. Clive uses local clay from Fremington, combined with slip from nearby Peters Marland (white and yellow) and the stream at the bottom of his garden (red).

He was born in Cardiff in 1943 and brought up in a terraced house in a working-class district. His affinity for art was quickly realized by his teachers, and at sixteen his choice lay between technical drawing and art college. It was resolved by the art master putting his name down for the entrance exam to Cardiff Art

School where he was accepted.

Four years at art school turned him out a painter and he left Cardiff to try his fortune in London in the early sixties.

He might have been a painter to this day if he had not gone to a dance at the Royal College of Art where he met a student called Alison Leach, daughter of the potter Michael Leach and grand-daughter of Bernard Leach, the founding father of Britain's twentieth century pottery revival. When Alison got pregnant, they decided that a cottage in Devon, near her father's pottery, was a better environment for bringing up a child than a London bed-sit. They settled in Appledore, near Bideford, where Clive continued painting and doing odd jobs.

One day he threw a pot for fun at Michael Leach's pottery and discovered a natural sympathy for the craft. "It worked the first time – I liked the idea of using my hands and making something," he told me. He signed up as an apprentice and worked at his father-in-law's pottery from 1965 to 1969. Clive was thus schooled in the Bernard Leach tradition.

BERNARD WENT TO JAPAN in 1911 after graduating from the Slade. He took an etching press with him, hoping to earn a living from teaching; instead, he began to study potting with a master called Kenzan the Sixth – in Japan the secrets of ceramic artistry were handed down from generation to generation. Pottery was closely allied to the Zen ritual known as the Tea Ceremony, a gathering of people whose every act was prescribed by the old Zen masters, including a formal appreciation of the artistry of tea wares – cups, teapots, water-jugs. Leach, who was an ardent admirer of William Blake and his spiritual art, found an instinctive sympathy for the Zen attitude to the artistry of everyday craftsmanship.

Bernard returned to England in 1920 where he built a Japanese kiln at St. Ives in Cornwall and fathered a revival of pottery making in Britain. He also became fascinated by British country potters of the seventeenth and eighteenth centuries, incorporating their slip trailing techniques with his Oriental styles. Clive has inherited both his interest in the British tradition and the Japanese aesthetic, which views the anonymous, functional pot, whatever accidents or 'errors' might have crept into its making, as a thing of beauty in itself.

Another influence arose when in the late sixties Clive read an article about Michael Cardew, who was then running the Wenford Bridge Pottery near Bodmin, and managed to scrounge an introduction.

Cardew was Bernard Leach's first and most famous pupil. He got to know and admire the traditional Devon pottery at Fremington during school holidays and, after reading Greats at Oxford, sought out Leach and became a potter himself. He took over an abandoned country pottery at Winchcombe in Gloucestershire in 1926 and began to make earthenware in traditional style, but his attempts to cure the innate porosity of earthenware and other defects quickly drew him towards stoneware – clay fired at a very high temperature. In 1943 he was invited to set up a pottery in Ghana, and worked in Ghana and Nigeria for the next twenty years, creating whole communities of potters who made stoneware from local clays. The undertaking was inspired by the idea of welding art and technology into a life-enhancing partnership. Cardew established the pottery at Wenford Bridge when he retired from Africa in 1965. At the time Clive first met him, Cardew was one of the only potters in the country using a wood-fired chimney kiln.

Meeting Cardew was a dazzling experience for Clive. "I shall never forget the smell of wood fires and real coffee at Wenford Bridge," he told me.

In 1971 Clive and Alison bought a run-down smallholding outside Shebbear with the aim of turning it into a pottery. They had two small children by then, Nicky and Dylan, and a third, Helena, arrived in 1976. After several years working on his own, Clive attempted to expand; his dream was to bring together a group of four or five potters who would continue the long tradition of country potting by working together to make anonymous, useful wares of the highest quality.

The dream ran against an immediate log jam. The capacity of the kilns he had built was sufficient for the output of four potters but there was no space to store such a massive output. He gathered three associates: his brother-in-law Philip Leach, an Irish potter called Tony Murphy and Martin Simpson, who had worked with Cardew. "In one week, if we all made pots, the workshop was full – there was no space left for potting – and we had no capital to expand sensibly." The others drifted away; only Martin Simpson is still associated with the pottery, working at Shebbear through the winter and travelling in the summer.

From time to time there are visiting potters from Japan, America or elsewhere in Europe, since the fame of Clive's work is widely spread. He has exhibited in most of the leading craft galleries in Britain, including the Victoria and Albert Museum. He has represented Britain in travelling exhibitions and lectured at home and abroad.

It's a far cry from that terraced house in Cardiff where he grew up. Most of his experience has been internalized, since he's not much of a talker. But, as Rosie points out, you must not be deceived by his silence into underrating the strength of his character. Friendly and gentle, he allows his vision to speak through his pots. While he remains true to his original ideal of the anonymous country potter by never marking them, the cognoscenti have no trouble in recognizing and admiring his work. ●

RICHARD BATTERHAM

Everyday patterns of creativity.

BY DAVID WHITING

IF YOU TALK OF A 'Leach School', a group of potters here and around the world who have embraced the philosophical and aesthetic ethos of Bernard Leach, then you speak of a good deal of imitation as well as genuinely individual exploration. In many ways Richard Batterham (b. 1936) is both the most faithful and least imitative of the Leachian potters – and has, more clearly than any other post war 'Anglo-Oriental' potter, developed his own distinctive and consistent language. And he has never been deflected from this path. This retiring man has never courted publicity, never set much store by exhibitions and general critical attention. Instead there has been, purely and simply, a complete commitment to the art and craft of potting. This sense of focus, of self-containment, is reflected in work which, quite by itself, un-bolstered by hyperbole, has achieved a special place in 20th century studio ceramics.

For forty five years now Richard Batterham has been working in the village of Durweston in Dorset, with his home and workshop on either side of a quiet lane, a few miles from Blandford Forum. Here he grows much of his own produce for the kitchen, tending a half-acre site in between making pots. Batterham's biography is exceptionally straightforward. He was introduced to the craft by Donald Potter, his remarkable art master at Bryanston School, close to Durweston. Potter, who had trained with Eric Gill and spent time at Winchcombe Pottery in 1940, was a persuasive advocate of ceramics, essentially teaching it as an aspect of sculpture. In 1957, after a period in the army, Batterham secured an apprenticeship at Bernard Leach's pottery in St Ives, attracted as he was to the idea of making good functional pots for the household. St Ives helped to instill these values – and a sense of responsibility and receptiveness to the materials, discipline and processes of the craft. Here he made lifelong friendships, notably with fellow apprentice Atsuya, son of the great Japanese potter Hamada (who helped to establish the workshop back in 1920), and with Dinah Dunn, also work-

ing in the pottery, whom he would later marry.

He set up his own pottery at Durweston in 1959, building a completely new workshop seven years later, for which he designed a four chamber oil-fired climbing kiln, based on the original Korean type also used at St Ives. With Batterham, it is important to consider his place of work, his kiln and the kinds of material employed, because he invests so much in each aspect of making – in the preparation of the clay, the progress of the firing, the varied character of the particular glazes he uses. Except for occasional forays into porcelain and salt firing, Batterham has concentrated on ash glazing his stoneware, investigating the extraordinary diversity of a few ashes derived from local trees, often used in combination with various slips and dark irons which give each pot added surface depth and density.

Mechanized tools are kept to a minimum. He throws on a kick wheel, mixes his own clays and collects the raw components of his glazes – not out of stubborn resistance to the realities of industrialization, but because the whole method of assembling and refining materials, of making and firing, is a matter of finding one's own unforced working rhythm. This is the staple empirical diet of this kind of potter and these kind of pots. Each stage of creativity is part of a wholly integrated process, a momentum that has gradually been attuned to the hours of the day and the seasons of the year, to the needs of his garden and the vagaries of the Dorset climate. Several weeks of throwing will be followed by biscuit firing, a course of glazing and then a final thirty hour period in the kiln (which is only lit five or six times a year). And Batterham gradually discovered how much more fluid potting seemed in early Spring and late Summer – a pattern of creativity was emerging.

Richard Batterham has produced literally thousands of pots for use about the house, from the kitchen to the sitting room. Concentrating on a particular range of forms, the shapes have quietly grown and evolved, a continuous process of refinement, not

Stoneware bottle.

Covered jar with lid. Photograph courtesy of the Crafts Council.

sudden changes. The experimentation with apparently familiar materials continues to yield surprises. Batterham has long recognized that one should follow and respond, rather than dictate terms. He has a very assured sense of design, as the critic Muriel Rose, an early admirer, was quick to observe. The pots of the sixties already showed that distinctive clarity and confidence. There was never any interest in fussy shapes or brush and resist decoration. Instead he has concentrated on clear strong contours, simply articulated through crisp turning, faceting and cutting, fluting and incising. They are pots which, though clearly indebted to early Korean wares and medieval English exemplars, are also quite definitely modern. Their quiet minimal language shows a true traditionalist's sense of the present.

His production ranges from various tablewares – cutsided teapots, casseroles and fine jugs – to the sculptural confidence of his tall elegant bottles and cutsided bowls. These are pots which, along with his individual, more decorated boxes and lidded jars, principally feature in his rare exhibitions, but there is no sense of hierarchy in Batterham's output. They are all everyday pots, with a particular stylistic cohesion. All share a marked economy, a resonant austerity that explores ceramic form at its most abstract – enlivened by matt or liquid covering ashes, ranging from a creamy white to olive and translucent celadon, and often combined with deep tenmokus. His glazes delineate and add movement to form. Occasional saltfirings have produced pots of particular understatement, but the nuances of the kiln create warm variations of surface and texture.

Batterham's pots change and transform in the shifting light of the day, in being moved about the house. Out of the particular rhythm of conception and making emerges a rhythm of form and colour in the work. Because Batterham has led a particularly undistracted and concentrated life, unconcerned with the ramifications of a wider craft world, this private, very independent craftsman has been able to channel his energies into what matters most – the making of beautiful pots for our use and contemplation, objects, as he once wrote, "to enrich rather than adorn life". ●

MAKING IN THE CITY

Craft is not just a country pursuit.

BY EDMUND DE WAAL

THIS ARTICLE IS a sort of sketch map, one of those maps where nothing is quite to scale and the notes and addenda keep doubling up. It's an attempt to map something inexact, a sensibility and an approach both to making pots and to living in a city: to being a metropolitan potter. I am a potter, making porcelain jars and dishes, and I live in London. It is a city that informs my work, a vivid background haunted by other makers and other presences. But it is still regarded as slightly unusual, the assumption being that I am stranded amongst this asphalt, awaiting a rural rescue. That there should be such a powerful assumption about where craft 'naturally' belongs says much about the dominant images of making over the last few generations. To reclaim craft and the city is hard work.

For instance, in Michael Cardew's treatise *Pioneer Pottery* there is a plan of a workshop. It is a decided and logical piece of work. Making, drying, glazing and packing are clearly differentiated. But the scale is huge: a collection, maybe, of farm out-buildings, byres, stables, barns. Bernard Leach has a considered view, too. In *A Potter's Book* he writes: "A friendly and inviting atmosphere in the rooms where pots are thrown and decorated, good lighting, reasonable orderliness and quiet, the tools and furnishings attractive in themselves, however simple, and a few specimens of first-rate pots against light-toned walls make all the difference to the mood in which the work is done."

This is a very particular territory. You look at the plans and read the sensible admonitions and it slowly becomes clear what pottery means. It involves plant, wood stacks for the flame kilns, raw material stores, slurry pits and drying areas for clay preparation, packing rooms, car parking. It's so obvious that it needs no comment: pottery, like clay, wood and passing trade, happens in the countryside. It is a grounded art. The images that emerge are heroic: Cardew surrounded by vast grain and cider jars at Winchcombe, Leach beside the new St.

Ives kiln. To call them ruralists is too partial an observation. It doesn't give the sense of absorption between these potters and their landscape: that English nexus of feeling between land, clay and maker, shot through with all the old serious words: settled, rooted, earthed. It's present in the pots, too, the confidence of belonging-to and owning-of linked together. The cultural history is still to be written that analyses just how deeply embedded is this connection within the sense of identity of English craft-culture.

The using of local materials, for instance, 'making them your own', is a litany throughout the English folkcraft revival. Tankards, mead-cups, chargers: the lexicon of forms is also a grammar of the country, a speaking English. Or, in Leach's case, the teabowls, an Oriental country argot. You can hear the different rural accents: place particular makers in particular landscapes with confidence. Of course they travelled, but they came home. Urbanism just doesn't fit in with this: earthed in London hasn't the same ring to it.

THE LONG TRADITION of making things in cities is interwoven with the equally long tradition of placing their value elsewhere. There is, as Raymond Williams wrote in 1973, "almost an inverse proportion between the importance of the working rural economy and the cultural importance of rural ideas." The weight of conceptual gravity hasn't altered in the world of handmade things. Making things in cities is overlooked. The Japanese potter Kenzan in the early eighteenth century, building his rural studio in the hills outside Kyoto, was the first *faux rustic* artist-craftsman to live authentically, near to his urban centre of patronage. It remains a powerful image. And there is the feeling that there is a profound disjunction between making and cities – not in the Leachian sense of cities as being places that infect makers' authenticity, but in a yet more serious way. Christoph Asendorf puts it simply when he poses as a polarity the domain of the

The Porcelain Room.

storyteller or the craftsperson (which he describes as the world of continuity, habit and sequence) with 'Erlebnis', or the discontinuous experience of the city, a place of adventure. To get to this polarity, habit versus excitement, you have to start at a place where craft is a signifier of being settled. But is this actually the case? Consider, crucially, how craft skills reach the city. This is Steen Rasmussen, the great Danish writer, on London: "In the sixteenth century the weavers in London were almost all of foreign extraction. Another wave of immigrants, who introduced silk weaving . . . settled in the villages of Shoreditch and Spitalfields. A colony of French hatters, who introduced felt hats, settled in Southwark, together with the Flemings who introduced the brewing of beer from hops. Printers from the Netherlands settled in Westminster, in Clerkenwell and elsewhere."

London is a city of emigré makers. It is haunted by people who arrive not with possessions, but with the most essential of all things, their skills. From the Huguenots to the Jewish Diaspora of the thirties to the textile artists from South Asia in the seventies, London has been endlessly renewed by these makers. And they have made the city, in just as complex a way as the rural geography of Britain has been made up by craft. Just as Bideford might mean cider jars, can you think of Spitalfields without the

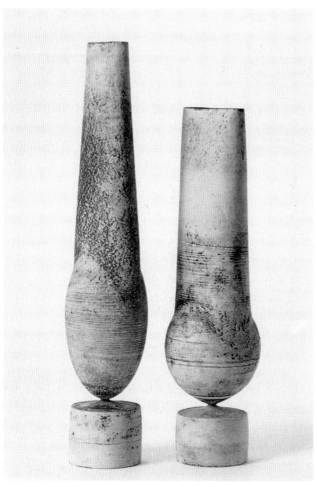

Two-lobed tube forms by Hans Coper.

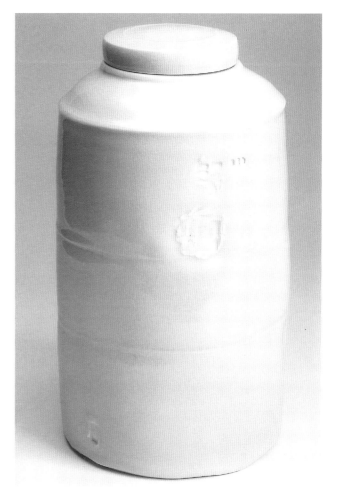

Porcelain container.

Huguenots or Bangladeshi textiles? Interestingly, in the sixteenth and eighteenth centuries it is the Guilds who try to stop these makers: it's the rooted, the 'authentic' owners of skill who turn against the newcomers. Skill has *always* been a good word to start an argument with. And you may argue that even if there is an emigré life of making within cities, it is not an emigré life of making *about* cities. But aren't making in the city and making the city closely entwined? How can you not do it? London is a theme in itself: Lucie Rie's and Hans Coper's pots of the 1950s are not just made in and for particularly urban settings; in their abraded textures and density of colours they are urban constructions too. They have the inwardness, the opacity of other great artistic meditations on London: David Jones' 'Pool of London' in *The Anathémata* or Frank Auerbach's *Primrose Hill* painted every day for forty years.

The images of Lucie Rie and Hans Coper sharing the studio in Albion Mews working on their individual work alongside a continuum of jointly marked tableware are also images of a making of London.

Their example has been crucial for me. The sharing of space as peers, despite their differences in age and experience, is part of it. Sharing a studio is an urban necessity: studios are difficult to find; they are expensive. But it's also the mythic lure of symbiosis: not a studio full of workers, apprentices, foremen but of another maker. Half the bills paid and an interrogative presence too. I share my urban studio for these reasons.

The things that I value in living and working here in the city are the tensions between the settled and the unsettled, the new and the habitual. I like the serendipity of people coming through London and dropping into the studio on the off-chance, the transience of the makers and artists in the yard of studios surrounding mine. I like the richness of possibility, however infrequently taken up, of the museums and the libraries. My morning walk to the studio through a mixture of Georgian streets, a council estate and a small, busy park, settles me into myself. It seems to be the right place to be making things, this odd and vital job of creating things of beauty. ●

JOHN MAKEPEACE

The process of self-discovery is central to design.

BY SARA HUDSTON

The Great Hall at Parnham House with table and chairs by John Makepeace.

IN THE HANDS OF John Makepeace natural materials reveal their protean qualities; English holly is spun into a web for a chair back, burr elm is twisted around oak as if it were a length of pale cloth, and carved lime becomes a sea-polished pebble. Wood is always his core material, but he often marries it with metal, leather and fabric. It has been said that John Makepeace feels about wood as a jeweller feels about gold. To him wood is a malleable material, infinitely precious.

Makepeace has an international reputation as a craftsman, designer and teacher. His pieces are commissioned by collectors and museums around the world. His work first began to attract public notice in the 1960s when he produced a range of retail products including a flat-pack table for Heal's furniture storc in London. These items suited the mechanized aesthetic of the times and sold well, but left Makepeace unsatisfied. He went back to handmaking and has been exploring the pleasures of craft and design ever since. Over the last forty years he has come to believe that design is the key to his art.

"Design puts expression back into objects. The things we have around our homes are very much part of us and we can feel deeply about them if they have a rightness about them. Good design is when an object expresses its role, its particular function, with delight. With furniture that delight means not just looking good but feeling good in relation to the body. Most chairs have been 'designed' but most chairs are uncomfortable. A designer cannot afford to ignore anything that affects the way you think or feel in relation to an object. It's a whole language and one which I think has been savagely impoverished in the twentieth century through Modernism."

In Makepeace's view, modern methods of production are to blame for severing the connections between designer, manufacturer and user. Design is reduced to a selling point for objects which are less well-made than they should be. There is also a social cost.

"There is a distinction between the trade and art of furniture making. Trade is about making something adequately which I don't think is fulfilling for anybody.

"If you design, you are affecting the lives of a lot of people: those who use the product and those who make it. People are happiest when they are designing and growing rather than simply following repetitive instructions on an assembly line. If you are going to make things using human labour, you've got to consider the social implications of the effects of repetitive labour on your workforce."

MAKEPEACE'S THINKING is strongly influenced by Ruskin, William Morris and the nineteenth-century Arts and Crafts Movement. Ask him if this comprises a credible strategy for the twenty-first century, and he sticks to his ideals. "It's about having values and facing challenges for the future in the way we live and work." He believes that with the aid of modern technology, the Arts and Crafts philosophy can finally come of age. This sounds convincing when it comes from a man who has studied the art of business and who is personal friends with the forward-thinking business guru Charles Handy.

He is putting his theories into practice at his home, Parnham House in Dorset. Parnham is a place of extraordinary beauty, a Tudor vision in honey-coloured stone which rises from water meadows in countryside made famous by Thomas Hardy. Before Makepeace bought it in 1973, the Grade I listed mansion had stood empty for three years. Makepeace bought it because he wanted to showcase his work in a historic property. This urge was not mere window dressing, but a part of his feeling of being rooted in a living English tradition.

"I am particularly attracted by woods that are grown in England, trees which have been grown over aeons and have come to thrive in our particular climate. That has a kind of wholeness about it," he says. Making these woods into modern pieces and then placing them in a space fashioned by generations of use would, he hoped, demonstrate the continuum between contemporary design and the past.

Parnham had another important purpose – to teach new craftspeople the skills of wood-working. Parnham College opened in 1977 and David Linley was one of the first students. The college was unusual because it taught marketing and business skills alongside craft techniques at a time when artists generally regarded the world of commerce with lofty disdain.

Makepeace says that he too once considered business beneath him until he came into contact with thinkers such as Norman Leyland and Clifford Barclay, who encouraged Makepeace to develop theories of training and self-development which lie at the heart of his work as a teacher. "To be fulfilled, individuals have to take up the challenges within their power. If they can find out what their purpose is and be guided to follow it, that is most rewarding."

"Some of these discoveries are intuitive, some are logical and some are unaccountable and in a sense spiritual. For me the process has been a case of passing through a sequence of discoveries which have now begun to complete a cycle."

"Coming to Parnham could have been a huge mistake, but all the signs were that there was a desperate need among students to learn not just about design but about the business dimension that makes real craftsmanship possible."

MANY OF THE Parnham students have been mature people changing career, or machine furniture makers keen to become true handmakers. Makepeace speaks of the rewards of observing people undergo the 'cultural revolution' of the Parnham workshops. "At first they won't understand that what you can't see matters. Once you get that through to them you can see them grow."

The process of self-discovery is central to Makepeace's philosophy as a teacher and craftsman. He planned to become a priest until it burst on him with the force of revelation that what he really wanted to do was to make furniture.

"At some point in your life you start to make decisions for yourself. Unless you take control, the decisions tend to be made by the people around you. My father died when I was eighteen. Four

Chair in English holly designed by John Makepeace.

years later I went to America and came back feeling that anything was possible. My choice to be a furniture maker was very much a vocation because everybody told me I would never make a living."

He's shy of discussing where this powerful sense of purpose comes from but he believes that it is not simply an exercise of will. "It's something outside oneself," is all he will say. Wherever his self-belief comes from, the effect on others is astonishing. His gift at communicating his convictions has won enormous financial support for various projects at Parnham and his newer venture at Hooke Park.

"I certainly believe in the leadership of vision. If your vision of life is well-resolved, then that becomes quite compelling for those you are able to bring on side."

Hooke Park is the culmination of Makepeace's aims and beliefs. Essentially, it is an ecologically-aware attempt to realize the nineteenth-century Arts and Crafts philosophy using twenty-first-century knowledge.

"It started with the realization that British woodlands are under threat. In the past they had been grown for agricultural crops and people managed them with a view to their long-term value. In the process they became an amenity and a high-quality part of the landscape."

Many woods are no longer managed in the old

Mollusc. Desk in washed oak and suede by John Makepeace. Photograph by Mike Murless.

ways and this has led to a decline in wildlife and in the health of the woodland itself. Makepeace was shocked to discover that because of the decay of manufacturing in the UK half of the crop that is felled is useless. "We treat as firewood what in France and Germany would be the feedstock of major industries and we import eighty-five per cent of our timber and timber products."

In 1972 Makepeace heard the German architect Frei Otto lecture on lightweight structures – that is, buildings which don't use materials with high environmental and energy costs. Makepeace had the idea of building with woodland thinnings – the part of the crop which in the UK gets burnt or thrown away. In 1983 The Parnham Trust acquired Hooke Park, 330 acres of mixed broad-leaved and conifer woodland four miles from Parnham House, with the aim of creating wooden structures which would house a craft community. Since then three buildings have been constructed, and a training programme is established.

It's too early to judge whether Hooke Park will achieve its aims. In 1994, difficulties with funding forced the student training programme to close. Makepeace has since embarked on ambitious plans to move Parnham College to Hooke and run a re-shaped course which he hopes will rejuvenate the furniture industry.   ●

DAVID DREW

Work and leisure, labour and pleasure, food and family are woven into one.

BY RICHARD BOSTON

I THINK DAVID DREW is about the only person I have ever met whose name is a sentence. It is very rare in this age of specialization to find anyone who personally carries out every stage of a job, and sees it through from start to finish. David Drew is one. He personally grows the willows which provide the material from which he makes the baskets which he himself sells from his own house without advertisements and without a middleman.

The 1911 edition of the *Encyclopaedia Britannica* says of basket-making: 'Essentially a primitive craft, its relative importance is in inverse ratio to the industrial development of a people'. At first sight the remark seems pretty condescending, but that's only if you think that 'industrial development' is necessarily what *1066 and All That* calls a Good Thing.

Certainly the way that David Drew lives and works is about as far from industrialization as is possible in twentieth-century Britain. Life at the thatched house at Higher Hare Farm, Somerset, can't have changed much since it was built in the seventeenth century. As for the way in which the baskets are made, this has continued unchanged since long, long before the industrial revolution.

Reading on in the *Britannica* it is soon apparent that in fact the author, far from being condescending, has a deep respect for and understanding of the craft. "No machinery is used in basket-making", he writes. "A considerable training and natural aptitude go to form the expert workman, for the ultimate perfection of shape and beauty of texture depend upon the more or less perfect conception of form in the craftsman's mind, and on his power to impress it on a recalcitrant material." I like that sentence very much. Consider the way in which its various elements, the 'considerable training', the 'natural aptitude', the 'ultimate perfection of shape', the 'beauty of texture' and the rest of the recalcitrant material is woven together – like a basket.

The most recent edition of the *Britannica* is more succinct. Its final sentence states that 'the essential

requirements have been available for at least 50,000 years: a simple awl, nimble fingers, and patience'. While David Drew has these three, he does in fact have a few other tools, though not many. Basket-makers' tools are hard to come by nowadays, and he has mostly acquired them from retired makers.

Like all craftsmen's tools, they are in themselves objects that give pleasure both to the eye and the hand. As well as the sharply-pointed rope-maker's bodkin there are the pick-knife, the shop-knife, the shears. His cleave (one of the last to be made) has a boxwood handle that fits snugly into the palm and has a brass head, the wedge-shaped edges of which split a rod into four.

His hands are large and powerful but far from clumsy. A slip with the bodkin or one of the sharp knives would make a nasty wound, but there are no recent cuts on his hands or, as far as I could see, scars of ancient ones. This is a sure sign of a craftsman who works with his tools and materials and not against them. Since his hands are his most important equipment, he takes as good care of them as does a violinist.

Whether or not basket-making favours the dextrous, it certainly demands dexterity. It also requires physical strength. David Drew is strongly built, but he works for very long hours and he works every day. He is always conscious of the need to conserve his physical energy and to use his strength economically. When he cuts a stick he does not just hold it in one hand and pull the knife towards him: that way, all the strain is taken by the arms. Instead he sits down, locks his left hand behind his knee (in what he calls the basket-maker's vice) and then draws the knife towards him. Now the strain is distributed throughout the body, the legs taking as much as the arms. It's a bit like the Japanese martial arts in which, instead of countering your opponent's strength, you use it against him.

Watching him put the border on a large basket I was astonished at how quickly what was to my eye a chaotic collection of projecting sticks was bent, twist-

David Drew. Photograph by Chris Chapman.

ed and woven into a perfectly finished object. As they say in conjuring circles, the speed of the hand deceives the eye. But, as with any good artist or artisan, the speed comes from skill, not hurry.

I was reminded of something Robert Pirsig says in *Zen and the Art of Motorcycle Maintenance:* "When you want to hurry something, that means you no longer care about it and want to get on to other things". Pirsig also quotes a gem of technical writing from a Japanese manual. It begins with the words, "Assembly of Japanese bicycle require great peace of mind". One's first reaction is to laugh. Then you think about it. What better advice could you give as a first step in putting together an object of great complexity, such as a motorbike, or a basket?

David Drew says he doesn't read much. This is not so much for lack of time (though there are indeed few waking hours left over from his work) as

that he is the kind of person who works things out for himself rather than by looking for solutions in books. Even so, I was a little disappointed when he said he had only got half-way through *Zen and the Art of Motorcycle Maintenance*. It seemed to me that the book contains so much that is in sympathy with his way of living and and working. When I got home I read the book again, and thought I could see a possible reason why he hadn't finished it. He knew it all already. Taoism is "the philosophy of Lao-tse that advocates a simple honest life and non-interference with the course of natural events". I learnt that from my dictionary. David Drew learnt it from basket-making.

Work and leisure, labour and pleasure, house, garden, food, drink, family: the different elements of David Drew's life are woven together into a whole which is greater than its parts – like a basket. ●

KAZUO HIROSHIMA

Kazuo Hiroshima is a master basket-maker in rural Japan.
With consummate skill and attention to detail he creates
a perfect marriage of beauty and utility.

BY LOUISE ALLISON CORT

EXCEPT WHEN HE HAS gone to the hillside to cut fresh bamboo, Kazuo Hiroshima can be found in his workshop on the main street of Yato, a small village near Hinokage, in Japan. The weathered grey wooden facade of Mr Hiroshima's workshop is unmarked. People know that they can slide open the door, step in, and find him there, making bamboo baskets. They chat about the weather and local events before placing an order for a new backpack basket or collecting a fishing creel that Mr Hiroshima has made for them.

Kazuo Hiroshima, born in 1915, is the last full-time professional basketmaker serving the town of Hinokage and surrounding villages on Japan's southern island of Kyushu. In his memory and hands he carries the measurements, proportions and constructions for more than eighty basket shapes with all their variations. When he began making baskets for a living in the 1930s, twelve men were working as basket-makers in the area. They supplied dozens of varieties of basket to households of farmers and fishermen to serve precise roles in the tasks that supported those families – harvesting forest products, raising and processing food crops on the terraced fields along the steep slopes, catching fish and transporting them to market.

Since the 1930s, the population in his region has declined as young people move to cities for employment, while the proportion of farmers has shrunk in absolute terms. Sweeping changes in rural life since the end of World War II have eliminated some farming tasks and transformed others by mechanization and new materials, with plastic and metal vessels replacing bamboo baskets. Dams and pollution have depleted the eels, crabs and fish in the Gokase River. Most tellingly, with most roads paved and most families owning cars or pickup trucks, people can ride where they once had no choice but to walk, carrying their tools, lunch and harvested products in a bamboo backpack basket. These changes in rural life have sharply reduced the variety of shapes that Mr Hiroshima produces on a regular basis.

KAZUO HIROSHIMA was born into a farming family. As the second son of eight children, he was not in line to inherit the family land, but he probably would have made a living through farming, had it not been for an accident at age three, when he dislocated his right hip. Local medical care could not correct the dislocation, which left him with a permanent limp. Walking to school was impossible, although he did learn basic reading and writing at home. The young man was repulsed by the prospect of living out his life as a dependant in the home of one of his siblings. At the age of fifteen, with his parents' encouragement, he became an apprentice to a basket-maker in a nearby village. His apprenticeship lasted two years.

His teacher was also lame, as were several other basket-makers who worked in the region. Basket-making was an accepted occupation for people with disabilities. Even so, Mr Hiroshima's teacher, Kudō Masanori, followed the physically demanding pattern of itinerant basket-making that prevailed until World War II, and Mr Hiroshima took up that pattern also. Each spring and autumn he made the rounds of nearly two dozen communities within walking distance of his home village. He might stay in one village up to a month, going from household to household to fill orders for new baskets or repair existing ones, using bamboo cut on the client family's land. He worked outdoors under the shelter of the farmhouse eaves, took his

Left and centre, storage baskets for dried fish. Right, creel. Photographs by Louise Allison Cort.

meals with the family, and slept in the house.

Although Mr Hiroshima learned his trade from Kudō Masanori, his 'heart's teacher' was Uncle Ushi, whose work set a standard he still aspires to attain. One day, as a new apprentice, Mr Hiroshima was alone in the workshop when he received a visit from a wandering basket-maker known to local residents as 'Uncle Ushi'. Everyone knew Uncle Ushi as a prodigious basket-maker who sometimes refused to fill a farmer's order if the quality of available bamboo did not meet his standards. On the day Mr Hiroshima met him, Uncle Ushi scrutinized one of Mr Kudo's colander baskets and remarked that the rim was wobbly and weak. "When Masanori returns, tell him to make a sturdier rim for this basket." To prove his point, he gave the young man a colander of his own making.

Thereafter Mr Hiroshima studied Uncle Ushi's

skills whenever a customer asked him to repair a basket made by the older man. In dismantling such baskets, he saw that Uncle Ushi did not take short cuts, even on aspects of construction invisible to the user. Mr Hiroshima also observed that each weaving strip of a basket made by Uncle Ushi was shaved to perfect evenness, sometimes only a millimetre in width, and he absorbed the lesson that a well-made bamboo basket begins with meticulous selection of raw materials and preparation of the basic units of construction. "I've never seen work finer than his – perhaps no one *could* do anything better."

Mr Hiroshima understood that the artistry of Uncle Ushi's baskets was not an end in itself; the baskets were not made for their beauty. A basket-maker bent his skills toward making a basket that suited exactly the needs of the user, and the next order depended on the customer's satisfaction with

the basket's utility and longevity. Details of skilfulness were significant for the basket's intended use, not as ornament.

WORLD WAR II brought permanent changes to Mr Hiroshima's working patterns. From 1943 to 1945 he served in a bamboo workshop in a nearby city, making containers that were in short supply. From experienced basket-makers in that workshop he learned the repertory of shapes for the urban market, along with the tools and techniques peculiar to their manufacture. After the war, however, he did not resume the old pattern of itinerant production. He married, and he and his wife settled along the Gokase River. There he learned to make the fish traps, creels and storage baskets required by fishermen. Moreover, he began to work out of his own shop, and customers came to him. When making the rounds of the villages, he had carried his tools in a bamboo backpack basket; after he opened his own workshop, he asked a carpenter to make a wooden tool-box. Now worn on the edges and darkened with age, the tool-box documents his nearly fifty years of working indoors in his own shop – something he dreamed about as a young man.

The course of Mr Hiroshima's career over seventy years as a basket-maker can be measured in terms of the steady acquisition of new shapes for his repertory, new tools to perform certain tasks, and new refinements in forms he already knew. He regrets that he has not been able to pass on his skills.

He tried to train several apprentices, but the younger men all found 'better opportunities' as farmers or shop clerks. He is the first to admit that basket-making has never been a lucrative craft. In order to support his family, he used to work from dawn to dusk, "from the moment I could see my hands until I couldn't see them any more."

Mr Hiroshima's career might have gone unrecorded had it not been for Nakamura Kenji, whose family runs a grocery store in Hinokage. After graduating from college, Mr Nakamura returned to Hinokage to help with the store. His experience made him take a new look at the crafts that still survived in his native area – vine baskets, bentwood boxes and rice-straw sandals, in addition to bamboo baskets – and he decided to sell them in the store, to tourists as well as to local customers. Conversations with Mr Hiroshima revealed the full scope of his repertory. Mr Nakamura placed a standing order for whatever basket forms Mr Hiroshima wanted to make. That opportunity to draw once again upon all his skills revived Mr Hiroshima, who had grown dispirited because of the dwindling demand for baskets.

In 1982, the members of a crafts tour that I organized visited Hinokage. In the Nakamura store we marvelled at dozens of different baskets made by Mr Hiroshima. Our enthusiasm inspired Mr Nakamura to begin a permanent record of Hinokage crafts. He contacted the National Museum of Natural History at the Smithsonian

Bamboo grove; women picking tea using hip-baskets; a fisherman empties an eel into a basket; fisherman using a creel.

Institution. When the museum's Department of Anthropology responded favourably, he commissioned M. Hiroshima to recreate all the basket forms in his repertory, and he asked local carpenters and blacksmiths to replicate the tool-box and tools that Mr Hiroshima uses. He collected a group of older baskets (including three by Uncle Ushi) from local households, and he even included some plastic and metal substitutes that have replaced bamboo baskets.

Mr Nakamura's father presented the group of 169 items to the National Museum of Natural History in 1988. Five additional items were presented in 1989. In November 1994, the Arthur M. Sackler Gallery of the Smithsonian Institution borrowed a selection of those baskets for an exhibition titled *A Basketmaker in Rural Japan*, fulfilling Mr Nakamura's dream to present Mr. Hiroshima's baskets to the world. Meanwhile, Mr Hiroshima continues to work quietly in his shop, pleased that the publicity about the exhibition has inspired his local customers to place more orders. ●

CULTURE OF
COMMUNITY

Why should one reject the perfect
in favour of the imperfect?
The precise and perfect carries no
overtones, admits no freedom.
We in our own human imperfections
are repelled by the perfect.
Beauty must have some room,
must be associated with freedom.
Freedom, indeed, is beauty.
The love of the irregular is a sign
of the basic quest for freedom.

Soetsu Yanagi

'Diamond in the Square' by unknown Amish quiltmaker, Lancaster County, Pennsylvania.

AMISH THREAD

Quilting is as high an artistic effort as painting or sculpting.

BY ROBERT HUGHES

STUDENTS OF AMISH have never been able to discover anything like a 'theory' of quiltmaking held by the Amish themselves. The Amish talk about quiltmaking as a purely practical matter: they do it to keep warm. This would seem to fly in the face of reason, since there are, to put it mildly, much easier ways to obtain a blanket than by patiently expending hundreds or thousands of hours on piecing, patching, assembly and quilting. What we have here is an activity that is in part practical, part aesthetic and part ritualistic, a social binder. It is not 'pure' creativity, but neither is it 'pure' use.

Amish quilts adhere to a strict repertoire of patterns but have no religious iconography in the real sense of the word. Quiltmaking falls under the general rubric of what the Amish call the *Ordnung* (pronounced 'artning'), an oral tradition of religious rules governing social customs, moral life and work that has descended – branching and changing as it went, throughout the various Amish subgroups – from the sixteenth century. It directs the Amish toward the cardinal virtues of their social ethic: humility and non-resistance, simplicity and practicality. Many details of daily life are covered in the *Ordnung*, from the length of beards or skirts to bans on harness ornament, 'showy' linoleum and radios. Apparently, though, the *Ordnung* says nothing specific about quilts as such, or their design.

Nevertheless, it has clearly affected both, because the *Ordnung* is an instrument of intense cultural as well as moral conservatism. There was a schism among the Amish in Pennsylvania around 1942, over the question of whether houses could have projecting eaves at their gable ends. The *Ordnung* forbade such eaves as showy and 'worldly'. A family of the Old Order, had bought a farmhouse from a non-Amish family. They did not want to saw off its eaves. The elders insisted they should. From this doctrinal wrangle (in the course of which one dissenting Amishman expressed his solidarity by building a doghouse with gable eaves sticking out, a radical gesture if ever there was one) a new subgroup, the Zook Amish, was born. However, the only difference between them was that one had eaves on their houses and the other did not. Societies like this are not, if one may so frame the point, rich seedbeds for stylistic innovation. Their designs tend toward a 'conservative' central-medallion form, whether Square, Bars or Diamond. Likewise, the cultural pressure of the *Ordnung* favours sober colours as emblems, not quite metaphors, of moral states.

Lancaster Amish quilts have a rich palette of saturated colours, which suggests both gravity and fullness and suits a culture that puts a tremendous premium on stable order and material adequacy. White and yellow are not used, though when the Amish moved west into America, to Iowa, Kansas and Nebraska, they began to put the brighter colours – some groups using oranges and yellows, others preferring white – into their designs. In the classic days of Amish quiltmaking, all designs were made from the kind of cloth used for dresses and shirts. Lancaster County Amish quiltmakers, in particular, would buy this cloth by the yard for their designs, just as an artist buys the paint he or she needs: they did not wait until suitable scraps accumulated. Under the black coats and capes Amish men and women wear in public, these shirts and dresses could be bright. But the colour of the quilts mirrored the sumptuary restrictions placed on the colour of clothes, and the *Ordnung* could be quite specific about that, if one can judge from one of its rare printed forms, set out in a tract by the Amish of Pike County, Ohio, in 1950: 'No ornamental, bright, showy, form-fitting, immodest or silk-like clothing of any kind. Colours such as bright red, orange, yellow or pink not allowed.' But if scarlet might suggest the Whore of Babylon to one group of Amish in Ohio, it did not to others elsewhere: 'turkey red', that deep singing red between carmine and burgundy that recurs in Lancaster quilts, was a favourite throughout Pennsylvania.

'Sunshine and Shadow' by unknown Amish quiltmaker, Lancaster County, Pennsylvania.

And so, Amish quilts in general are not conceived as collages in cloth, full of micro-images snipped from the flux of daily life. They are distanced, august and austerely geometrical. The Amish central medallion, a Centre Square or Diamond, was opposed to the repeated-block design common among American quilts of the period. It confirms, one might say, 'conservative' liking for figure-ground relations as against an 'advanced' preference for all-overness. The almost liturgical grandeur of a 1930s Diamond quilt from Lancaster county, seems to look back to the architectural inlays of the Tuscan quattrocentro, whereas the repeated-motif blocks of popular non-Amish quilts might appear, if you care to stretch a point, to predict Andy Warhol and his rows of soup cans. Even where the Amish were influenced by repeated-block designs a nostalgia for their medallion would often persist: the bright red 'cross' centres the whole design and deprives it of its all-overness.

The dislike of 'worldliness' – for which read 'showiness' – means that the elaborate detailing of other American quilts is repressed in Amish work. One can readily see why: it would look as though the maker had spent too much time on the quilt, at the expense of her other social and domestic duties;

it could suggest idleness or, worse, a certain frivolity, both repugnant to the *Ordnung*. The stricter the group, the more common the process of 'saving' will tend to be: thus Old Order or 'Nebraska' Amish quilts are apt to incorporate more worn, recycled material than those of less conservative groups, which used new cloth, scraps of bolts rather than scraps of clothing. But the skill of Amish needle-workers is always on parade in the quilting in those precise, unwavering curves, sometimes though not always drawn out with standard templates, through which the lines of running stitch describe the stylized forms of swag, leaf, rose petal, basket, urn and spray, the figurative counterpoint to the abstract grandeur of the large colour design.

In any case no custom, however strict, is going to suppress an artist's inventive powers. The Amish did not make crazy quilts for some decades after the general vogue for them in America peaked, but when they did they could give the form an entrancing visual gravity. In their complexity, visual intensity and quality craftsmanship, these works simply dispel the idea that folk art is innocent social birdsong. They are as much a part of the story of high aesthetic effort in America as any painting or sculpture. They deserve our attention and abundantly repay it.   ●

71

A TALE OF TAPESTRY

At the Wissa Wassef Art School in Egypt vibrant rhythms
are woven into a dance of life.

BY CLIO MITCHELL

PICTURE A WOOLLY paradise in which flocks gambol and graze in a luxuriant landscape rich in palm trees, crops and foliage, flecked with the brilliant flashes of flowers and birds. Perhaps the domes of a biblical-looking village nestle in its lush folds, and shepherds enjoy a picnic in their pastoral idyll.

Allow your mind to explore every inch of this joyous world, wander in its palm groves, bask in its sunlight and let your eyes rove across its delicately gradated shades. Feel the energy of the vibrant rhythms suffusing it, magically transmuting the patterns imposed by the loom on which it is woven into a pulsating dance of life.

Then reflect that this elaborate paradise inched its way up the threads of that loom directly from the imagination of its creator, without any form of sketch or model, and that its creator comes from a background whose deprivations we more normally associate with the hellish than the heavenly. For such is the provenance of the tapestries made at the Ramses Wissa Wassef Art School near Giza in Egypt.

THE LIFE WORK OF Ramses Wissa Wassef (1911-1974) was governed by his preoccupation with the effects of industrialization on human wellbeing, and the need for a radically different approach to education. Trained as an architect, the young Egyptian turned to indigenous traditions of architecture – notably the mudbrick vaults and domes of Nubian villages – to give his own work a greater empathy with Egyptian climate and lifestyle.

Looking beyond architecture, Wissa Wassef also lamented the fact that industrialization was leading to the gradual dying out of craft traditions. His ideas on education added particular force to his regret at this loss.

He believed that "every human being is born an artist, but these gifts can only be brought out if artistic creation is encouraged by the practice of a craft from early childhood." He saw modern education as crushing this innate artistic talent, through imposing its own conventional norms.

In 1941, Wissa Wassef was commissioned to build a primary school in old Cairo and saw the opportunity to try out his theory in practice. He obtained permission to install some looms in the school so the children could learn the weaver's craft. Weaving was chosen because, by enabling the production of pictorial images, it offers more scope for creativity than most other crafts. The fact that it is relatively complicated as a technique also meant that the children were less likely to become bored.

As Wissa Wassef wrote, his experiment soon demonstrated that "the sense of colour and rhythm, the instinctive feeling for the play of shapes and composition are the innate gifts of the child." Encouraged by the results and wanting to pursue this project further, in 1952, Wissa Wassef and his wife Sophie set up the Ramses Wissa Wassef Art School in Harrania near Giza. They located the school in a poor rural village so their young weavers would come to them free from all taint of a formal education.

The children – aged about eight to ten – were not selected in any way. Those who wanted to learn were shown the basic techniques of weaving and then left to work out for themselves how to create an image. Three simple rules were observed. They should not work from preparatory drawings, so their creativity could find direct expression in the craft medium itself. They were never exposed to other works of art to copy, as Wissa Wassef believed that being influenced by another's work would lead to the loss of contact with one's own emotions. All criticism or intervention by adults was banned, so the children's creativity remained able to run free of any such censorship.

AFTER A WHILE, as they expressed the desire to produce more diverse and lifelike imagery, the

'The Wedding' by Sayed Mahmoud. Photographs courtesy Ramses Wissa Wassef Art Centre/Werner Forman Archive.

young weavers were told stories and taken on trips around the school's large garden, to the Nile, the desert, the zoo, or further afield, and shown how to look at their surroundings. The only notes they ever took were mental.

These experiences they translated into their work, which gained steadily in complexity and imaginative vision, until today, those first generation weavers still working at the school, now under the supervision of Sophie Wissa Wassef, are consummate masters of their difficult art. (As an experiment, some of the weavers were once given pencil and paper. They could not create a coherent image by this means at all.)

As Wissa Wassef wrote: "Far from weakening, the miracle of this creativity's incredible vitality has been continually renewed in spite of outside disturbances. It went on through the age of puberty, which we had been led to fear, and even through marriage and adulthood."

Another two generations of weavers, as well as cotton weavers and batik artists, have since been trained by the Wissa Wassefs' daughters Suzanne and Joanna, to similarly spectacular results. One of the original principles behind the school was that the children should receive a salary from day one, so this craft activity could be seen as a means to contribute to meagre family incomes. The first generation therefore viewed the time they spent at the loom as a job. Inevitably, with time and the growing renown of the school, their successors have a greater awareness of their identity as artists, and the weavers and their families tend to live a little more comfortably than the other villagers.

When I visited the school, their life did actually seem almost idyllic. Wissa Wassef's award-winning mudbrick buildings are set in large gardens. Here the plants, used for making the dyes for the wool, are grown. Twice a year the great dyeing ritual takes place. Everyone joins in and the colourful wools are then draped around the garden to dry. A vaulted and domed museum houses some of the finest works, while a gallery displays tapestries and batiks for sale.

The looms are set up in the various alcoves of a large whitewashed studio, as well as in small cells around a courtyard. In this yard, I watched the weavers at work, one or two to a room, with the doors open to let the sunlight slant in. The weavers' children play around them; a baby lies asleep in a nest of cloths in an upturned stool,

'Birds' by Thorya Hassan.

while its mother weaves nearby. During my visit, wild drumming and ululations suddenly broke out in celebration of a young weaver's engagement.

WATCHING THE QUICK fingers flying to and fro across the tapestry was dazzling – they moved so fast I could not see them. It seemed almost inconceivable that the emerging picture, with all its complex entanglement of flora and fauna, did not exist anywhere

outside the imagination of the weaver. Somehow the weaver knew that those fragments of coloured shapes were the lower halves of palm trees, flowering shrubs, a flock of sheep and a group of villagers.

That the weavers are Muslim, the Wissa Wassefs are Copts and many of those who buy the tapestries come from wholly different cultural and social backgrounds serves to emphasize the fact that the feeling inspiring these images at the most basic level – this

celebration of nature and human life in harmonious co-existence – is an eternal part of being human. We all understand it, we can all respond to it and we always will.

In these images of earthly paradise created by people living in an Egyptian village the underlying common love of life flows forth uninhibited. The true, creative urge is linked to this deep joy at the wider Creation, and can tap into its energies and reflect it back to us, regardless of material hardship.

How much more joy there would be in life if the many po-faced artists around the world could allow themselves to access this and to express it simply, to accept that it is enough – that it is all art need do. Creativity explored free from the theories and rigours, the intellectual snobbery, the vicious critical apparatus of modern art and thought, has a timeless message of joy for us all.   ●

LIVING TRADITIONS

"We have separated the cloth from the weaver.
We praise the beautiful cloth but ignore the weaver."
HAKU SHAH interviewed by SATISH KUMAR

HAKU SHAH IS AN ARTIST and a lover of indigenous people and their art and craft. He comes from a small village, rich in folk traditions. He has spent many years of his life among rural and tribal people.

What motivates the village people in Gujarat to spend so much time making beautiful things?
It is love for oneself, for one's own village or country or even the universe. The tribal people have sheer love for doing things, and that is why the things become fantastic. Schooling or academic knowledge can't create these kinds of things.

What is the use of these embroidered clothes?
They are used for dowry, for the daughter. Before she gets married, the mother, the aunts, everybody in the family starts embroidering skirts and blouses. The daughter herself from the age of 7 or 8 starts embroidering. They don't see these things as art objects, they are for use. For them there is no distinction between art and non-art.

And what is the process of learning?
It is just like the way the child learns to speak. The mother will be sewing and the daughter will learn from her. Through generations it was given like that. So learning was not an imposition but a natural outcome. Even in the formal teaching of craft in India the teacher keeps the students at his workshop and asks them to observe and do whatever he says. Observing the master at work and serving the master in every way including cooking and cleaning; these two combine in learning the craft. There is no distinction between the work of learning the craft and the work of everyday life.

What about the mirrorwork on people's clothes?
The small pieces of mirror reflect the light. People use mirror on clothes and on clay walls. They say that if we light one lamp in the house, we get hundreds of lamps. It brightens the whole house. It also reflects the colours. Run of Kuch is rather sober, it is a desert land, so the bright colours go very well in this landscape. That is why you see more mirror and more colour in Kuch. Sometimes people talk of poverty and think that the village people are poor, but when you see their costumes, their embroidery, their mirror work, you cannot say that they are poor. But modern values are different. We think that whoever has a car is a rich man, and whoever has a mud house is a poor man. That value judgement is wrong.

Is craft of high quality, available in plenty?
No, it is not. This sort of exquisite work is rare. There are some people who promote it for money and do marketing, but this sort of good work cannot come out of money motives. It was the sheer love for the daughter which was inspiring them to do such beautiful things. You know, they will have 400 or 500 mirrors in just one dress. We don't have even patience to see them doing it, never mind the patience to make it.

They not only used mirrors, they sewed cardamom seeds and cloves on to the clothes. When we see textiles, we only think of colour and texture. But these village people think of smell. Look at this clay horse. The stomach is made like a pot, the head is another pot, the leg is like (if you cut it in two) a roof tile. The potter told me that he makes a soul out of eight pieces.

We all had cultures based on crafts. But do we respect craftspeople? We give much greater importance to those who are intellectually clever, never mind if they can do nothing of substance.

Spinning is a symbol of all crafts but we have not understood it. We see handwoven cloth as something separate from the craft of weaving and more importantly from the weaver. We praise the cloth but completely ignore the weaver.

Photograph by Stephen P. Hulyer.

Banjara women, Maharashtra. Photograph by T. S. Randhawa.

How did you get involved in tribal art and culture?
I did my master's degree in painting but while studying I used to observe the terracotta horses in my own village. I developed an attachment with them. I felt more and more that academic study is not enough. I could see that my village had more to offer than my university. The tribal and rural art gives more knowledge of totality, of wholeness to the people and it enriches life. The rural people live close to the soil and so they are capable of expressing their natural love in their art and craft. If you go off the main road in the interior of the countryside, you find beautiful things.

What sort of work do you do with village people?
I go around meeting people and mixing with them. That makes me happy. I have been working closely with one person. It so happened that one day her husband came to me saying, "Haku, I need some money." So we started to talk. During our conversation I said "If your wife can make one appliqué for me I will be most delighted." I said it gently and in passing. I was very happy that she liked the idea. So, she made it. Gradually we developed a relationship and then she made two and a third and a fourth. She was more and more in it. She is a rare craftswoman. I made an exhibition of her appliqués in San Francisco and it was very well received. Then she made some very big appliqués and now she is

flourishing and says to her husband "You don't know what I am making!" I don't tell her address to anybody, and I don't allow the fashionable art dealers to make a media star out of her.

In fact, some pressmen came to me and they were very disappointed when I said that giving recognition to one or two craftsmen creates wrong feelings among them. Journalists say that in no time the whole thing will go: the city mind, the industrial mind, will wipe it out. But then I told them that people have something inherent which is love for natural things. People will have to return to the source of life. This cannot be done by writing about it. We have to live it.

The city culture is dominating our education in such a way that students think that this is the only culture. For example, look at this photo: here this young tribal girl has made a pipe out of a leaf, which she is smoking. We think she is uneducated, primitive. But why don't we see a pipe which is being made out of a leaf? It is a craft by itself, but we don't see that. And she is nearer to her own self. She was grazing cattle when I saw her. She was about 14 years old. So, you see what I mean when I say that we city people should give up this idea that our civilization is better and the rural people and the tribal people are uncivilized. City civilization and rural culture should learn to live together and particularly we, so-called educated people, must learn to respect the great qualities of the village traditions which are our roots.

Tell us about the tribal people.
I went to visit one of the tribal communities called Rathwas. They have beautiful paintings in their houses. The head of the village had a big house, he had cattle, he had a farm and he had paintings on the walls but when I saw him he wore only a loin-cloth and he was smoking a clay pipe. Now there are government people, city people who would like to do something for the rural folk, they would like to bring development to the villages, they would like to give them clothes which they don't need.

In New Guinea they gave clothes to the tribals and then whenever the officers came to visit, the tribals would put them on and as soon as the officers had gone, they would take them off.

We misunderstand the real values of these simple people. Their wealth is their lifestyle, their art and their culture which we must learn to respect. These people are much happier in themselves. As they are, they are fantastic. For example, they don't lock their doors. You go to any house, it is not locked. When we go to their house, they give us food. They are extremely hospitable. These tribal values are seen wrongly or not seen at all. If they make a painting on the wall, we don't see that. Who will see it? The archaeologists will see an old monument, the architects may not even reach it, the sociologists will say "Art is not necessary; food is necessary."

Each year the tribal people celebrate for a full day, the ancestor worship day. With flour paste they make forms. These forms have a very natural beauty. I took one painter to that area but he couldn't see any beauty in them. He said "Why did you bring me here? There is nothing!" Then I took some photographs of them and presented them as an exhibition. Then, of course, many artists, art critics and newspapers said: "Oh, these are fantastic paintings!" For the tribals, these are not paintings as such. They say, "We make a new day, we make a new wall, we feed the ancestors, we feed the wall." If they have to feed the ancestors, the have to feed themselves, they have to feed their cattle, they have to feed their wall, so they sprinkle flour paste because this is the unity of life. There is a strong relationship between us, our ancestors and everything else. We say that they are wasting the food, why do they sprinkle it on the wall? They should eat it. So we, the civilized and city people, do not understand the tribal traditions.

Are you saying that it is better not to bring so-called 'development' to the tribal people?
No. What I am saying is that before we make any judgement we should see that tribal people are doing things in their own way, we have to recognize them as they are, we have to see that, before we bring roads or modern education or whatever. We have to have a proper regard and respect for them. But it is difficult for so-called 'educated' people to get near them. We have to go to them, we have to see their death, we have to see their birth, we have to see their marriage, we have to see everything, but we only want to see them as museum objects. So, we do not really see them. We think that they are backward.

But I am always confused as to who is backward, who is forward. People always say "He is backward because he has a mud house, because his house has no doors." In India you don't have to close the doors and windows all the time, but the houses which are closed are considered to be the houses of a 'forward' people. But if you go in a village and see a mud house without doors it would be considered that they haven't any money for doors. And do you know that the huts without closed doors have some relationship with the outside environment? Those mud houses were being made through generations. Whereas we would like to impose on those people our knowledge of some four or forty years, the knowledge that is there for four thousand years we neglect.

For example, the tribal houses are made of cow dung and clay. It is such a fantastic subject and a lot of good ideas could come out of it but it has not been studied very well. Cow dung and clay keeps the air not too hot, not too cold. It is a natural insulation against heat and cold. If it is too hot outside, it will be cooler inside a cow dung and clay hut, if it is too cold outside, it is warm inside. This way the cow dung and clay together provide air conditioning.

Look at the storage jars. They are made of cow dung, clay and straw. These jars keep the grain very well. We have yet to find an alternative to cow dung and clay. There is nothing. Not one solution has been found which is as good. Particularly, a cow dung and clay house is most suitable in India. Out of cow dung and clay the whole culture came into being.

When they paint the walls of their houses the off-white colour has first to be applied by unmarried girls; only then the artists, the Lakharas, come. First they take a vow to be faithful to the ancestors and to each other. Then the musicians play music while the artists are painting. Then the trance man, the holy man, comes to approve and bless the painting and then the whole village dances and feasts. Sacrifices are offered to the painting. They feed the figures. One of the tribal men said to me: "We feel at night as if the horses of the wall paintings run." So it isn't just a wall painting, it is God, it isn't space and colour and texture, it is Life itself. Ritual makes these people, they live by it. ●

Women preparing trays for silkworms in the Rishi Valley, Andhra Pradesh.

Mandanas, or floor designs, are painted for important occasions. Photograph by Stephen P. Hulyer.

ALL HANDS TO WORK

A craft economy makes peace possible.

BY SATISH KUMAR

TODAY PEOPLE ASK if we can afford to have an economy based on handicrafts. But according to Gandhi's long term and comprehensive understanding of economic principles, the opposite is true: we cannot afford not to have one.

Industrialization brings many costs. In the context of India, Mahatma Gandhi presented an alternative. He envisioned a mode of production which was home-grown, people controlled, small-scale, decentralized and locally driven. He named it *swadeshi*. This was an economy dependent on craftspeople, artisans, small-scale farmers and businesspeople. *Swadeshi* brings wealth and enrichment in many forms.

When India was colonized, her economy underwent a great change. The British believed in centralized, industrialized and mechanized modes of production. Gandhi turned this principle on its head. In his words, "Not mass production, but production by the masses."

By adopting the principle of production by the masses, village or town communities would be able to restore dignity to the work done by human hands. There is an intrinsic value in anything we do with our hands, and in handing work over to machines we lose not only the material benefits but also the spiritual benefits, for work by hand brings with it a meditative mind and self-fulfillment.

Gandhi wrote, "It is a tragedy of the first magnitude that millions of people have ceased to use their hands as hands. Nature has bestowed upon us this great gift which is our hands. If the craze for machinery methods continues, it is highly likely that a time will come when we shall be so incapacitated and weak that we shall begin to curse ourselves for having forgotten the use of the living machines given to us by God. Millions cannot keep fit by games and athletics; and why should they exchange the useful, productive, hardy occupations for the useless, unproductive and expensive sports and games?"

Mass production is only concerned with the product, whereas production by the masses is concerned with the product, the producer and the process.

The driving force behind mass production is a cult of the individual. What motive can there be for the expansion of the economy on a global scale, other than the desire for personal and corporate profit?

In contrast, a locally based economy enhances community spirit, community relationships and community well-being. Such an economy encourages mutual aid. Members of the village take care of themselves, their families, their neighbours, their animals, lands, forestry and all the natural resources for the benefit of present and future generations.

Mass production leads people to leave their villages, their land, their crafts and their homesteads and go to work in factories. Instead of dignified human beings and members of a self-respecting community, people become cogs in the machine, standing at the conveyor belt, living in shanty towns and depending on the mercy of the bosses. Then fewer and fewer people are needed to work, because the industrialists want greater productivity.

The masters of the money economy want more and more efficient machines working faster and faster, and the result is that men and women are thrown on the scrap-heap of unemployment. Such a society generates rootless and jobless millions living as dependents of the state or begging on the streets. In *swadeshi*, the machine is subordinated to the worker; it is not be allowed to become the master, dictating the pace of human activity. Similarly, market forces serve the community rather than forcing people to fit the market.

Gandhi knew that, with the globalization of the economy, every nation would wish to export more and import less to keep the balance of payments in its favour. There would be a perpetual economic crisis, perpetual unemployment, and perpetually discontented and disgruntled human beings.

Potter in Jandali village, Punjab. Photographs by Mark Edwards/Still Pictures.

Woodcarver's hamlet in ludiya, Gujarat. Photograph by Stephen P. Hulyer

In communities practising *swadeshi*, economics has a place but does not dominate society. Beyond a certain limit, economic growth becomes detrimental to human well-being. The modern world view is that the more material goods you have, the better your life will be.

But Gandhi said, "A certain degree of physical comfort is necessary, but above a certain level it becomes a hindrance instead of a help; therefore, the ideal of creating an unlimited number of wants and satisfying them seems to be a delusion and a trap. The satisfaction of one's physical needs must come at a certain point to a dead stop before it degenerates into physical decadence. Europeans will have to remodel their outlook if they are not to perish under the weight of the comforts to which they are becoming slaves."

In order to protect their economic interests, countries go to war – military war as well as economic war. Gandhi said, "People have to live in village communities and simple homes rather than desire to live in palaces." Millions of people will never be able to live at peace with each other if they are constantly fighting for a higher standard of living.

We cannot have real peace in the world if we look at each other's countries as sources for raw materials or as markets for finished industrial goods. The seeds of war are sown with economic greed. If we analyze the causes of war throughout history, we find that the pursuit of economic expansion consistently leads to military adventures. "There is enough for everybody's need, but not enough for everybody's greed," said Gandhi. *Swadeshi* is thus a prerequisite for peace.

The economists and industrialists of our time fail to see when enough is enough. Even when countries reach a very high material standard of living, they are still caught up with the idea of economic growth. Those who do not know when enough is enough will never have enough, but those who know when enough is enough already have enough.

Swadeshi is the way to comprehensive peace: peace with oneself, peace between peoples, and peace with nature. The global economy drives people toward high performance, high achievement, and high ambition for materialistic success. This results in stress, loss of meaning, loss of inner peace, loss of space for personal and family relationships, and loss of spiritual life. Gandhi realized that in the past, life in India was not only prosperous but also conducive to spiritual development. *Swadeshi* for Gandhi was the spiritual imperative.

Historically, the Indian local economy was dependent upon the most productive and sustainable agriculture and horticulture and on pottery, furniture making, metalwork, jewellery, leather work and many other economic activities. But its basis had traditionally been in textiles. Each village had its spinners, carders, dyers and weavers who were the heart of the village economy. However, when India was flooded with machine-made, inexpensive, mass-produced textiles from England, the local textile artists were rapidly put out of business and the village economy suffered terribly. Gandhi thought it essential that the industry be restored and started a campaign to stem the influx of British cloth.

Due to his efforts, hundreds of thousands of untouchables and caste Hindus joined together to discard the mill-made clothes imported from England or from city factories, and learned to spin their own yarn and weave their own cloth. The spinning-wheel became the symbol of economic freedom, political independence, and cohesive and classless communities. The weaving and wearing of homespun cloth became marks of distinction for all social groups. Thus reclaiming the textile industry on the most local level possible, i.e. home spinning, was a powerful part of the political movement for independence and national self-determination.

According to Gandhi, economics and politics should not simply be concerned with material things but should be the means to fulfillment of cultural, religious and spiritual ends. In fact, economics should not be separated from the deep spiritual foundations of life. This can best be achieved when every individual is an integral part of the community; when the production of goods is on a small scale; when the economy is local; and when homemade handicrafts are given preference. These conditions are conducive to a holistic, spiritual, ecological and communitarian pattern of society.

In Gandhi's view, spiritual values should not be separated from politics, economics, agriculture, education and all other activities of daily life. In this integral design, there is no conflict between spiritual and material. It is no good for some people to close themselves in a monastic order practising religion and for other people to say that a spiritual life is only for saints and celibates. Such a separation of religion from society will breed corruption, greed, competition, power mania and the exploitation of the weak and poor. Politics and economics without idealism will be a kind of prostitution, like sex without love.

Someone asked Gandhi, "What do you think of Western civilization?" He simply replied, "It would be a good idea." For Gandhi a machine civilization was no civilization. A society in which workers had to labour at a conveyor belt, in which animals were treated cruelly in factory farms, and in which economic activity necessarily led to ecological devastation, could not be conceived of as civilization. Its citizens could only end up as neurotics, the natural world would inevitably be transformed into a desert and its cities into concrete jungles. In other words, global industrial society, as opposed to society made up of largely autonomous communities committed to the principle of *swadeshi*, is unsustainable. *Swadeshi* for Gandhi was a sacred principle – as sacred for him as the principle of truth and non-violence. Every morning and evening, Gandhi repeated his commitment to *swadeshi* in his prayers.

Swadeshi enables people to make, live with and use beautiful things through which they gain cultural richness, because their economy is in their hands, and they are not in the grip of a system of mass production. ●

A Thuri couple making mats, brushes and rope from grass. Photograph by T. S. Randhawa.

MADE TO MEASURE

The renaissance of the local shoemaker.

BY ROGER DEAKIN

I T IS NOT so very long since every town and village in this country had at least one shoemaker – 'shummackers', as they were called here in Suffolk. In my own village, the neighbours who live in what was once the shoemaker's cottage still find odd bits of leather in corners, or dig them up in the garden.

Boots or shoes were always hand-made, and cost a couple of weeks' wages, so most country people only had a single pair, which they generally had re-soled once a year. Younger children often went barefoot. Boots only came down in price when they began to be mass-produced in the factories of Northampton. Sold in town shops, these were known in the villages as 'bought' boots, as opposed to the 'made' boots from the shoemaker. 'Made' were superior to 'bought' in comfort and strength, and kept out the weather better. The town or village shoemaker 'had the measure' of everyone, and enjoyed the same kind of lifelong relationship with the parish people as the vicar or schoolteacher. A good pair of boots was essential to anyone working on the land.

Following the almost total eclipse of these local shoemakers by cheaper mass-produced shoes, it was, until recently, only the makers at the top end of the market who survived. John Lobb's in St James's have been making boots and shoes for the Royal family since the 1860s, and a pair of their traditional brogues will cost you well over £1,500. James Taylor & Sons have made bespoke leather shoes in Paddington Street since 1857. "Getting the customer's first pair right is the hard part," says Peter Schweiger, who inherited the business from his father. "It takes several fittings, and people can be impatient." The upper is stretched wet around one of the hundreds of carved beechwood lasts, each numbered and labelled with the name of the customer whose feet they represent. They are a powerful physical presence, panelling the walls of the workshops.

The firm makes about 350 pairs of shoes a year, and each will take from three to eight months or more to make, costing anything from £895. (A shoe factory may make as many in an hour.) Customers tend to stay for life, and about half the

shoes made are repeat orders, which are generally easier and a hint less expensive to make. The old shoemakers' pun 'We get to know our people body and sole' expresses the particular intimacy of their craft.

IN RECENT YEARS the tradition of the local shoemaker has been re-invented in Devon by Green Shoes of Totnes. The firm was founded in 1981 by Alison Hastie to hand-make shoes to a high standard. Alison had graduated in English from Exeter University, but had a passion to design and make shoes. She began by working for another firm of independent shoemakers in Totnes, Conkers, which had begun life in the late seventies originally making just four or five pairs of shoes a week. Alison later opened Green Shoes with a partner, and all the shoemakers have always been women for the perfectly simple reason that the half-dozen of them have always worked well together in an atmosphere you recognize the minute you enter the shop as at once convivial and creative.

In the workshops behind the shop and upstairs, Alison, Flora, Liz, Steph, Mirren and Gillian work amongst stacked rolls of coloured leather: green, blue, grey, plum, brown, red. Another member of the group, Hilary, makes leather bags from home. A radio plays. Jam jars overflow with buckles, rivets, eyelets or ski-hooks. Skeins of shoelaces hang around the walls, pale blue lasts are pigeon-holed in rows, and on another set of shelves is an array of children's lasts. Liz is seated at a sewing machine stitching the uppers of children's T-bar sandals in green, apricot and red. Customers' orders, with drawings of their feet attached, lie beside a cutting board. Even the Apple Mac computer sitting in one corner does nothing to detract from the robust air of low tech about the place.

All the Green Shoes are custom-made to last from carefully selected leather, traditionally stitched so they can be resoled or repaired. The great bonus of such individually-made shoes is that they are just too comfortable to take off. I know this from many hours, and miles, of happy walking. They become, quite simply, a second skin. Comfort, indeed, is what the handmade shoemaker is principally selling: it is what brings the customers back. "We have no interest in making shoes that are 95% fashion and restrict the wearer, but we do make innovative and challenging shoes that enable our customers to be brave and make a more individual statement," says Alison Hastie.

I discovered the shop in the High Street near the top of Totnes hill a couple of years ago, tipped off by a Norfolk couple who have ordered twenty pairs of boots, shoes and sandals between them in recent years. I live in a pair of donkey-brown sandals from Green Shoes day and night all summer, and the firm's handsome ten-hole Dartmoor boots in winter. I have yet another pair, chocolate brown, warm and figure-hugging, which I wear about the house.

Prices are much more modest than in the West End of London, ranging from £45 to £250. New customers have their feet measured and drawn, or are instructed how to send in their measurements and a pencilled outline of each foot by post. People tend to come back for more shoes, or bring in purchases of an earlier vintage, nicely worn in, for resoling. You will always see several high-mileage

Shoes decorated by indigenous people from around the world, from the Camper Shoe Company in Majorca.

Hand-made shoes from Green Shoes.

specimens on the workbench being resoled with Vibram, crêpe or cleated rubber ready for a new lease of life.

About 60% of the customers live locally and most other sales are by mail order. Alison Hastie finds that customers much prefer knowing the people who make their shoes – as they always used to do in the days before trainers, global brands and throwaway footwear. Whoever met the maker of their Nike or Adidas trainers? The delight of Green Shoes is that they are the very opposite of trainers: not mass-produced in some anonymous, miserable sweatshop on the far side of the globe but made close to home by real craftspeople you can get to know, actually enjoying their work, taking delight in the pleasures and fruits of their skills

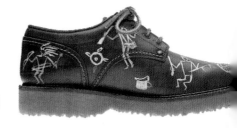

and in the well-being and appreciation of their customers.

What a difference there is here, and what a future our rural towns and villages could have with many more such small-scale, independent enterprises creating better quality products for people they know and like! The American poet Wendell Berry expressed the principle succinctly:

"Spend your money with your friends." Green Shoes is significant, because it proves that you can still make things locally on a modest, human scale and offer personal service over the long term – and that you can do it successfully. There's nothing new about the idea, but I hope it catches on – and wasn't it a man called Schumacher who said "small is beautiful"? ●

WILLOW WORKERS

Somerset's culture is documented by the painter Kate Lynch.

BY OLIVER LOWENSTEIN

REG HECTOR MAKES HIS WAY up from his terraced cottage, and greets his friend, Kate Lynch, and me. He ushers us towards a small collection of sheds. In the dimming light of dusk are bundles and bundles of willow rods. Retired for some years, Reg may not be as agile as he was, but willow-growing is in his bones and he isn't about to stop just because he's eighty. He's one of the very few remaining Somerset willow growers who still ply their craft, which has been around for thousands of years. But the decline in willow crafts reflects the recent changes in agriculture: a century ago, before agriculture's industrialization, Somerset was the epicentre of rural willow-growing.

I've been brought to meet Reg Hector by Kate Lynch, who over the last three years has instigated a wide-ranging documenting of this continuing tradition, focusing on the lives and work of the once widespread Somerset willow industry. Soon after moving to the Somerset levels, Lynch, a painter, attuned her interest in land and landscape towards a particular community connected to the terrain of her new home: the small band of makers who have maintained an unbroken connection between the craft of basket-weaving and the watery flood plains of this mid-south-west British county.

In 1999 Lynch began painting these mainly older and, with one exception, male willow growers and weavers while they worked. Since that time she has produced a broad canvas of paintings, charcoal works and drawings, evocatively documenting the different stages of the craft process: from harvesting the willow, through the various stages of preparation, be it stripping or boiling, to the stage when the willow is turned and woven into baskets and other rural artefacts. Her enthusiasm and energy have in turn led to Lynch recording the thoughts and memories of the willow workers.

The paintings evoke an atmospheric, dark and muted feeling of Somerset life: not surprising, as many, executed during the winter months, are of darkened attic interiors where the slow, meditative

repetition needed for a basket to gradually form often happens.

Perhaps people know something of willow's long-standing place in the Somerset wetlands as they whisk along the motorway to the holiday destinations of Devon and Cornwall. There is Serena de la Hey's great willow man running along the motorway, ever present to remind motorists that these flatlands are willow country. Somerset's watery channels fed nearly 3,000 acres of annually harvested acreage until at least the end of the nineteenth century. Some parts of Norfolk and Lancashire aside, Somerset was the centre of basketmaking for the whole country.

The willow was harvested all through the winter months and stored until it was needed. When the orders came in from late spring onwards, the withies of brown willow were first boiled; this process released tannin within the bark, which stained the inner wood the ruddy brown colour. After the boiling, the rods would be left to dry, before the brown willow was graded and sorted. A few willows were left growing in water-heavy soil until April, when, with the sap naturally beginning to rise, they could be harvested and the bark could be peeled off, exposing the distinctive creamy white willow. There was a short period during May when the whole community was involved in this white willow harvest. Up until the 1920s complete families would turn out for the crucial month of the willow year, May, with even the school holidays organized to fit into this seasonal cycle. This white willow was used particularly for making laundry- and bread-baskets, as well as cribs.

Today there are still four working boilers, and this tradition has continued, albeit in modified form. It is this story of a whole way of life that Lynch's exhibition fully relates.

Up until the interwar period, willow was the mainstay of the basket industry in Somerset, just as it had been in Roman times. But as the war years approached, plastic arrived and things changed for basketry; once the habits of the modern 'throw-

Eddie Barnard tapping the willows down tight.

away' society were well entrenched with the dubious pleasures of the disposable plastic bag, even the long permanence of a well-kept wooden basket paled against its short-term rival.

Although Lynch cautions against any description of willow basketry being an almost dead craft, today the number of working basketmakers on the levels can be counted on two pairs of hands. Of these, all are over thirty-five; and for most, the skills have been passed on from within families, sometimes through four or five generations. That said, there is a thriving national willow basket society with a newsletter that goes out to a thousand members worldwide.

The acreage of willow land in Somerset remains constant at around 300, and there has been some diversification. The Coates family opened the Willow and Wetland Centre, which has thrived; another family, the Hills, has been making Cameron balloon baskets for the ballooning fraternity. Willow has also been reintroduced as a natural stabilizing material on riversides, and is a proven ecological alternative to concrete in this respect.

Lynch talks of how those few basketmakers she knows are in touch "with something that was very old, the way of weaving being the same as it was late in the Iron Age." ●

THE WAY OF THE COOK

Good food on the table represents skill, experience and practice.

BY JULIA PONSONBY

LONG BEFORE WE great apes needed to craft clothes, homes, furniture or boats, we needed to make tools to help us find food. We began to poke grubs out of holes with sticks, and we began, sometimes, to wash the earth off our root vegetables. It was the beginning of the craft of cooking. Long afterwards, we began to use fire to transform our food from raw to cooked. We began to create pots to hold the hot food, and to carve spoons to stir it. Who knows at what point we began to spice it up by adding herbs, salt from the sea and other seasonings.

Over thousands of years the uniquely human activity of fire-centred cooking has proliferated all over the world alongside the expansion of human life. Rich local diversity of cooking skills and recipes evolved, reflecting the variety of habitats and the nature of their productivity and people. This in turn was reflected in the development of an enormous variety of cooking techniques and tools.

Once upon a time you had to travel to a particular place to eat of its cuisine. Not only lack of ingredients, but lack of skill in another place made it difficult to replicate the dish out of its native context. Nowadays this true authenticity is being undermined over and over again. The last century has brought freezer ships, air transport and the internationalization of ingredients. But despite this, the association of place with food remains strong.

If I think back over my life I can associate the making of certain foods with certain places, and they are always the traditional foods of the region. As a child I was taken to Mont St Michel in France,

and as we climbed the holy mountain our ears were assailed by the rhythmic guttural pulse of crepes being tossed high by expert crepe makers. It was the first time I had eaten pancakes (as I knew them) with anything other than sugar or lemon. It was the first time I had seen these large circles of egg, flour and milk produced so finely, and the first time I had seen them fly so high in the air. How much care and attention must be involved in such a process! Likewise, though pasta is now a staple part of the diet in the UK and worldwide, it took a visit to Tuscany to appreciate the full diversity of fresh handmade pasta in its original context. As I sat in medieval Siena eating pasta with wild mushrooms and freshly grated parmesan, I reflected on the craftsmanship involved in spinning these threads of spaghetti and how this must have long been the job of local professionals.

If I think of trips to India I recall the skills involved in rolling of chapatis at Rishi Valley School and other places, seeing these small rounds of wheat being spread out and stacked high before cooking. I have never been entirely happy with my attempts to reproduce local specialities I've eaten abroad, but continue to want to try to make these different breads. It is not just the mechanical process you have to get right, as the whole ambiance feeds in – the sun, the mood of the people (which reflects the culture), the subtle differences in the nutritional content of the grains the land gives rise to, high or low gluten etc., and the kind of oven that is used. I always wonder how much experience and practice is involved in all this.

A noodlemaker in Tokyo. Photograph by Satish Kumar.

In Mexico, corn flour is used to create tortillas which can be eaten hard or soft – the south American version of chapatis, perhaps. Although simple metal taco presses are now commonly used, you can still see women patting out their tortillas between their hands, flipping the expanding disc from one to the other. Such everyday tasks become part of life's cyclic gesture, as much as the swirling of prayer wheels in Buddhist Ladakh or the counting of Catholic rosary beads. Indeed, in Hindu India the traditional appointment of high caste Brahmin as household chefs acknowledged the indelible bond between tasks of nurturing the spirit and nurturing the body.

Staying on the island of Karpathos in Greece, our landlady served us bread for breakfast that was still baked on a weekly basis in large brick bread ovens shared by the community. At the beginning of the week the bread was fluffy inside and crusty. It needed to be sliced carefully so as not to squash down. By the end of the week you could cut leathery slices as finely as you liked and the almost lemony tang of unbleached flour had matured. It was like eating two kinds of bread. One day we chanced upon a baking session and were fascinated to see the large rounded ovens being stuffed with wood and set ablaze. The charred wood and ashes were then removed and the bread and pasties carefully stacked into the open mouth of the smouldering hot oven. As we left the scene, an old Greek lady in black tapped our shoulders and pressed into our hands two piping hot pasties. We walked back over the hills by small white washed chapels and olive trees blowing on our pasties and gradually nibbling them up. Rarely do I remember anything tasting so good as that spinach and potato pasty. I realized that baking of bread and pasties was not only a fine art but also a fine way of life.

But the craftsmanship in cooking lies not just in local skills, fresh local ingredients and recipes – no two cooks ever cook exactly the same. They are the composers of gastronomic symphonies for our tastebuds. Taking the same recipe, one person can produce a masterpiece that you can't eat enough of, whilst another person will produce a dull, boring tasteless flop. What is the difference? As with all

A potato basket (maund) by Raymond Skinner. Photograph by David Baker.

crafts, some people have more of a nose for cooking than others. They enjoy it more and put more love into it. They are elegant with their knife-work, and care for what they are doing. They long to share it and give pleasure. They taste again and again and have a good intuitive sense of what a bit of this or a bit of that will do to a dish. They do not put theory before deliciousness or let information deter their fingertips from adding that crucial tad more of this or that. When it comes to serving the dish, they seem to have an almost instinctive sense of what to accompany it with to obtain a nutritional and aesthetic balance. There is a synergy between what is healthy and what delicious – and they have tapped into it!

The role of the cook as an artist or craftsperson is sadly being undermined by the growth of the fast food industry. The impersonal robot chefs that mass-produce snacks for general consumption have no concern for how many bags of crisps or bars of chocolate we buy or what other food we accompany them with. Preservatives and other additives that would horrify a household cook are the name of the game. The rise of the fast food market in the west is part of a process that is destroying the fine profession and pleasure of cooking. Cooking becomes a hobby or a TV spectator sport, and it becomes difficult for many to maintain any sense of balance in their diet, despite modern insights into the effects of eating carbohydrates, proteins, sugar, salt, fat and vitamins. The temptations are too great. In a sense, the limitation of food in former times helped to focus cooking and consumption in a way that was more appropriate to our lifestyle and we were able to develop suitable techniques and skills. Now, sadly, the craft of regular, house-

Soups at Schumacher College. Photograph by Nick Philbedge.

hold cooking (from scratch) is fast disappearing.

Going back to aesthetics of food, an experiment in a prison showed that when food was served on beautiful pottery dishes, prisoners ate more and digested better. For me, school meals associated with worn white plates and oversize stainless steel serving dishes never tasted good. Another aspect of the good cook's aesthetic lies in choosing vibrant colour combinations and creating interesting shapes. With it comes a determined wish to avoid mechanization of the process of food making. Although when catering for large numbers it is tempting to grate all your carrots on a food processor, we cannot pretend that the quality of the experience for the cook is as satisfactory.

Direct fingertip contact with the raw materials is lost and the jangling sounds of machinery invade the peace, so how can you put as much love into your recipe? Likewise the furniture makers who do all the sawing, sanding and polishing by hand may feel more in touch with their creations. The result will have a more harmonious feel to it.

We often think of professional cooks as chefs: it sounds much grander. Chefs may have been trained in cordon bleu cookery or learned a specialist task like pastry making. I prefer the word cook. They nurture family and friends. The former wear great white hats, and may have teams of sous-chefs and kitchen-maids and potato scrubbers supporting their great banqueting work! The latter, meanwhile, try to remember to tie their hair back and often work on their own or with one or two friends or family to help. Cooks can turn cooking into an art if they have their favourite tools and the goddess of the hearth, Hestia, working with them. ●

95

CARING
FOR NATURE

Through touching materials
and working with them
I get an understanding of those
materials which you can
only get through touch.
I understand snow, leaves, feathers,
mud, sticks and stones around.

Andy Goldsworthy

'Little Sparta', by Ian Hamilton Finlay. Photograph by Andrew Lawson.

97

TREADING LIGHTLY

A new counter-culture of sustainability.

BY ALEXANDER MURDIN

THE IDEA OF environmental responsibility in craft is something that has developed in the last twenty years as a reaction to changes that have made our society predominantly urbanized and industrial, both conceptually and demographically. For many craftspeople this alienation from nature started with society's unquestioning acceptance of a dispassionate science that refused to become involved with the reality of nature. The mechanistic world-view of Newtonian science, one of cause and effect, encouraged a world-view where we believed we were ultimately in control.

With the emergence of the new biological sciences of the past fifty years this world-view has been effectively challenged, with ecology, holistic biology, energy economics and the study of complex systems through chaos theory revolutionizing traditional science. Previously, science's position had been one of the observer theorizing with no moral or cultural context, in a quest for a utopia that would be realized through technology.

However, the environmental sciences have now shown that science and technology cannot exist in isolation, unaware of the consequences of innovation and development. Ecosystems are robust and have been built up over vast periods of time but are vulnerable to human, short-term solutions and pressures. At the beginning of the twenty-first century this holistic world-view of ecology is claimed as the new metaphysic: where we can break free from the culture of the self and become part of a spiritual world again. Environmental theories reintroduced untidiness and mutability to our culture, the reductionist debate of art versus science turning in favour of the artistic experience. Art and craft informed by environmentalism have entered the scientific and technological sphere to criticize and illuminate. In return, science now acknowledges the validity of human subjectivity in scientific observation, thereby admitting human creativity back into the mainstream of society.

Within the art world, this breakdown of materialistic values has been paralleled by the decline of modernism which emphasized an individual and non-relational art, supported by the art market. Craftspeople, by the very nature of what they do, are involved in the new counter-culture, producing work that is made on a small scale and frequently selling this work on a one-to-one basis to the consumer. As the craft critic Gloria Hickey puts it, "Craft occupies an ironic position: that of a commodity that rebels against the marketplace." But sustainability is not just about 'opting out' of normal economic patterns; it affects materials used in creation of work, methods of production and it also has a spiritual dimension.

The materials used in the creation of work often form a backbone to a sustainable approach to craft. For instance, many furniture-makers are insisting that their materials are from sustainable forestry and are avoiding imported hardwoods such as mahogany. Guy Martin, a furniture-maker from Somerset, creates chairs, tables and boxes from local coppiced woods such as willow, which will go on producing wood year after year with no detrimental deforestation; this raw material is from the Somerset levels where he works, and does not require energy-consuming transportation. The finished piece of work will last ten times longer than a factory-produced equivalent. Martin, however, does not stop there, and reflects the origin of the material in its appearance, developing a transparency of design that creates a monastic purity in the work, or, as he says of his designs, "to achieve a balance between the physical, mental and spiritual needs of people".

Some makers take their low-impact responsibilities even further, and prefer to use recycled materials. Tony Mann creates toys or automata on this basis, utilizing found objects that are incorporated into work as much for their aesthetic value as for their ecological soundness. In doing so, other associated ideas about industrial history and the vanish-

'Throne' by Paul Anderson. Photograph by Paul Wilkinson.

ing values of quality and longevity are dealt with.

The use of indigenous materials can also have importance when creating work for a specific place. In a time when the predominant form of vernacular architecture is the ubiquitous sterile box, it is more important than ever that design and materials for buildings break free from the norm. Craftspeople can contribute a sense of identity for architectural projects by creating unique designs that reflect the nature of a particular location. There is a whole range of interventions that artists can make, from wrought iron railings to street lighting, mosaic paving to sculpture in the square. The environmentally sensitive approach is demonstrated by Jill Smallcombe and Jackie Abey, two artists who use cob, a mixture of earth and straw, to make powerful sculptures. The use of this material is an ancient practice that creates well insulated and functional buildings. Abey and Smallcombe reflect this history in their sculpture by constructing monumental towers and columns, using the differences in the nature of the earth at a particular location in order to give each work certain visual characteristics.

However, it is not only in the production of work itself that sustainable ideas can be expressed but also in their functionality. An initial impression of the lighting designs of Mike Stevenson would lead most people to conclude that here was work that was part of an industrial design process, using high-tech materials, and that was inherently profligate with energy. In spite of this appearance, the work actually uses low-voltage light-emitting diodes that are much more energy-efficient than usual light sources. They are also being run off a water wheel, demonstrating how even the most sophisticated technology can be worked from an environmentally friendly energy source.

In 1940 Bernard Leach, the famous St Ives potter, wrote that craft "since the day of William Morris, represents the chief means of defence against the materialism of industry and its insensibility to beauty." Perhaps, sixty years later, the widespread acceptance of the need for environmental responsibility has finally confirmed this point of view and contemporary craft will reach the larger audience it deserves. ●

GUY MARTIN

Materials must be loved for their own sake.

BY SANDY BROWN

I HAVE BEEN included (with some pride I must admit) twice in Pseud's Corner in *Private Eye*, and have a fear that it could happen again with what I am about to write. Nevertheless . . .

I am often aware that I feel my response to works of art as a physical, visceral sensation in my body. For example, if I admire the technique in the making of a table, or if I like the clean lines, then I can feel it in my frontal temporal lobes, and not anywhere else in my body. But it is not enough to have a visceral response only in my head: I want my whole body to feel something.

And that is why I love Guy Martin's work. In particular a Dining Chair made from willow and ash. It has heart, and soul. Which means that my response to it is – all right, I'll come out with the phrase which could get me into *Private Eye* again – something I can feel in all the *chakras* of my body.

The sensation in the base *chakra*, an earthy groundedness, is there in the wholesome use of the ash in the legs of the chair, the wood beautifully rounded and sensual. Also, I am aware that the chair has heart too, in the way the materials are loved for their own sakes, the ash undisguised, unpainted, unvarnished, just being itself: and the willow in its willow-ness, honest, naked, visible, celebrated. And something magical happens in the overall chair which I can feel everywhere in my body, glowing. It is an extraordinary synthesis of intuitive design, an implausible construction of bendings and joinings, with a transformational halo curved around its back. It is a chair which looks as if it has evolved out of drawing in wood in three-dimensional space.

I imagine Martin enjoys playing with the complexity of construction. He has a great knowledge of how materials behave, of how they can bend, and also a pleasure in inventing new methods which bring in elements of weaving, of ancient hurdle-fence-making, of modernism, of cross-word-puzzle-devising, and of what looks like the simple pleasure of inserting the joinings, various metal pins, in an obvious way.

What I find most inspiring about his work is that he is bringing a tradition forward and making it contemporary. We do not have enough appreciation of this in our culture, which all too readily searches for the sensational and the new in art. I have nothing against being new and sensational if the new and sensational is truly wonderful, as Jackson Pollock or the brilliant ceramic artist Peter Voulkos were. They shook up a world which needed shaking up.

But it is much easier to break down a closed door. When all the doors are open, as they are now in art, it is impossible to make the impact that comes through an initial sensational breakthrough. So, in our search for the new and sensational, we forget that eternal values like those expressed in Martin's work can be remarkable for their ability to re-interpret something as old as the chair.

Martin is very much a modern artist: he was shortlisted for the prestigious Jerwood Prize – the most important prize open to craftspeople. He studied and later was a tutor for many years at the renowned Parnham College (set up by John Makepeace and famous for its understanding and promotion of ecological concerns).

Martin exhibits in the real world, and has a website, and yet he lives close to where his willow and ash grow. That is a true, real image of a modern artist. I use the word 'artist' for Guy Martin, as of course he is an artist. There are those who believe that you cannot be an artist and a craftsperson as well. That is absolute rubbish. Of course craftspeople are artists – if they are artists, that is. Not all so-called artists are artists, either.

And to take me neatly around in a spiral, I will say that for me the way to distinguish an artist from the crowd is the quality of the visceral response in the body. So I urge you to watch out for yours, learn to observe your responses. Be aware of your body, how it feels in the presence of art, and learn from it. ●

Dining chair made from coppiced willow. Photograph courtesy of the Devon Guild of Craftsmen.

LIVING STRUCTURES

Sculptures which grow with the seasons.

BY JON WARNES

LIVING WILLOW is an exciting medium to work with to create a sculpture or structure that can grow and change with the seasons. Willow's unique properties of easy rooting, pliability and fast growth make it ideal for large-scale work. Over the last few years living structures have become very popular due to the upsurge of interest in gardening and the use of natural materials and growing environmental awareness.

Freshly cut willow rods can be pushed straight into the ground and will root easily in a wide range of soils. The rods, which are usually one or two year growth, can range from several feet long to over twelve foot depending on variety. Their length and pliability means that the long rods can be interwoven to create a full size structure so that there is an immediate impact before any growth has occurred. Subsequent growth can be woven in, left to grow wild or pruned back in the autumn.

There are many varieties of willow, with a range of stem colour, leaf shape and catkins. Growth rates and pliability also differ between varieties, many of which were developed for use in basketry. Basketry varieties tend to be shorter and slower growing, so are used less in large structures. Much of the recent work has been made using biomass willow such as Bowles Hybrid. Biomass willows have been bred for exceptionally fast growth. They are grown on a short rotation and coppiced (cut down) every several years. The willow (biomass) is then burnt in wood-fired power stations to create electricity. They tend to be very straight, quick growing and are available in long rods (twelve feet plus). They are also easily available because they were planted by farmers for government-sponsored biomass trials, which ended several years ago. However they do have disadvantages, such as rust in older growth. Some varieties may also attract wasps, a problem in public places!

With the recent growth of interest it can be difficult to get hold of good willow. A way round this is to set up your own withy bed. I have found that half an allotment provides plenty of material and when a mulch mat is used to control weed growth very little maintenance is needed. Good varieties include Viminalis X Mollisima and Continental for long, fast growing structural rods. Albas provide colour, Britzensis is a bright red and Vitellina a bright yellow. The mauve coloured Daphnoides have lovely catkins and grow well in poor soils.

Work on living sculpture is usually done from late autumn to early spring when the leaves have fallen and the willow is dormant. This is the ideal time as there is no water loss through the leaves before roots form. Willow is cut during this time, usually every one or two years, and in the following springtime stools send out new shoots. Ideally the rods are not cut until needed; otherwise they should to be stored in a shady corner with the ends in water.

Choose a suitable site, not too dry, and use freshly cut material, carefully selected for a range of colours and textures. Avoid sites where the structure will be shaded in the summer, as willow likes a lot of light to grow well. Knowledge of basic techniques is important for a long-lasting structure. A range of skills is used from basketry and horticulture. Consequently people from different backgrounds and with different skills have become involved in living willow work. Careful planning of the structure is important. Upright rods will tend to grow mainly from their tops. Including diagonal members will encourage lower growth and give strength. Planting the living rods through a mulch mat keeps down weeds and grass which benefits the first year's growth and makes maintenance much easier. Chipped bark is an alternative, but tends to blow away. Basketry techniques can be used to weave the willow together, especially where non-living willow is used. The two most useful strokes are 'pairing' and 'randing' (an in-and-out weave).

Split willow 'God's eyes' and willow ties can be used to hold the rods together. String or thin rubber tubing can also be used. As the willow grows and expands, fixed ties will need re-tying as otherwise they will cut into the stem and may eventually kill the plant. Tying stems firmly together may result in them growing together, 'grafting' so that they

Living willow chair, by John Warnes.

Chris Drury, the landscape artist, has used willow in his sculptural work, creating living domes such as 'Covered Cairn' in Denmark (1993). Chris Drury writes in *Found Moments in Time and Space* of the unseen hazards: "The dome was woven from hazel running in one direction, willow in the other. While the hazel would die, the willow would strike and grow. The work would be allowed to go its own way, and I predicted that in time there would be a thicket of willow surrounding the fallen boulders of the cairn. . . . Unfortunately it reverted to chaos sooner than anticipated: the deer in the park ate it in the spring and butted holes in it during the rut."

An alternative approach is to grow your sculpture into its final form from small cuttings, grafting and training it over a number of years. This approach seems to be favoured by people with a more horticultural background. It is great fun growing a chair. A simple project is to nail a stick chair together, plant it in the ground and wait for it to grow, weaving in new growth to replace non-living parts. Alternatively and perhaps more elegantly, plant willow rods and then train them into a chair as they grow.

An interesting variation is the combination of living and non-living elements. Stephanie Bunn has created bowers and fences with living uprights and diagonals and used basketry techniques on a grand scale, weaving horizontally. She incorporates a great range of varieties in her work and shows knowledge of how stem colour will change, often dramatically as the willow dries and ages. She also uses climbing plants in her work, such as sweet peas, honeysuckle and golden hops. A recent collaborative piece where Stephanie and I worked together was at Wakehurst Place in Sussex, a stunning arboretum holding the overflow collection of Kew Gardens and also home to the Millennium Seed Bank. The project involved designing and making a sixty-foot sculptural fence which used freshly cut willow to give a range of colours and textures. The willow dried quickly in the warm spring sun keeping some of their colours and mellowing as the fence aged. The fence screened the large scale composting area but had a number of windows or 'portholes' to look through and view the composting process. One of the notable things about the project was the interest shown by the public and a real desire to have a go – in my opinion, a basic need for people to create and make.

Don't forget your maintenance, unless you want your structure to become a wild and secret den. Some of the new growth can be woven in to strengthen the structure. Stem colour is strongest on one year growth and fades with age, so heavy pruning will help to keep colour. Catkins on some varieties form on two-year growth, so a little care when you prune may be rewarded!

So have fun with your willow, and get to know your material! ●

become one. A good example of this is the 'Glade Arcade' by Clare Wilks (in the RHS Garden at Wisley in Surrey) where the tightly bound stems have formed pressure grafts. This structure also incorporates metal formers to give shape to the archways. Another well established example of a structure that has grafted is the 'Living Tree' by Ian Hunter (Rawtenstall, Lancashire), a giant representation of a tree with tunnels through the trunk and branches for children to play in. Both structures have been maintained to keep their original form.

Structures can range from the functional to the sculptural. Good examples of well made and very functional structures are the range of lattice fences, domes and tunnels at the Henry Doubleday Research Gardens near Coventry. These have been made over a number of years on courses led by Steve Pickup. Examples of very large-scale work are at the Earth Centre in Doncaster. They were planted in 1999 by Jim Buchanan, and were used for landscaping and shelter. Very vigorous varieties were used for immediate impact.

GROWING WITH GRATITUDE

Gardening is also a craft.

BY BRIGITTE NORLAND

WHY SHOULD GARDENING be included as a craft? Nothing is made, flowers bloom and drop, vegetables are grown and consumed, and a garden's lifetime rarely extends beyond that of its maker. Yet without the practice of growing most of human life could no longer be sustained. We have been gardening since we began farming, when the habit of keeping useful plants and animals close at hand became widespread. The culture of the settler came to view the outer environment as difficult, while the garden was the source of sustenance, and even the mirror of Paradise with bubbling fountains and scented flowers. While small gardens nourished generations, garden culture was also developed by the wealthy and powerful for display, for collections, for privacy; all of which have left their mark on post-imperialist gardening. In some parts of the world the garden is now a different kind of oasis, where trees, birds and ecosystems may flourish as the impact of our built environment and an urban, industrialized way of life really sinks home. Gardening is one of the most inclusive of human activities; like painting and singing, it can be practised from childhood to old age; a small patch of earth, light and water gives the gardener the raw material of his craft, which literally has a life of its own. Continuing generations, abandoning the mores of inadequate social and political systems, have been reclaiming this habit, from city farms in Western Europe to the Eastern European summer gardens, feeding families whose incomes have been so devalued as to be worthless. Gardening is not only the practice of a skill, it is an important agent of social and environmental change.

The most important part of gardening is the soil. If you nurture your soil then your garden will grow and you can enjoy the fruits of your relationship. Soil is a truly miraculous phenomenon, made up of particles ground down out of mountains, washed by sea, rivers and rain, bound together with organic matter of all kinds, decomposing leaves, roots, worms and the myriad mysterious bacteria whose existence the gardener only knows of by their absence. Soil is nurtured by returning everything you take from it; every weed pulled out, every pruning taken and what you eat should be returned in the form of composted manure. These cycles become extended in modern urbanized living, but the principle holds true, and the craft of the gardener lies in an understanding of the soil and locality as well the manipulation of the growing environment.

The most important quality of a gardener is to observe and remember. Even if as I do you remain in one place, bound to the rhythm of season, England brings an extraordinary variety of climate and growing conditions. To live at the fiftieth parallel with our minimal winters is a unique climactic phenomenon. We can grow plants from all around the temperate world, from the Mediterranean, the Himalayas and the antipodes, and can be tempted into mania of all kinds: the perfect lawn, the representative collection, the largest leek, the blackest tulip. If a craft is the harmonious relationship between maker, material and purpose then these activities could be considered for inclusion given that purpose extends beyond physical needs. We garden not only to eat but also to celebrate our existence as creatures in nature. Our view of ourselves and of our connection to nature has changed as our populations multiply, and the purpose of

Photograph by David Baker.

gardening has come to be more significant as we desire to reconnect with nature. How we handle our materials, soil, space, light and water are indicators of our skill, and can be ends in themselves. Our purpose then becomes simply the way we conduct our existence.

Maintaining the integrity of your eco-system is a priority. All gardening is an intervention, and our violation of the earth can be softened. Nature abhors nakedness, so a good gardener keeps the soil covered as much as possible and returns everything taken out through good cultivation and composting. Not doing can also be an important aesthetic judgment. I leave the summer's growth standing until the spring, when fibrous stems have become papery and worms have dragged amazing quantities of dead leaves into the soil. In the vegetable garden I sow with mustard, rye or clover and mulch perennial planting with shredded prunings. When weather conditions allow, the first cultivations begin, compost is forked in, and soon weeds will start to grow around the crops. They are hoed off and their drying forms maintain a turnover at the soil surface. conserving moisture and promoting the activity in the soil. Larger quantities of weeds can be composted along with kitchen waste and ideally, human waste to complete the cycle. Compost heaps need a flexible representation of dryer fibrous matter, also fresh green sappier material and an aerated environment within so that heat can develop and the bacteria can convert the debris into humus. A good gardener returns what is taken out, erring on the side of generosity; nothing is wasted and the benefits are to the soil in increased diversity of structure and activity have an impact throughout the growing community.

A garden cannot be viewed as though it were in a little aesthetic bubble, unconditioned by all that is around it. The surrounding buildings or open spaces are also a part of your garden and together make up a communal environment. When I arrived, our garden was already mature, even congested; outgrown hedgerows with mature oaks and limes enclosing remnants of orchards and thickets of shrubs where birds, snakes and small mammals all made their home. From 1920 the garden had ben cultivated with distinctive ambition by an erudite spinster, a Miss Marker. Bereaved of any younger relatives by the First World War, she poured her love of beauty and industry into a garden of many parts. Forty years after she died in her nineties, those inhabitants of the garden that could really survive here remain. Around them the vernacular of English woodland has spread and multiplied; foxgloves, buttercups, campion and bluebell follow the daffodil, lungwort, primrose, snowdrop and aconite. All we did was weed out nettles, dock, hogweed and brambles; we watched and waited, and old plantings reappeared. I spent many hours walking round it, waking and day-dreaming, trying to visualize change and renewal, and planting trees. When you come to a place of such legible history all you have to do is nurture the soil and the soul of a place can breathe.

How the garden looks is gloriously ephemeral, and is only one part of its integrity. Our garden can be most enchanting in the early morning, or at dusk, in mist, rain, frost and snow. The passing beauties of flower and colour are amply represented, and yet nothing lifts the spirits more than fragrance. My desire for integrity prefers the older inhabitants of the countryside; the delicate scents of appleblossom and briar rose, the sweetness of honeysuckle and the pungency of hawthorn are all native, but it is hard to imagine a garden without jasmine, mahonia, wintersweet or azalea, to think of a few. Feeling and memory are evoked in a scent, offering a moment of transcendence.

The art of planting a garden involves thinking in time and space; seasonal beauties can give way to one another in the same spot, and all the space from the tops of trees, the volumes around them and the ground beneath them all await your acknowledgement. Every locality has its vocabulary of vegetation, and if you do not stray too far from type your garden will flourish effortlessly. The benefits of raising your own plants are recommended; you can understand something more closely when you have observed it from its first root and shoot, be it the obliging curly kale or the reluctant colchicum, which flowered for me sixteen years after I sowed the seed. Best practice means planting for minimum future disturbance; the right conditions for the right plant will reward you.

As a gardener I can claim no other expertise than my own practice in the cool temperate maritime climate of the West of England. My first teacher was the fertile red soil of East Africa where my father taught English on a Roman Catholic mission and my mother grew fruit and vegetables. In the heat of the equatorial sun and the regular rainfall it seemed as if anything would grow. Beyond the bungalows of the white men the Africans grew cotton and bananas, and women would cultivate their gardens through their pregnancies, returning immediately with the tiny baby tied on to their backs. Fertility seemed effortless. Back in England at the age of nine my interest was fostered by my grandmother, a resourceful woman whose family farm had been eradicated in the trenches of the first World War. She helped me plant my first patch and opened my eyes. All around me I looked at what people did with their new suburban plots on the dry chalky soil at the edge of Cambridge, cycled miles searching for diversity in the industrialized farmland, admiring

'Little Sparta', by Ian Hamilton Finlay. Photograph by Andrew Lawson.

the trees that survived and celebrating the appearance of honeysuckle and scabious in the verges. My school adjoined the university botanical gardens and I escaped whenever possible to become acquainted with the greenhouses, the magnolias, lilies and irises; going further across the university meadows and discovering the embodiment of the English tradition in the many college gardens.

Gardening and mothering proved inseparable for me; in ensuring that my children should eat well I began to grow food. I gave my attention to revitalizing the sandy soil of the vegetable garden, its integrity somewhat compromised by the use of a rotavator and too much chemical fertilizer. Twenty years on, with a dressing of compost at almost every replanting, the soil stands up to the interventions of crop growing with cheerful resilience. Growing

food plants in Devon is a delightful pageant of foreigners; potatoes, onions, carrots, pumpkins, beans and tomatoes have all been imported over centuries and we grow them with gratitude. Our location demands that we make the most of the light and warmth of spring and summer, when sowing and planting must be done, cultivating air and light around the growing crops. Maintaining the vegetable garden is an extensive practice; the hours given may seem lengthy but the garden's productivity rewards amply and we have been able to raise children who know the real value of food. While working I enjoy the poetry of seasons, the sounds of our valley, the continuing strength of a used body and the discipline of repeated physical activity that eventually gives way to longed-for self-forgetfulness. ●

BUILDING LIKE GARDENING

With the emergence of vernacular architecture, our houses will be as various, as imaginative and as well cared for as our gardens.

BY BRIAN RICHARDSON

D O YOU MOW IT?" This remark comes to everybody's lips when they first approach our house. The question became so predictable that I used to become irritated by it and look for a smart answer, but I have come to value its use as an ice-breaker. People who would be hesitant to plunge into a discussion on architectural style are not at all shy of talking about our grass roof.

Why?

Because they are in the realm of gardening, where they are comfortable.

Another question that regularly gets asked, once the house itself is the subject of conversation, is: "How long did it take you to build it?" This also made me uneasy. All I could do was look round at the countless unfinished details, let alone the alterations and repairs already needed, and say: "We started in 1976, and began to move in around 1980 . . ." But this risked the even more difficult question: "When will you finish it?"

One day it occurred to me to brazen it out and say, "It will never be finished", and to make this seem less startling, I added, "You wouldn't expect me to say when the garden would be finished, would you?"

This led me to ponder further the similarities between gardening and self-building, and then to claim that self-build could become the breeding ground for the new vernacular architecture.

I use R. W. Brunskill's definition of vernacular taken from his *Illustrated Handbook of Vernacular Architecture:* "The ultimate in vernacular architecture will have been designed by an amateur, probably the occupier of the intended building, and one without any training in design; he [or she] will have been guided by a series of conventions built up in his locality, paying little attention to what may be fashionable on an international scale. The function of his building would be the dominant factor, aesthetic considerations, though present to some small degree, being quite minimal; tradition would guide constructional as well as aesthetic choice, and local materials would be used as a matter of course, other materials being chosen and imported quite exceptionally."

But 1 would add that the vernacular building would be intimately related to its site. An essential part of the ordinary usage, as described in the dictionary, is 'native to the place'. The regional and local climate are prime formative influences, as are the geology and topography of the site.

I also accept Brunskill's judgement that vernacular house-building had died out by the end of the nineteenth century, but I am not as pessimistic as he is about its revival. I would rather try to revive the vernacular here and now, and align myself with Nicholas Habraken's suggestion that: "[We] might begin by allowing a return to the unsophisticated spontaneity of people building their own places to live." So I put my faith in the self-build movement.

We lost vernacular architecture when we lost control of the housing process.

With the enormous increase in the power of the modern state, those activities of ours that threatened the state and its business allies have been suppressed. Building our own houses was one of them. There is enormous profit to be made from housing, and we have allowed it to be taken out of our hands so that the powerful can make money out of us and shape our lives into patterns that perpetuate their domination. Since the Industrial Revolution and the emergence of mass production (with mass politics) in Britain, most housing has been

Maureen Richardson watering the garden of their house in Brilley, Hay-on-Wye. Photograph by Mike Trevillion.

provided by municipalities or speculators. They are now known by the unpleasant, but in a way apt, name – volume builders. The technical and management professions have connived in this exploitation and made a mystery for themselves. We are led to believe that they, and only they, have the special knowledge and skill to provide us with houses.

As a result we now have a housing disaster brought about by professionals serving their political and business masters, and a dearth of vernacular buildings. We have lost control over building but, on the other hand, we do have a wealth of gardens.

BECAUSE OF THE nature of gardens – their unsusceptibility to industrial exploitation and their reliance on intensive manual labour – there is little money to be made out of them. The State has not felt obliged to take gardening over, as it has housing, and we have been allowed to continue gardening.

Gardening is anarchic without being threatening. Architecture, once our pride and joy, has been surrendered and we are surrounded by ugliness, waste and decay, but gardening thrives, and up and down the country there are myriads of lovely, well cared for and productive gardens – the pride of

their owners and the subject of great interest and satisfaction to the community.

There are no Gardening Regulations equivalent to the Building Regulations and gardeners are free of planning control. There is no Health and Safety in the Garden Act. There is no need – gardeners are expected to be responsible for their gardens and themselves, and they are.

There is no government control and no gardening disaster. Gardeners have even escaped the nonsense of 'set aside'.

Gardens are vernacular, literally by being rooted in the place, and created by local people.

The ordinary commonplace gardener fits very well with Brunskill's definition of a creator of vernacular architecture, except that Brunskill assumes it will be a 'he', and our gardener is just as likely to be a 'she' who will be an amateur, probably the occupier of the intended garden without any training in design (other than self-motivated learning):

• guided by a series of conventions built up in his or her locality, paying little attention to what is fashionable on an international scale;

• the function of his or her garden would be the dominant factor – aesthetic considerations, though present to some small degree, being quite minimal. (The parallel doesn't fit Brunskill so well here,

One of the sites of the Lewisham Self-Build Project, designed by Walter Segal. Photograph by Jon Broome Architect.

because gardeners are keenly appreciative of the look of their flower gardens and shrubs, but it holds for the vegetable garden. Even in the flower garden one could say that its beauty is part of its function. Anyway, this is the most questionable of Brunskill's vernacular axioms. The degree of aesthetic care of any vernacular builder cannot be known or reliably inferred. I am inclined to think that the 'folk-art' element is strong in much vernacular building.)

• local methods would be used as a matter of course, other materials being chosen and imported quite exceptionally.

HOW CAN HOUSE-BUILDING become as popular as gardening? Through self-build, much of the gardening approach can be adopted.

The simile is not exact, because it has to be acknowledged that building is more difficult and more demanding than gardening. Humans are very tender plants and have become accustomed to a great degree of modification of the natural environment, so there is more work to be done making a house than a garden. For instance, temperature and humidity have to be held pretty constant whatever the climate and the season, and elaborate structures are needed to achieve this. Mistakes in building are less forgiving than in gardening: the home must not leak, it must be warm enough for infants and elderly people, and it must be hygienic and convenient to run.

But the knowledge and skills to create structures to do all this are still relatively simple and there need be no mystery about how it can be done. There are a small number of self-builders quietly demonstrating this all the time. The small numbers are not so much due to the difficulty as the lack of opportunity: to acquire land and finance, and get access to the fairly straightforward body of knowledge required. Many more people want to do it than ever get the opportunity to. This is a shame, as it has been noted that successful self-builders not only get good, affordable accommodation but also a sense of empowerment. They become more self-confident as individuals and citizens. They are generators of bottom-up energy. They inspire others to take on the daunting task of house-building. They are inventive and resourceful.

The top-down response to this that is needed from politicians and professionals is not to thwart it, or try to take it over, but to enable it to happen freely. Room must be made in the broad planning framework (which we persist with in its present form in spite of its evident failure) for bottom-up initiatives to emerge. Proper planning has to originate at grass-roots level. Only the people living the plan out can see the whole picture. Good plans depend on the local knowledge and experience

The self-build house at the Centre for Alternative Technology, Machynlleth. Photograph by Jon Broome Architect.

that exist everywhere but which the present system so largely ignores. We have allowed top-down planners to distort the supply and value of land. This often has the result that people can no longer afford to live in their own locality. Plans made at grass-roots level would certainly include arrangements to remedy this. The success of vernacular buildings of the past was largely due to the good sense the local people had of place. They knew where was the right place to build. Nowadays others purport to know more than we do about our own locality and its needs. We are more planned against than planning.

The other hurdle in the way of the self-builder is more easily overcome. That is the degree of knowledge required to master the technicalities of building – to ensure stability and good environmental performance generally, and incidentally satisfy the Building Regulations. Just plain common sense is not quite enough any more. Influenced by Walter Segal and people like him, there are architects who are prepared to set aside the top-down attitudes the profession is trained to adopt and instead put their experience and expertise at the disposal of self-builders – helping and advising them where they are needed, but not taking over the direction of the enterprise. Also it is a common experience with self-builders that, unlike local authority planners, the Building Inspectors take a

helpful stance and give constructive advice, actually helping self-builders get round difficulties.

There are books and magazines available which provide a resource for self-builders training themselves – nothing like the scale of the gardening scene yet, but one can see it growing. There is the Walter Segal Self-build Trust – a charity offering information, support, advice and training to people in housing need. The general D.l.Y. information field is still expanding, and most builders merchants have adapted to the situation and are now keen to advise and trade with self-builders. Although nobody should underestimate the degree of hard work involved, the act of building is as enjoyable as gardening.

I am confident that bottom-up planning and housing are coming. The old hierarchies and giant organizations are poised for change. Everywhere there is a stirring towards decentralization, lateral connections, small-scale business and energy efficiency. The ecological imperative for sustainability forces change, and the top-down system cannot cope with it in the old way. The great untapped resource at the grass-roots level will have to be given free rein.

As a natural outcome and expression of this release of energy a new vernacular architecture will emerge and our houses will be as various, as imaginative and as well cared-for as our gardens. ●

EARTH SCULPTORS

Topsoil is beloved of gardeners, but subsoil is the cobbers' delight.

BY LORNA HOWARTH

Cob shelter at the Eden Project.

THE MYRIAD COLOURS of subsoils: the yellow clay of North Devon, the red ochre of the South Hams, and the stark white of the chalk downs all lend themselves to cob sculpture. Subsoil reflects the locale of the cobber and imparts a texture and smell that are evocative to all those who love the land.

This ubiquitous yet unfamiliar material beneath our feet – subsoil – mixed with straw and water, was once the basic building material for homes, barns and byres throughout southern Britain, and more than 50,000 earth buildings are still inhabited in the south-west of the UK. Earth buildings combine thermal mass, sculptured beauty and probably the lowest embodied energy of any building material. Sadly, subsoil is now considered of little value: a waste product of the building industry something to get rid of, to hide away.

Yet in the heart of Devon there are two women who have created stunning sculptures from this so-called waste product. A few years ago, a pile of 400-year old cob, the remains of a barn on Jackie Abey's land, had to be cleared away as her farm was part of the local Chagford Festival Studio Trail. Whilst moving the cob, Jackie and her friend Jill Small-combe decided to keep with the spirit of the festival and created some sculptures from the old cob, remixing it with straw and water. This gave them a taster of the creative pleasures in sculpting with cob and led them to try their hand at other ideas.

Comely figures appeared in the corners of friends' barns, conical cob spires camouflaged amongst garden trees, spiral walls with wine-bottle windows took shape and, some time later, summerhouses became a speciality. Jill and Jackie, with backgrounds in art and design, had found a medium that responded to the moulding of their hands and feet, a material that is abundant, recyclable, and ultimately – during the course of hundreds of years in the case of larger buildings – biodegradable.

ALL THE COB sculptures and the larger 'built' installations – the summerhouses

Cob seat for Devon Guild of Craftsmen.

and staircases – are constructed using the traditional method: the cob is mixed by hand and the first 'lift' is forked on to a firm base. It is then stamped down with feet or mallet and left to set over a day or two. Dry weather is essential: cob building traditionally takes place between the time the swallows arrive and when they leave at the end of the summer. Once the first layer is set, it can be pared into shape – sculpted into whatever form the material inspires.

Jill and Jackie both agree that this natural pace – a day of relatively strenuous physical work, followed by a few days of rest and reflection on the object taking shape – enables the craftsperson's preconceptions about the work in progress to evolve with the natural variations of cob. "No sculpture ever ends up as we originally envisaged," remarks Jackie.

The golden rule with cob is that it must have dry feet (a solid foundation) and a 'hat', as exemplified by the thick, overhanging thatch that is the traditional finishing touch to cob buildings throughout Devon. In Jill and Jackie's work, the hats on their sculptures range from cedarwood shingles on walls and stairs, to thatch on summerhouses and even gold-leaf on some of the more delicate work.

As their work became more diverse and inspirational, Jill and Jackie received commissions from various organizations, including the Devon Guild of Craftsmen, to create installations for mythic gardens and contemporary galleries. The Eden Project in Cornwall commissioned them to build a Visitor Facility, and this enabled Jill and Jackie to build on a larger scale. The building is designed in the shape of a woman so that they could create gracefully curved walls and give a sculptural feel to a functional building. It was important for the Eden Project for the building to be as environmentally friendly as possible, not only as an educational experience for visitors, but as part of their overall ethos. Cob buildings fit this remit perfectly being very low in embodied energy, but Jill and Jackie used recycled products wherever possible, and included solar panels on the roof too.

Another recent project has been the development of earth tiles. Earth tiles have traditionally been used in Arizona and New Mexico in the USA, but now Jill and Jackie are adapting the technique to make cob tiles for use in the UK. The cob is sieved with several different binding materials, including straw, hemp and flax and then rammed into moulds. The tiles are allowed to dry naturally, and then the tops are sealed with layers of linseed oil and a final layer of beeswax. Using subsoils from different areas of Devon has created tiles with an interesting range of hues and subtleties. Despite moving towards more complex designs in their own work, Jill and Jackie insist that anyone can create from cob. Even in the smallest garden, the subsoil excavated from a wildlife pond or child's sand-pit could form a beautiful sculpture – and in bigger gardens there are no limits: a cob-walled potager with inset recycled glass windows; a luxury henhouse with roosting and laying compartments; standing cob monoliths; beehives; domed shelters or shrines. Jill and Jackie delight in the fact that they haven't yet scratched the surface of the possibilities of sculpting with cob and that every undertaking is a unique and pleasurable experience. ●

COB

MADE OF MUD

Throughout history in all parts of the world, people have built earth houses. They are ecologically sustainable and aesthetically enchanting.

BY IANTO EVANS

Wall in Cottage Grove, Oregon, by Cob Cottage Company.

WHEN I WAS AT architecture school in the 1960s I lived for a while with a group of civil engineering students. My world revolved around built places and how to perfect them; the subtleties of human building were of consuming importance to me. Yet to the engineers I must have appeared a strange fanatic – idealism was low on their list of priorities. They prided themselves on being pragmatists who believed that only that which can be measured can have measurable effect.

One night an intelligent and eloquent engineer called Tony cornered me in an argument. Why, he asked, did we think that quality of place was important? He could quantify precisely the effect of faster highways, bigger sewers, broader streets. The results of better engineering were well-documented, yet he asserted there was not one scrap of evidence that architects improved anything at all. He accused me and my profession of hoodwinking the public by promoting unproven assumptions about the effects of buildings on human behaviour.

Markers Cottage summer house, National Trust, by Jill Smallcombe and Jackie Abey.

115

Interior of a cob cottage in Texas.

My artistic family background and several years at architecture school had swaddled me in the unquestioned assumption that quality of place has a direct bearing on human behaviour. One needed no proof. Quality in buildings was self-apparent and as such must inspire people, raising the tone of their lives and ennobling society.

With the idealism of both youth and the era, I had entered the profession with a social conscience; it was to be my contribution to the betterment of society, to improve the face of Britain through better design.

IN THE SEVENTIES I was privileged to work extensively in Latin America, in village communities, and in the eighties my work took me to Africa: Senegal, Lesotho, Kenya, Bourkina Faso.

The contrast between new buildings in our industrial societies and those in traditional societies was stunning. In general the industrial buildings were square, hard and boxy with flat walls and boringly repetitive features; their structure was usually hidden. Traditional buildings came in soft shapes,

irregular, illogical and unpredictable; they had odd dimensions, surprise nooks and little towers. There was usually no secret about their construction. The building might reveal every detail of its structure, yet many of its functions were often obscure.

Industrial societies build for predictability, to allow machines to take over much of the construction and maintenance, to cater for modular furniture. Ceilings are usually eight feet high, doors six feet eight inches. Four by eight sheets of plywood, the International Building Module, codebooks, building permits, drafting tools and bulk-buying all conspire to create a predictable building. There are government regulations that dictate the height of windows, the size of a bathroom, how many nails a board must be held by.

Living in Guatemala, Nepal and Africa, it came to me that humans need sculptures which surround their daily activities, not boxes to fill with furniture. But the sculptural offerings of brick, steel, concrete, even wood, are governed by the rectilinear shapes of those parts. It's hard to mount an oval window in a concrete block wall, against the

116

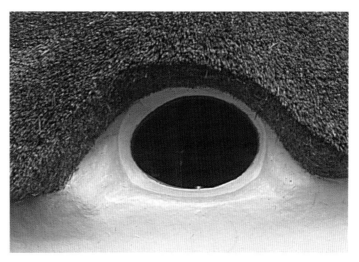

Cob and thatch with window set directly into the cob, Denmark.

nature of the materials, you might say. Flowing curves in stud frame and waferboard are expensive, structurally suspect, and artificial-feeling.

In *A Pattern Language* Christopher Alexander pleads for a material "small in scale, easy to cut on site, easy to work without the aid of huge and expensive machinery, easy to vary and adapt, heavy enough to be solid, long-lasting, easy to maintain, and yet easy to build, not needing specialized labour, nor expensive in labour, and universally obtainable and cheap". There is one material that meets nearly all these criteria. That material is, of course, earth.

About half the world's housing stock is built of earth. Not just simple mud huts, but large and elegant palaces, castles, factories, mosques and apartment blocks, castellated ten-storey skyscrapers, pavilions and manor houses. Are they all in the Third World? By no means.

The county of Devon in England boasts more than 20,000 houses built of earth, and as many again barns, sheds and outbuildings. Many have been inhabited since the fifteenth century, are in good repair and look good for another half-millennium. Thousands more stand in Cornwall, Somerset, Norfolk, Wiltshire, and probably every county in England. In Wales they ride out Atlantic gales; in Scotland they survive at the latitude of Kodiak Island, in weather no better.

IN 1989, WITH LINDA, my wife, I built a tiny cob cottage in what is left of the world's biggest temperate rainforest. We used a carefully-proportioned mud and straw mix. We trod with bare feet, built with bare hands, every last handful. Through complete ignorance, we produced a harder, stronger material than the mediaeval English, the Africans or the Mexicans. Our cottage was solar heated, with sixteen-inch walls and a built-in heated earthen

daybed. We lived in it through four winters and three summers, through temperatures from 5 to 105 degrees Fahrenheit, in snowstorms, gales and months without sun.

At once it was clear that here was the flexible healthy cheap building material we had lacked all those years. In spring 1993 we built a second one. And then in the autumn began another.

The new cob cottages we built in the Oregon rainforest exploded all the rectilinear inhibitions of a lifetime. The sculptural potential of earth sprang right out of our hands. Almost uninvited the house grew earthen bookshelves, alcoves, niches. Eyebrows sprouted over windows, arches sprang across glass, a natural refrigerator sank itself into a north wall. The very shape of the foundation revealed the flowing shapes of human movement, a dance with the Earth.

Linda and I live now in one of these. It is tiny in terms of square feet ("round feet", one creative visitor called them) but because there are no corners, it feels spacious. Experienced builders coming here estimate it to be twice its actual size. But most important, we built it to enclose our activities.

We don't build with earth because it is cheap, but it is. We're not only concerned with saving forests, yet earth houses accomplish that. And we never set out to build in teams with little children and old people, but that has turned out perhaps most rewarding of all.

It's clear to me now that Tony the engineer was wrong. It is those very emotions which can't be quantified which make life worth living. Who in their right mind would set out to quantify humour, inspiration, joy or ecstasy? On the other hand, I was wrong about architects too. Their record as leaders in aesthetic structures is abysmal. Yet many unlettered peasants in the villages of the non-industrial world consistently create wonder-filled buildings which are magical and joyous. ●

SAVING THE SWILL

Oak baskets are useful and beautiful.

BY MARY BARRATT

AN OAKSWILL BASKET or 'swill' was a speciality of the Furness Fells in South Cumbria, and is famous for its durability. It is made from native materials: oak and hazel. Rent oak strips or 'smarts' are rendered pliable by boiling, and split or 'rived' by hand to produce 'spelks' and 'taws', which are woven round a hazel rim or 'bool'.

The Swill Basket Makers of the Furness district were known locally as 'Swillers', and some believe that the origin of this title comes from their fondness for ale. However, it is more likely that the name derives from the Anglo-Saxon word 'Swilian', which means to wash, for an expert Swiller was able to make a watertight basket.

Some were used locally, but many went to Scotland and other parts of Northern England, ironmongers being the main distributors. They ranged in size from 16 to 40 inches in length, and had many uses, the most common being potato-picking. They were also to be found in the charcoal pit-steads, smelting furnaces and coal mines, and used during the war for transporting gun cotton and by seed and tobacco merchants. Samuel Gawith's snuff factory has used them since 1792 and still does today. They were also a common sight in the cotton and bobbin mills. Farm and domestic uses included feeding stock, carrying laundry, firewood and refuse, and even as babies' cradles. Today they are still in demand by farmers, gardeners and tourists, but the industry has virtually disappeared.

Swills have been known in south Cumbria since the Middle Ages. Towards the end of the 19th century, Broughton-in-Furness, surrounded by plentiful supplies of suitable timber, was one of several Furness villages in which the industry flourished. By 1890 there were 5 swill basket firms in Broughton alone, employing 25 men in all. Men worked often up to 14 hours a day, and having completed the 7 year apprenticeship, were paid according to the number of swills made per week, which could be as many as $3\frac{1}{2}$–4 dozen. But it must be remembered that much of the swillers' time was used in preparing the timber before weaving the baskets.

Today, with the development of the forestry business and its emphasis on large scale soft wood production for timber and pulp mills, and for high financial returns, the careful coppice management of the native woodlands has been neglected, with the result that in a comparatively short space of time a wealth of knowledge, skills and crafts has virtually been lost. Local surnames such as Barker, Cooper, Turner and Ashburner still reflect the importance of these traditional industries.

The first swill basket I came across in 1980 was old and dilapidated. The bottom spelks had worn right through and the handles, riddled with woodworm, were polished smooth after years of use. It fascinated me, and I went in search of someone who knew how to make them. I soon discovered they were few and far between. I could find only one elderly swiller, George Coward in Cumbria, still regularly making swills. As I watched him at work in his little shed, I was inspired. He worked with vigour and enthusiasm, and to him a repetitive chore was a continual creation. He used simple basic hand tools and primary raw materials to create an object not only of intrinsic beauty, but of great practicality in everyday life – a traditional product which for centuries was produced in large numbers and had a multitude of everyday uses, but which had now virtually vanished and been replaced by metal and plastic containers. It was an industry with an ecologically sound basis, closely linked with the coppicing of native broadleaved woodlands.

I persuaded him to teach me, and set about the challenge of converting a standing tree into the finished article. I soon realized that even choosing a suitable tree was an accomplished skill, as not just any oak would do. The age of the tree, the soil, the area, the appearance of the bark, the time of year – all had to be considered. I found myself being brought into close contact with the natural forces

Oakswill baskets.

that are often obscured by modern living.

Faced with a heap of 6ft logs and a 10ft boiler, it seemed a daunting and crazy task to convert them into weavable material. Yet I felt a strong, almost subconscious sense of purpose. As I rived the steaming laths amid clouds of smoke, steam and sweet smelling oak, I gradually developed a feel for the nature of the grain and found I could respond to the suppleness and 'personality' of the wood. It was tremendously satisfying. Each piece of wood was different and was used according to how the grain ran and the positions of the various knots, curves and twists. Once riving was complete, each spelk and taw was dressed with a drawknife and shaped individually with a paring knife before finally being woven together round a hazel hoop bent into shape after steaming.

Two years later George finally gave up due to ill health. I felt I had met him just in time to learn the secrets of his trade. I was fortunate at this stage to meet Stella Dawson. She too became inspired in the same way as I had, and she set about constructing a primitive workshop deep in the woods in North Lancashire. Her enthusiasm was a great encourage-

ment and we began working together with the help of Jack Singleton, another elderly long retired swiller from the village. When I first met Jack, he seemed to have forgotten a lot about swill making, which he gave up 40 years previously when coppice oak became scarce. When we invited him to the workshop to help us, things started to come back to him and he showed us many tricks and techniques.

I would like to see the revival of not only swill basket making as a local traditional woodland craft but many other related coppicing skills. Already I find it exciting to see how things have developed. Public interest too is encouraging, and many woodland projects are being started all over the country, but unless our native broadleaves can once more be shown to have economic potential, they will continue to disappear and be replaced by more profitable monocultures of sitka spruce.

There is no comparison between traditional and modern methods of timber production and use. In traditional coppice management, every tree was treated as an individual entity, being used for the trade to which it was best suited, according to its shape and measurements. Nothing was wasted. ●

119

TINO RAWNSLEY

If you go down to the woods, near Liskeard in Cornwall,
you will meet a great bodger of our time.

BY PETER BUNYARD

GONE ARE THE DAYS when a craftsman or woman could guarantee that he or she had a ready-made market. Cheap labour overseas, mass-production, multinationalism and globalization have put paid to modern society's need, if not desire, for hand-crafted products. If we want a brand-new wooden chair with a rush seat and we don't give a thought to the young Chinese hands working under nigh-slave conditions to gather and weave the rushes, we can have what we want for £50 or less. A chair made from local British hard-woods, elm, beech, ash and possibly oak, will cost four or five times that, and justifiably so, because that is the minimum a craftsman or woman will need to live.

Nonetheless, in a globalized world where the laws of comparative advantage are God, it is difficult to resist the temptation to go for a bargain, even though we know in our hearts that we are profiting from the cheap labour and raw materials of another country, while turning a blind eye to the environmental damage caused by long distance transportation and by the mass exploitation of a natural resource. Here lies the dilemma: we can choose to support the trade in cheap goods irrespective of the conditions under which they are produced; or we can choose to pay a premium to protect our own heritage of traditional skills and local crafts.

That is where craftsmen and women like Tino Rawnsley come in. They are the 'salt of the Earth'. They add that ingredient of intelligent use which, with skill and commitment, enables them to fashion wood while encouraging the forest to grow up around them. Tino is a craftsman who can turn wood into a sleek boat that literally cuts its way through the waves, or make a longbow that would have done proud the yeoman who possessed it at the Battle of Agincourt.

He has now resurrected a mid-nineteenth-century high-backed Cornish Windsor chair, reproduc-

ing the one example in the High Wycombe chair museum with precisely the same mix of woods – sycamore for the seat, ash for the legs, spindles, bow, and elm for the arms – that served the original. Tino's chair, ordered by the Duchy of Cornwall, opens the possibility of a future collaboration between craftspeople in Cornwall and Devon and the managers of the Duchy woodland, covering some 1,000 hectares in Cornwall alone. Adding 'craft' value to its timber would certainly be a departure from the Duchy's current practice and would benefit the local economy.

In addition to making his living out of wood, Tino sees his mission as helping to bring back the woodlands that a couple of centuries ago provided tens of thousands of people throughout the length and breadth of the land with a way to sustain themselves and their families. Some twenty per cent of the population of England now lives in the countryside, and according to trends the proportion is forecast to rise. "It is a matter," as Tino puts it, "of restoring life to the countryside, which in the current political climate is increasingly seen as an attractive playground for the urban masses."

We certainly have a thorny problem on our hands. By pitching ourselves headlong into the global economy and opening our doors to every kind of cheap import, whether food, silicon chips or timber, the countryside and the rural economy are getting a beating. And were we to protect local prices in trying to shore up the local economy, that would be against world trade rules.

That is where the quality of the product and its attractiveness come into the picture. The market may be a specialist one, but if the consumer can be enticed to purchase products that are local in origin and have been fashioned locally, then that will serve, as nothing else will, to sustain rural living and consequently the local environment. Indeed, the challenge is to revive the good quality of the past so as to compete with the mass-production of

Tino Rawnsley.

the present, a return to many of the principles embodied in William Morris's social artisan revolution of a century ago.

In 1997 Tino returned to Cornwall from building, repairing and sailing classic boats. He had a small chunk of time on his hands and a small tongue of woodland jutting out from the River Ruthern, in a pleasant valley in the heart of Cornwall. The river itself, with its salmon, trout and increasingly the otter, is now recognized as an important component of Britain's wildlife heritage, helped in no small way by the thin line of woods on both banks.

Years of neglect meant that the woodland wasn't good for much, but Tino believed he could get some hurdles out of it, perhaps a stool, and certainly some charcoal. Having built himself a shaving horse for paring down staves, and other ingenious tools, he was soon in production. On site steam-generation for bending, a pile of staves, a charcoal kiln – the woodland was coming back to life, at least from a human point of view. Most important, that brief experience gave Tino the courage and determination to make a living for himself in Cornwall,

of which, part, at least, was to be from working in woodlands.

The timing could not have been better. The notion of 'sustainability', particularly since the 1992 Rio Conference and Agenda 21, has been bandied around ever since at every level, from central government to rural development schemes.

To realize Tino's dreams is virtually impossible without outside support, and in recent years a number of organizations with dedicated, inspired people have emerged with the sole task of supporting people like Tino. Silvanus Trust is one such organization; Working Woodlands is another; the Duchy of Cornwall is also getting in on the act.

Tino, on the other hand, has been helping Silvanus put on special courses. As Lynsey Faulkner of the Trust points out, "Tino is a dynamic craftsman who empowers people and especially children. He is brilliant at painting a picture in the head of what is going on in the woodland and bringing it all to life. Children find themselves absolutely fascinated."

It is all very well to make the product but it needed a market, and Simon Humphreys of Notterwood Designs in Liskeard, Cornwall, is one of those people with a broad enough vision to realize how to make the link between the growing trees and the final crafted product. Simon worked for many years as a forester in Wales and then, in 1983, worked for the Dartington Action Research Trust which was seeking to restore neglected woodlands. Restoration needed some justification and it did not take any great leap of the imagination to appreciate that if a market could be generated then the rest would follow. But how?

The conventional approach is for a craftsman or woman to seek out the raw materials to accomplish some pre-conceived design. Simon, although not exclusively, has turned all that on its head: instead he finds an attractive piece of timber and looks to see what design would best do justice to it. He then looks for the right craftsperson to do the job for him. It's a principle which is working well in the South-West, where the timber may often be of lesser quality. But Simon has managed to turn many of those 'flaws' into features, such as 'cat-paws' of oak and elm, giving the finished product a distinctive quality all of its own.

"Over the years", says Simon Humphreys, "we have become increasingly remote from the raw materials that go to make up our world. I want to help regenerate those connections by creating a business that generates a demand for local wood, which in turn makes us look after local woodlands. And if we take care of the landscape because we are part of it, then that will benefit wildlife. In the meantime we will be producing products that people enjoy and which last. The slogan should be: grown here, made here, enjoyed here." •

BUILDINGS LIKE TREES

Architects need to meet the challenge of ecology, economy and equity.

WILLIAM MCDONOUGH interviews TIM STEAD

I N A WORLD where most of us just hope to do less harm to the natural environment, William McDonough says we can act beneficially. While we scurry to find ways to recycle, he promises to trash the concept of waste altogether. Named a Hero for the Planet by *Time* magazine and recipient of the first and only Presidential Award for Sustainable Development, this bright-eyed architect delights in turning accepted ideas inside out and inventing new language to express his philosophy of eco-effective design.

The buildings he has created speak for his revolutionary vision better than anything he can say about them. The Adam Joseph Lewis Center for Environmental Studies at Oberlin College has been described as one of the most environmentally intelligent buildings in the world. Then there's his work with chemist Michael Braungart to spearhead the next Industrial Revolution, designing products – such as carpeting and shoes – that cycle back to their manufacturers instead of to the landfill. But McDonough's redesign of Ford Motor Company's huge River Rouge plant may be the ultimate demonstration of his vision for the built environment, and the ultimate test of his principles of ecology, equity, and economics.

How rigid is the common definition of 'green' or 'sustainable' design?

Sustainable design and green design are not the same thing. Green design describes a process that honours the natural world to the optimal extent. The things that are green in the world celebrate diversity; they are powered by the sun. The whole notion of the single photosynthetic cell multiplying itself, transforming into new species, learning how to have sex, creating mammals and humans, for example, is the magic and wonder of a green world. Things are fecund. Growth is good.

But in the modern world, when commercial actors talk about growth being the engine of commerce and environmentalists talk about growth being the structure of the world, we realize that we've adopted a machine mentality. In green design we are now looking at the idea that there is such a thing as a living machine.

For example, at Ford's River Rouge facility, we are designing an assembly plant that will have 454,000 square feet of habitat for native species on the roof. We are using plants to absorb stormwater, make oxygen, sequester carbon, fix nitrogen, and so on. But if all we end up doing is taking plants and using them to serve human purposes, then we're using plants as machines. I think that the question of green design today is ultimately about how humans pick up tools of nature.

In that context I would say that the argument that growth is bad for the environment is a silly argument – because the real question is, What do you want to grow? You can grow a tree – that's good. We grow asphalt – that might not be good. But to grow things that are fecund and generative, that's good. If I can design a building that makes more energy than it needs to operate, then I'm designing a building like a tree. And it could be fecund – but only if, for example, I make sure the species on the roof are natural species that evolved through the place. On the roof of The Gap in California we planted the native grasses of San Bruno, so that the birds flying overhead look down and say, "Oh my god! It's our people. They're back!"

Now sustainable design is not green design. Green design is part of it, a third. The other two factors, equally important, and equally creative as zones in which to work, are the social equity issues and the economic issues. We don't really use the word sustainable very much in our work because sustainable is not that interesting. I mean, who wants to celebrate

The Oberlin Environmental Studies Center. Photograph by Barney Taxel.

> We should design a landscape that is a life support system
> for people who work, instead of a work support system
> for people who don't have a life.

maintenance? We want to celebrate the abundance of the world and the generosity of spirit. So we are looking for a sustaining strategy. Then you can have all the hot water you want, so long as it's solar-heated. The philosophy of the work I do is really about community. When we begin a project, we don't really think of ourselves as designing buildings; we think of ourselves as creating an environment for a community. And we start with the idea of all species in that community. Instead of simply saying, 'How can we begin loving our own children, even for seven generations?' we ask, 'How do we love all the children of all species for all time?' In that sense it's a fundamental act of restoration and regeneration.

And the next question we have to ask is, 'When do we become native to this place'?, because that changes the way you think about community, and it changes the way you design. For example, this renovation at the River Rouge – it's a two-billion-dollar project with a twenty-year plan. And I realized that Ford had declared themselves native to Dearborn. By saying they are staying, that they are going to clean up their own mess – not just leaving it behind, but transforming it from an icon of the first Industrial Revolution to an icon of the next – what a phenomenal act! It's an indigenous declaration.

You put forward three components of sustaining design: ecology, social equity, and economy. How might a building honour all three equally?

Affordable, profitable things that build diversity and mixed use and connect to the natural world in ways that are fecund and healthy – that would meet the criterion.

One of the things we are looking at is how we can design communities with homes that are very, very low in toxicity, very high on the solar energy front, and still affordable. Affordable, say, for the carpenters who built them, who may come from cheap, terribly insulated, double-wide modulars set on three-quarters of an acre, and whose families need two cars costing them $12,000 a year after taxes because they are so remote from culture. But maybe they could get alternative transportation so they don't need two cars, and end up with a solar-powered house that's worth twice as much. That's the kind of strategy we're developing on the affordable front.

I also think our communities need to enjoy much more diversity of provision. Our society focusses on just one part of the market, as if everybody wants to live in a three-bedroom house. Actually, young people want to go to cities and wear black clothes and find mates; young families might need some space where the kids can play outdoors; and then older people want to be part of a community again, maybe one that's pedestrian. If we don't engage all these people in a mixed-use way, we're not being socially intelligent. We're not even being economically intelligent.

The Herman Miller facility you designed seems to exemplify how architecture can build stronger ties between people, the buildings they inhabit, and the landscape that surrounds them . . .

When we designed the building, we thought about all these issues. We curved the building so that the water moving off the site created wetlands and travelled for hundreds of yards before it actually left the site. So it provided the optimal amount of habitat for as many species as possible. The people who work there really get to celebrate that. They get to look at this fecund place that is constantly changing colour. It's full of butterflies. They call the building "the greenhouse" now, and the gift they give visitors is honey made from the site.

Inside, we designed a street where all the office workers and the factory workers convene. The coffee and the training rooms and the bathrooms – all the places you go – are on a sun-filled street full of glare and plants and sculptures. Does it produce productivity? Well, yeah. The performance of the company went up 24% after they moved. This means that the building is being paid for about every three months by the increase in business.

The stories are quite astonishing. Sixteen people left for higher wages. If you're in business, you know that when you lose an employee, you've lost something that you've invested in, and you have to invest more to replace that person. Well, those sixteen people all came back. And when the President of the company said, "Why are you back?", they said, "We want our jobs back because we had never worked in another factory before. We couldn't work in the dark." In a market where there is almost no unemployment, Herman Miller has a waiting list. If we can design a landscape that becomes a life-support system for people who work, instead of a work-support system for people who don't have a life, perhaps we become the employer of choice. That's more valuable than just about anything in the economic sector. It's also phenomenally valuable in the social sector.

Is sustaining design currently an affordable choice for small businesses and nonprofits?

We actually work with lots of little organizations. The Oberlin Environmental Studies Center, the building we're doing with David Orr, is definitely a not-for-profit project. It's a research project, and was done with grants from foundations – and it's only 15,000 square feet. We're doing the new Woods Hole Research Center, with George Woodwell and his scientists – people tracking global warming, the carbon balance, and so forth. Their building again is small, and, like Oberlin's, will make more energy than it needs to operate. We do small schools, we do houses for families . . .

But the larger commercial projects have the resources that allow us to experiment on a large scale, so what we do there appears dramatic to other people. When I put a grass roof over a whole building as habitat, people think that's interesting. When we make our office buildings with windows that open, we get written up in the *Wall Street Journal*. I told their reporter that we had reached a low point of Western civilization when a window that opened was news. It's terrifying.

In Palm Pilot's new headquarters in California, we're designing the building to have outdoor offices. Here you are in San José, one of the most beautiful climates in the world – this is almond country, for heaven's sake! – and they've trapped these young software types in gas chambers. Everybody's sealed up, with the air conditioning running. So we're designing our building with windows that open and outdoor offices. Why not? Sit outside under a tree and do your work. Why is it that we have to lock everybody up in a grey rectangle to think that they are working?

In 1992 you created a list of nine principles of sustainable design for the 2000 World's Fair, including rules like 'Insist on the rights of humanity and nature to co-exist', 'Recognize interdependence', and 'Eliminate the concept of waste'. How can these principles serve organizations and communities as they consider their responsibilities towards the larger world?

The Hannover Principles are really meant to help someone understand their relationship to the natural world, to technology, and to hope. You see, there's a kind of fierceness here. When it says, eliminate the concept of waste, it doesn't say, minimize waste. It doesn't say, please recycle.

What's exciting is that once these protocols start manifesting themselves, you see that all sustainability is local. It becomes a system that divests itself to the local level. So the products that are preferred and the ones that have economic benefit are local products.

We're going to get back to the ability to have pedestrian communities and mobility services, and we're going to benefit from the multiplier effect of an urbane situation. We're designing a town now where

there is a day-care centre, health-care centre, and elder-care centre, all connected in the centre of town, so that we bring these generations back together. And it's a transit point, obviously, so they can get wherever they need to go. Then it has a botanical garden where people, especially elders, can spend their winters in a beautiful greenhouse full of delightful plants, which are purifying the water of the public laundry, which is serviced by the transit system. And it's all solar-powered and the water is purified, so the community's effects on global warming and on water quality from their laundry are zero.

I think that sustainable development starts, though, with the restoration of our cities. The rebuilding of existing communities is our most urgent opportunity. The next level would be the regeneration of the brownfields, for a lot of reasons.

I'm also concerned about our highway system. All these highways that slice through cities or cut off the waterfront really have to be looked at as some kind of strange detritus from a moment of high cultural amnesia. We're doing a project for the Fuller Theological Center in Pasadena where we're proposing that they actually cover over the Pasadena Freeway for a whole block. There's all this air over these stupid highways that could be fantastically viable as parks and all sorts of things. And it would knit the city back together, connect the two sides again.

As our transportation systems become pollution-free, all of a sudden the highways could be in tunnels. They can be buried, just like when New York City switched over to electric locomotives – they put the trains underground and they got Park Avenue, some of the most valuable real estate in the world.

Your work bespeaks a great optimism. Do you really believe we can design our way out of problems such as deforestation, toxic waste, social injustice, and mass consumerism, or are there limits to what human ingenuity can accomplish?

Well, we're all on the planet for a certain period of time, and you can decide what you want to spend your time doing. If the existing trajectories play themselves out, then we have huge tragedies in the making. All we're saying is that we'd rather spend our time on a strategy of change that allows our children a story of hope. And I don't know that we can stop it. Much of the past has already determined the future. Global warming is underway, bio-accumulation is a serious concern, persistent toxins are persistent.

There is no answer for everything. I just think that if we model ourselves on a system that's had 15 million years' experience instead of these 100-year-old experiments that are taking place without any control, the bet might be a little bit better. We say this very humbly because it took humans 5,000 years to put wheels on their luggage. So how smart are we? ●

ENDURING SKILLS

The sound of a mallet or hammer
is music to my ears when it is
used rhythmically, and I can tell
by sound alone what is going on.

Barbara Hepworth

'Hieratic Head', appliqué embroidery by Frances Richards.

POETRY OF PRACTICE

Homage to mentors. BY JOHN MOAT

WHEN I LEFT SCHOOL I wanted to be a painter. Our neighbour, an old general, remembered a 'young artist chappie' who'd served under him in the First World War. The General commanded. 'Young Kapp,' he said, 'I'll have him look you over. He'll know what's best for you.' 'Young Kapp' was then sixty-five – Edmond Kapp, distinguished painter and draughtsman. He was living in France, but by chance was due to visit London and was so amused by the General's orders that he agreed to see me.

We talked for some ninety minutes, and because the reality I encountered was so unfamiliar to me I felt that I was in a dream. Finally he said that if after our talk I was still drawn to painting, I could if I chose come and live near by for a while and work; that I could, for a fee, come and talk with him for three hours once a week.

Those ninety minutes with a person who spoke from his being as an artist was live information I'd never been exposed to. In him there was no division between experience, knowledge or practice. No division between means and ends, or between life, living and the imagination. Above all, no division between living and learning.

Edmond Kapp was an extraordinary mentor. The house, his and his wife's, was full of painting, music, literature, argument and laughter. And everything – making an omelette, the relish of an anecdote, lighting a cigar, writing a letter – appeared to be unpretentiously but exactly part of an artistry. I felt I was experiencing a liberation from years of grey self-denial. But then came a problem: Kapp was fiercely critical of any shortcomings in my painting. I began to lose my way. I realized I was unsure of what I wanted to do; I began to fear that I wouldn't pass the examination that would qualify me for this way of life. I became depressed. But at the same time I began to write more, though secretly because I hadn't forgotten what school had taught me – that that sort of diversion was beyond me. Here was a crisis: I couldn't paint any more. Then somehow Kapp got out of me that I was writing. He insisted on seeing the work and was immediately enthusiastic. Soon we were

spending more time talking about writing than painting. The result was that by the end of the year I'd written a little book of childhood memories. An old friend of Kapp's was David Higham, the eminent literary agent. He sent my book to Higham, who was enthusiastic. So, at nineteen, I had a distinguished agent. The book came near to being published but – thankfully – wasn't. Higham advised me that at Oxford I should for the time forget about writing and just live to the full being at university, which is what for the most part I did. I had outstanding tutors, including Nevill Coghill, but there was nothing I learned that had bearing on my own writing, or in any direct way on the practice or craft of writing. And it is significant that Kapp, for all his detailed encouragement, had not been a writer.

When I came down from Oxford I made the common mistake of thinking that if I went away for a year to write I could prove one way or another whether I was a writer. I wrote two drafts of a novel, which David Higham and his readers thought promising, but not ready for publication. I was (familiar story) suddenly nowhere – exhausted, depressed, helpless and, even among my friends, profoundly lonely. Then, again by chance, in London I met John Howland Beaumont, the deaf South African poet. Beaumont made a scanty living as an occasional correspondent to *The Times* and as an inspired copy-editor. He agreed to read my novel. He returned it with polite encouragement. When I pressed him for his opinion he said that it was fine but that I needed to learn to write. I was, to say the least, taken aback, but managed to bite down enough of my indignation to ask whether in that case I could come and learn from him. He agreed, and so a kind of apprenticeship began. I visited him in his small single room in Kilburn two or three times a week. Always we worked on something I had written, maybe as little as a paragraph. He concentrated almost exclusively on three things: alerting my ear to the difference between reporting and what he called 'writing at first hand'; the economies that allow accuracy in the essential art of writing by implication; and, for him I think the most necessary skill, a command of syntax. So

Illustration by John Moat.

'Squalentem Barbam', painted inscription by David Jones.

entirely had these disciplines of elementary craft been neglected in my education that at first I was afraid I lacked any sense that was alive to what he demonstrated. But after a time – and he was patient, uncompromising and persistent – I realized with first-time excitement that my ear was beginning to come alive. From the moment I'd begun to write I'd known that I had a distinctive ear that could hear a certain music; I had assumed that was all the gift one needed. And syntax? The word meant detention and a Latin primer. For Beaumont, though, command of syntax was chiefly what enabled a writer to be a magician. Where there was the ear and the skill, syntax could be the fusion of cadence and meaning and narrative drama. It controlled the heart-catch. In any sentence it could make for the unfolding of life. And was as essential to poetry as to any form of prose. And for any writer was the key that would unlock the voice. I was sent away time and again to redraft. Gradually I became alive to what he was on about. And very gradually (in fact a process that has never ended) the new deliberation became seemingly more effortless, more spontaneous and, whether in description or mood or feeling, more accurate.

I came to see that the only person who can teach the technique of writing reliably is an experienced writer. That is because the teaching is proved by experience that is whole-hearted and profoundly relevant. It is the authority that can relate the specifics of technique to the spirit of writing. Which means the authority in a specific art of one who has been 'in it with all his or her heart'. A Sufi writer, Mouni Sadhu, has said:

> There exists a mysterious spiritual *siddhi* or power which only a perfect master can possess. It is the ability to help and promote the evolution of his disciple's consciousness. It is actually unexplainable, but I believe it to be something like an invisible radiation that reaches to the deepest recesses of the disciple's soul. Then, if the man is able to tune this consciousness to the vibrations of the master's spirit, he knows many things that remain hidden for others.

My first experience of this was with Edmond Kapp; here the transmission, or awakening, related to the artist's total commitment. The second was with John Beaumont; and here the authority included and conveyed something specifically related to writing.

It may be that complete mastery is available only to complete authority. Even so, a limited mastery is also powerful, to the measure of its limited authority. Anyone who has worked in sympathy with a more advanced practitioner of his or her craft must have experienced what Mouni Sadhu is getting at.

So, apprenticeship to craft in the full, live context. To experience the writer's gnosis, the live authority. The authority that has been proved by imagination and is able to inform another. Then there is practice. The apprenticeship over, then it's work on one's own – the whole package, which most often is the unfolding wrangle between survival and commitment. ●

130

ROMAN LETTERS

All things need their space – trees, butterflies,
plants, children and even lettering.

BY KEN SPRAGUE

AS A KID I GOT myself a job in a lithographic printers. I wanted to be an artist. Not one of those who lived in a garret and painted masterpieces, but one who painted big signs and illustrated stories. Colourful cinema posters and daily newspaper cartoons were my guiding stars.

For months I stood at a deep sink and ground big litho stones to the required texture. I swung a heavy cast-iron disc round and round, grinding each stone with sand made wet from a big brass tap. The instructions: "Timing, distance, balance."

The iron disc had an offset handle and if my timing was off, my fingers got caught between the handle and the sink's metal sides. If my balance was off or I misjudged the distance, my head cracked on the brass tap. For a couple of weeks that sink, designed as a practical working space, was a very painful space.

It makes me smile when I hear people say, "I need my space." All things need their space, from animals to trees, butterflies, plants and children. Space, combined with art, can give a certain living quality even to inanimate things. Take lettering for example.

I graduated from the sink to a drawing-board and drew each day a single letter of the alphabet with pen, brush, charcoal and chalk. The journeymen printers would tell me how wrong the letters were; how badly I had placed them.

An old Italian lettering artist began to take an interest in me. He said my brushwork was good and he explained that the Roman alphabet had an underlying structure. He showed me that the little tails on letters (called serifs) were there to allow the chisel to be driven into the stone in ancient times by the letter cutters. Lettering was art!

One day the old man took a four-inch high letter 'R' that I had drawn, pinned it to the wall and announced to everyone in the workplace, "The boy's an artist!" The whole room cheered: the foreman, the journeymen and all the sink boys.

I was put to making words and learning 'letter spacing'. If the letters were too close to one another, they looked crowded and unreadable; too far apart and they looked disconnected and unreadable. I worked hard at it for many weeks. Some days went well – the eye would flow along the words and letters – but then a too big space, a too thick letter, a too clumsy curve would block or offend the visual effect and destroy the balance.

I had spoiled a day's work, torn it up and been told off for "throwing away good paper and wasting good ink".

The old Italian asked me to get him a cup of tea. I was pleased to do so; anything to get away from that damned lettering. The kettle was always on the boil.

"Fill the cup to the brim," he called, and I did so. Carrying it back, I slopped some into the saucer. He sent me back several times to refill it.

I didn't resent him sending me back over and over again; I guessed it was some kind of test! The works bell had sounded and within seconds the place had emptied. We were alone; the old man had chosen his moment with care. On about the fourth attempt he shouted, "Timing, distance, balance." I remembered my bruised knuckles and made it to his board without a drop being spilled. He was waiting with his own special cup in his left hand. "Now, watch," he said. "This cup represents the space between each letter – any letter in any word – the liquid in your cup must, when poured, fill the space exactly – EXACTLY – between any letter in any word."

In the days that followed, in my imagination I poured the cup full to the brim between each and every letter I drew, and enjoyed doing so. It felt right and, when the line was finished, it looked right. The boss himself said so: "It lives," he said, and my old friend winked and added, "Get us all a cup of tea, Ken." ●

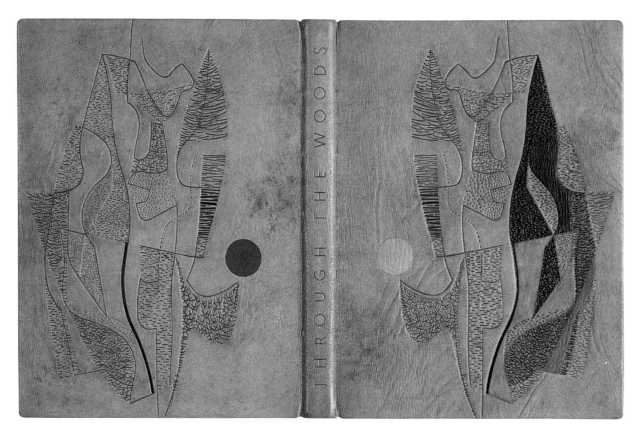

Binding of H.E. Bates, 'Through the Woods' by Edgar Mansfield.

BOOKBINDING

LIFE OF BOOKS

Binders pay attention to detail with an appreciation of beauty.

BY MAUREEN DUKE

MANY YEARS AGO a wag introduced me at a party with the never to be forgotten words, "Maureen is a book-maker". The hushed amazement with which this introduction was received can be compared with the general non-pulsed reaction to saying "I am a bookbinder".

I am a bookmaker – I make books, from any kind of paper or other flexible material, rag pages, parchment etc. But more often I am engaged in re-making books that have degenerated and need rejuvenation, so the nomenclature 'bookbinder' is more usual.

Bookbinding has been a craft practised since written material became portable in codex form. A codex is a folded sheet as distinct from a scroll. The earliest European codex are on parchment or vellum, animal skins stretched and scraped smooth to accept ink or colour. The gelatinous skin is susceptible to humidity; it is unstable so requires weight to keep it flat. So, the introduction of wooden covers with clasps. They in turn were wonderful surfaces for decoration and since most of the texts were of a religious nature, the decoration was elaborate and valuable. Here we look for the first time at the dependents of the bookbinder. The wood worker for the cover boards and the tanner, the parchment maker, the silversmith and so on.

The other two required participants are the

author and the reader, the author is a person of ideas and information, which the reader will read and enjoy; between them is the bookbinder, thus the book as a physical object, has to serve both parties. It should be legible and easy to read, open and close well. Knowing and understanding that position requires the binder to have a training and skills, which can be called upon to resolve physical book problems for books come in all shapes and sizes.

With the setting up of the first paper mill in England during the thirteenth century – a whole new prospect for the author, binder and reader was introduced. No longer did the volume require board stability. The paper could be printed, folded and assembled in book form with a speed hitherto unimagined. The extraordinary change from the laborious writing by hand and consequent times of production compared with the printing of numbers of copies, in fact an 'edition', was incredible. More people were at work with the introduction of movable type. But it was that material – paper – which changed the aspect of life and books.

Paper was of course handmade until the industrial revolution, when machinery was introduced to assist the production. In the early days, cotton and linen rags were boiled, macerated into pulp and made into paper. Added or applied to this paper was a size made from cooking vellum pieces for their gelatinous content. It was not until the demand for paper was so great that other fibres were added, some for bulk and some for strength. While there are now huge paper mills (not as many as there were) producing paper at unimaginable speeds, there is still the requirement for handmade paper, by fine printers, print makers and watercolourists.

Once the paper is printed and folded into book form the pages have to be secured by sewing with linen, cotton or synthetic thread. Much research has been undertaken to test their lasting qualities. There is virtue in the study of old books whose structures have stood the test of time, and not only the types of sewing but also where the stresses arise. A book is a mechanical object whose function is to open so that the reader can enjoy its content without fighting to keep it open. When the binders are selecting materials they will chose appropriately to fulfil those functions. A paper, which is flexible with the grain running from head to tail, will flow while one that is stiff, heavy and with the wrong grain will behave in the opposite manner. Perhaps the most horrifying prospect for the binders of the future is the restoration of the contemporary paperback. Many titles are now printed in that form, the paper is often poor, the margins are small and as in other paper ephemera they are not produced to last.

Once the text has been sewn into book form there are a great many ways to bind it. The construction will depend upon not only the physical aspects of the volume but also what is required of it. A large cookery book, a slim volume of poetry or a garage manual, a photo album or music score. Each has a given set of requirements to be acceptable and perform as expected.

In training the binder begins by learning very simple structures the varieties of adhesives with a basic over-view of materials used in covering. The progress through what used to be a seven-year apprenticeship is hard and concentrated work. At present there are no full time courses and training opportunities are rare. The would-be binder has to take advantage of part time learning when available.

Part of the heredity of bookbinding is the awareness that skill includes attention to detail with appreciation of beautiful papers, printing, leathers and so on. Our tools have changed little over the centuries, our presses of wood and iron, our tools of steel, brass and bone. We owe a debt to the medical profession for our scalpels and hypodermics, which are so much part of the conservation scene.

It is because the conservation of books and libraries has been recognized as part of our heredity that the bookbinder instead of being another artisan has become a skilled craftsperson, consultant and solver of practical deterioration problems.

The tanner has to provide leather which is tanned by a vegetable process and is thus not waterproof. Gold tooling requires particular types of skin. We use calf, goat, or sheepskin imported from India, Africa and Europe, some home grown. The textile manufacturers making book-cloth, the gold beaters and many more provide us with our stock in trade. We listen to each others joys and woes, our dialogue sometimes engenders new products and tools.

Unless it is a limited printing, seldom do binders work with books in sheets; the general run of work is re-binding. Books are special to each one of us. Since the scene is now set on a search for roots and a connection with the past, books have become even more precious and those who prophesy their demise are proven wrong. The costs of warehousing printed material affect the time any book is actually in print. Once it is out of print, after much use it falls apart and cannot be replaced. A binder is needed to put it back in condition. It is a strange interdependence that the economics of storage should have such a spin off for bookbinders.

Books are special to each one of us, and bookbinding, as perhaps any other craft, is a way of life as well as a profession. ●

BILL PHIPPS

The pleasure of making plain silver spoons.

BY MARGOT COATTS

ONLY ONE WORD springs to mind when the name Bill Phipps is mentioned: spoons. Big spoons, small spoons, fat spoons, slim spoons – and every one of them a beautiful object and a well-balanced tool. They are dead plain, made of forged Britannia silver, shimmering and white. Their forms result not from endless preparatory models or drawings but from the force of the hammer's fall, spreading the silver slowly on the anvil and the stake. Throughout this process Phipps pays particular attention to the thickness and weight of the metal, and almost unconsciously arrives at his special forms. But what lies behind them?

Born in Berlin in 1936, the son of a British diplomat, Phipps was brought up in London and educated at Ampleforth. He did not begin his apprenticeship in silversmithing until he was 24. Before that he completed his National Service in the Royal Marines and served in the Royal Canadian Navy for three years – an unusual situation for a British National. Phipps was a diver locating and identifying mines, maintaining underwater rails and other engineering structures, or searching for dead bodies. This work called for heightened manual dexterity, accurate metalworking skills and, above all, a strong sense of touch when working in deep, black water.

On returning to London in 1960, a deepening interest in music, coupled with his skills, led him to apply for an apprenticeship in hand making flutes at Rudall Carte in Islington. The firm went out of business before he could take up the offer, and instead he found an apprenticeship in the Clerkenwell workshop of Michael Murray, the ecclesiastical silversmith who worked predominantly for the Roman Catholic Church.

Phipps recalls with a chuckle that he was unprepared for the exacting craft of silversmithing: "I just about knew what a ruler was." In the workshop they made various sconces, crosses, chalices, patens and other items of worship, normally working straight into the material from only a sketch. Phipps was first put to work in nickel, which, like stainless steel, is hard and unyielding, and then in copper. Murray used copper for his very large crosses and one of the most important examples produced by the workshop was a Christ the King, measuring 2.7 metres in height and made for the Church of the Holy Rood, Oxford.

It was not until over a year into his apprenticeship that Phipps was put to work in silver. He was completely unused to the material and when asked to tap in the 'MM' monogram punch (Michael Murray) into a piece nearing completion, his strength was such that he went right through the silver. Phipps values his training greatly and recalls it as anything but strict. Most importantly, Murray put Phipps up for membership of the Art Workers' Guild. It was at a meeting there in 1963 that he first saw a demonstration by Roy Wilkes, a spoon forger from the London firm of C. J. Vander Ltd. It so impressed him that it was to influence his own workshop practice from that date.

In 1963 Phipps gradually began to make individual spoons. He left Murray, but continued to work for him one day a week. At this point Phipps worked predominantly from his home in West London, in the same workshop he uses today. He had collected special tools while working with Murray, as several casts had been taken from the unusual stakes they designed and made in the workshop; he had also bought machinery from various Clerkenwell firms which were closing down, including a handsome anvil and a very old wire-drawer's bench.

Bread-and-butter work at this time took the form of such commissioned pieces as candlesticks, altar crosses and other church work, probably resulting from recommendations by Murray. His

portfolio shows that Phipps was an expert crafts-man, producing 'contemporary' streamlined designs by traditional bench techniques, not from spinnings and pressings. He also worked for the antiques trade, repairing silver of all periods and styles. During the 60s he also taught metalwork at the Christopher Wren School in White City, London, for one day a week – a tough job in which he had to both outwit and win the confidence of some difficult boys before any classwork was achieved.

Phipps returned to Clerkenwell, setting up and working as a full-time silversmith in his own right, and began participating seriously in exhibitions in the early 70s; his first notable show at Cameo Corner, London, contained engraved, decorative eggs, and was a huge success. He went on to attract private clients and participate in many gold-smithing and silversmithing selling exhibitions.

The making of plain silver spoons has absorbed Phipps forever, but it is a very difficult craft. Each spoon starts as an intractable stumpy bar of metal – some are nine millimetres thick – which, when heated up, grows evenly under the hammer into a tapering lengthy form. One end, the bowl, has then to be spread wide, flattened into a paddle shape, hammered onto a rat-tail mould, then dished, filed, evenly planished and polished. The handle must be shaped to balance and support this perfectly, and similarly finished. The two parts are one piece; the one piece is two dissimilar forms – what a timeless conundrum the 'spooner' is faced with.

The most noticeable thing about Bill Phipps's spoons is that he has never fudged or felt limited by the formal issues, nor engaged in trendiness. He works steadily, wearing his intense devotion to sil-versmithing lightly, explaining with a minimum of words, talking through gestures and exhibiting a concern for touch above visual gratification. He is a man who always calls a spoon a spoon – but who enjoys it for much more. ●

GWEN HEENEY

With the female artists of today, we are seeing something new
in the history of western art.

BY SANDY BROWN

SOME OF THE most astonishing and ambitious ceramic work being made in this country is that of Gwen Heeney. When I first met her, about fifteen years ago, she was in the middle of a life change, having given up making production pottery (she was bored with it after twelve years), and ecstatic because she had secured a postgraduate place at the Royal College of Art. It was a fresh start for her.

I stayed with her in London for a couple of days during that time, and she was bubbling with effervescence, enjoying having Sir Eduardo Paolozzi as her tutor. That was a good opportunity, as in many colleges the ceramics students are separated from the fine art and sculpture students, and this leads to lack of understanding and appreciation of each other's culture. Paolozzi, a sculptor and an artist working in many different media, was inspirational for Heeney and encouraged her to use ceramics in public art.

After obtaining her MA she became involved with the Ebbw Vale Garden Festival in Wales in 1992 and made an amazing, large Mythical Beast. It was one hundred feet long – a huge, dramatic scale; magical, inventive, full of fun. It was made in a way I had not seen before: by carving brick, a method which Heeney has made her own. She works closely with factories which produce the large bricks, on site where they are made, so she can work to a big scale.

Her enthusiasm has inspired a great deal of co-operation on the part of the brick factories. While the bricks are still drying – having a similar texture to that of soap or cheddar cheese – she carves them. But not one at a time: rather, as one huge mass of bricks. She piles up the unfired bricks, to make a sort of massive block, and then carves away the surplus to reveal the sculpture inside. It is as a marble sculptor works.

I have watched Heeney carving: she attacks the bricks with a spade, hacking away corners, removing chunks. Gradually throughout the process the tools get smaller. She is effectively drawing in air, in large sweeping movements of her arms, carving away with her wire cutter. By keeping her arms loose, by making long movements as she carves, the forms retain a relaxed sensuality in the curves. She says it is possible for her to remain relaxed and intuitive while carving precisely because it is on such a large scale.

I have tried it myself, and I found it very strange. It is a very different way of working from that of most ceramic artists who use clay. Usually we add on clay, starting small and getting bigger. If I make a figure, even a life-sized one, I start at the feet, then add coils, as if I were making a big pot. Painters are the same: they start with nothing and end up with something. Adding something to the artwork is fundamentally the opposite of taking away. When you add something, you are dealing with what is necessary. When you take away, you are removing what is unnecessary. So it involves noticing different things, seeing differently. And another thing: once you have removed it, you can't put it back. You don't get a second go. So Heeney can see where she's going: she knows what is inside the form.

THE SCALE OF WHAT she is prepared to do is quite breathtaking. It is immensely hard physical work; and it is also mentally challenging to see how the form will go while all that is visible is the basic dull geometrical shape of the bricks. Heeney says that one of her grandparents was a stone sculptor, and she feels it is natural to her, as if it is in her genes. She has the most wonderful natural intuitive sense, fuelled by the Celtic myths of her Welsh ancestry. So the subject matter is goddesses, dragons; her inspira-

138

'Bid Ben Bid Bon', carving wet brick in studio.

tion has been the tale of Bronwen from *The Mabino-gion*, Dylan Thomas's *Ballad of the Long-Legged Bait*. She often depicts large strong female figures, in a stylized form which is smooth, with long curves.

With such female artists we are seeing something new in the history of Western art. Female figures were almost always depicted by male artists, up until fairly recently. Now, we are seeing female artists showing us what it is like to be female. And the interesting thing is that, unlike all the stick figures you see in fashion magazines, women artists make figures that are monumental. Huge.

Because she works mainly to commission, Heeney mostly draws on paper first, but she loves the opportunity to carve blind: to not know what the outcome will be, but to see it emerge in front of her eyes. She is currently planning a huge thirty-foot tall artwork for Cardiff docks, which will be two figures, one male, one female. In this way she represents the future of ceramics, in which the old categories of art and craft are becoming blurred. It's all art anyway, and always has been. •

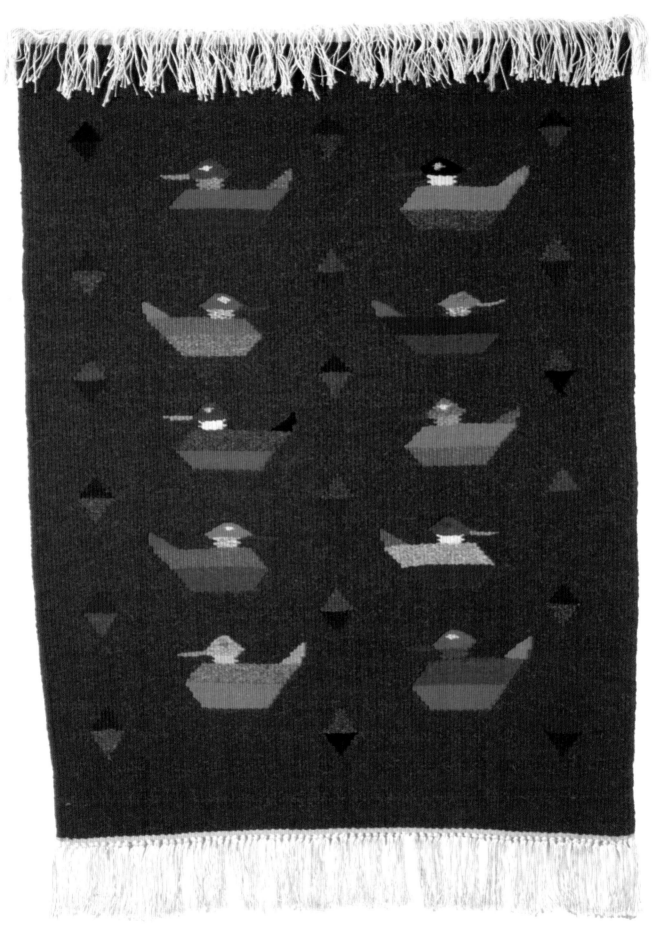

BREON O'CASEY

A jeweller, weaver, sculptor and painter.

BY KITTY CORRIGAN

ARTIST BREON O' CASEY is in his Cornish studio, set in a small orchard of apple, pear and mulberry trees, explaining how his father, the playwright Sean O'Casey, had longed to be a painter. Prevented by poor eyesight, probably caused by malnutrition in the Dublin slums of the 1880s, he turned to the theatre instead, his most famous legacy a trio of plays still regularly performed in the West End: *The Shadow of a Gunman, Juno and the Paycock* and *The Plough and the Stars*. Breon, 73, describes him as a loving and supportive father, who helped him through his ten 'wilderness' years after art school.

"I was directionless, living with my father in Torquay, helping to organize art shows. Then one day I saw a film about the mariner painter Alfred Wallis who had lived in St Ives, and I realized that was the place for me. I packed up my orange Ford van and went."

The thriving colony of artists in St Ives, at its peak when Breon arrived in the late 1950s, included the potter Bernard Leach, the painter Ben Nicholson and the sculptor Barbara Hepworth. Although he had yet to prove himself, Breon felt accepted at once, inspired by "the sheer love of true craftsmanship and a devotion to patient, skilled, exact finish. None of us had any money. You drank only half pints and hoped someone would buy you another."

He started by making jewellery two days a week and supplemented his income with shifts at the St Ives telephone exchange. The sculptor Denis Mitchell employed him as a part-time assistant and then recommended him to Barbara Hepworth, who took him on for a trial period of three weeks that stretched to three years. She proved a tough taskmaster but a great inspiration. As Hepworth's assistant, "There was no nonsense about expressing yourself. You did what you were told." He still remembers her advice that he should spend some time in his studio every day, whether or not he had an idea, to keep the rhythm going. One of his tasks was to smash her unwanted sculptures with a sledgehammer – "very satisfying". In Hepworth's studio there was constant pressure to produce enough work for exhibitions, and he still rises to that challenge, mounting at least two major shows of his own a year, each with about 100 paintings, etchings and sculptures.

The diversity of talents and influences at St Ives in the Fifties and Sixties may explain why Breon O'Casey developed and excels at so many crafts. He is an acclaimed jeweller (for 30 years this was his main source of income), weaver, sculptor and painter. As we sit by the fireside after dinner in his stone farmhouse near Penzance, he modestly mentions that he made the hearth and mantelpiece, on which rest his tiny bronze primitive sculptures and silver spoons; the walls are lined with his abstract still-lifes and etchings, and at our feet is a handwoven rug ("not good enough for export"). Now that he walks with a stick he can no longer manage the loom (he made his first one from a bed frame in the Sixties), but at an age when most people would allow themselves to slow down a little, he has set himself new goals. "On my seventieth birthday," he says, "I gave myself the present of 'no more jewellery' in order to concentrate on painting." He finds it harder than anything else, which is perhaps why he is determined to continue. "There is a mystery about it," he says. "Painting is like fishing – however expert the fisherman, he cannot be guaranteed to bring home a fish. To paint is to wait and watch."

He describes his work as abstract still-life. While the broader landscape provides his themes, what interests him is the detail: "not the wood, not the tree, not the branch, but the leaf". Everything for him is defined by pattern. "If one looks at the natural world closely enough," he explains, "all is symmetry. Nearly every living plant or animal can be split down the middle into two very nearly identical halves."

And so, recurring in his art are satisfying circular, square and triangular shapes representing the furrows in a ploughed field, birds on the wing, a leaf or a fish. He uses earthy pigments to build up layer upon layer of paint until he is content with the effect. He may have six paintings in progress at any one time (acrylics on board and paper are his preferred media) and abandon nine-tenths of them. "If it comes too easily I feel I'm cheating," he says.

He moves from one studio to the next – in one he paints, in another he sculpts and in the third he stores his jewellery materials and implements, many of which he has made himself. He no longer makes jewellery to sell, but still works with silver, creating small sculptures and bowls.

His driven nature was evident as a young boy at school near Totnes in Devon where he attended Dartington Hall, renowned for its liberal regime, its encouragement of the arts and physical activities. "I learned to saw and hammer, to think with my hands as well as my head," he says. Though not a boarder, he sometimes stayed at school until 10pm

and had a room for use at weekends; during the holidays he worked as a labourer at the school for 6d/hour mending chairs and windows.

His father had moved to Totnes in 1937, never to live again in his beloved Ireland, following an adverse reaction to his play about the Great War, *The Silver Tassie*. The formal letter of rejection from WB Yeats of the Abbey Theatre, Dublin arrived on the day Breon, Sean's first child, was born. Despite having a father so involved in Irish politics (born a Protestant, John Casey, he changed his name to Sean O'Casey to identify with his Nationalist comrades) and an Irish actress mother, Breon considers himself English because he was born in London and brought up in Devon. He acknowledges, however, that his Celtic blood may explain his love of

Cornwall. "As I get older," he says, "I am more drawn to Ireland." His wife, Doreen, is from Portrush, Northern Ireland, and their children have traditional Irish names – Oona, Duibhne and Brendan.

He works tirelessly in a windowless space with large skylights so as not to be distracted by views of the garden and the fields beyond. He hates holidays or being taken away from his work for long periods – when he has to visit London he returns as soon as possible to his own sanctuary where he lives quietly and privately. "Village life suits me," he says. "I am more at ease in the country. Living in the midst of greenery is bound to have an effect on my work, but where influences come from, God knows." ●

MARTA DONAGHEY

A journey from ceramics to silver.

BY SANDY BROWN

I HAVE KNOWN jeweller Marta Donaghey for many years – in fact since she took over the running of the potters' shop and gallery Contemporary Ceramics (in Marshall Street, London). She trained as a potter, and made some striking bold teapot forms using slip-casting in a dynamic way. In some ways it is a shame she did not develop them. But slip-casting is a laborious and indirect way of making things, as the creativity is in the preparatory

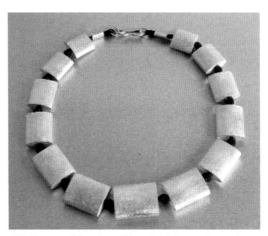

Hollow oval bead necklace by Marta Donaghey.

drawings and the original idea more than in the making process. Marta is too direct a person to be satisfied by that for long.

Now she expresses her love of ceramics by being surrounded by them and selling them every day. Her house is full to bursting with pots: she uses teacups and plates and lidded storage jars by the top potters in the country, and her enthusiasm is a joy to behold.

It is often the case that, when an artist has reached a sticking point, changing the material can release a fresh energy and a new lively approach. And that is what happened with Marta when she moved to silver and started making jewellery.

She says she started doing so for personal reasons: "I wanted to make it for myself!" And she does wear her jewellery all the time. Her clothes are mostly black, and her jewellery looks striking against it. Every time I see her I want what she is wearing for myself. I think it is because we both have a similar approach to our materials. When I use clay I leave all the fingerprints, I work spontaneously, and my pots are chunky and bold. So it is with Marta's silver. She loves the material, and works with it directly, boldly.

She says, "I like fluid, free forms with a scratched, unpolished surface, giving a warm colour and a feeling of softness." In fact, she works like a potter does. She makes stamps herself, which is what a lot of potters do, and these stamps are impressed into the silver to form a simple decoration. They are not fussy and delicate, they are clear, such as chevrons, squares. You can see that Marta has simply hammered in the stamp to make its mark. And it is so simple. Currently I have fallen in love with some earrings of hers which are a big chunky square of silver, with the hand-beaten hammer marks on it, and punctuated by one textured square stamp in the middle. That's it. No fiddling about, no fastidious little pretentious details, just basic metal. And somehow a hard material looks soft; fluid, even.

I have a brooch of hers that was made in a similar way, breathtakingly generous in its form. It is a big rectangle of silver, with three stamps punched into it. I just love it. I buy navy blue clothes so that I can wear it, together with the bangles I have (and necklaces from Charmian Harris, another favourite jeweller).

I have been told by a jeweller's partner that he thought the reason his wife had so many clients was because she made her customers feel good about themselves. That is a lovely aspect to making jewellery, that a maker such as Marta gets the pleasure of seeing women (and some men) light up, feel more special in their very being when wearing her work.

To write this, I asked Marta to give me her CV. Reading it now, I am reminded that she, being Polish, went to University in Warsaw and did a degree in Mechanical Engineering! So her interest in metal was actually there from the start, before she did pottery when she came to England. Now she looks to African and pre-Columbian gold for her inspirations, and I am still waiting for my earrings. ●

THE HARMONY IN HAND TOOLS

Work is not only a source of livelihood; it is also a source of spiritual and aesthetic fulfilment.

BY JOHN BROWN

MY GRANDMOTHER used to tell me that most of life's ills were caused by men chasing money. Even fifty years ago, the poor old dear could not understand what all the rush was about. She had a theory that the heartbeat hadn't altered since time began and that the pace of life should be regulated by this fact. I didn't take any notice of her at the time, but recently, I've had cause to recall her words. The speed of modern life is out of synchronization with the human body. If we could slow our lives down a little, think of quality before quantity, there would be more time to savour the pleasant things before we are forced to rush on to something else.

Woodworkers are not excused from this malady. Every bit of literature, every handbill or periodical to do with the craft is packed with advertisements for machines. A young man interested in making things out of wood can be forgiven for believing that machines are a fundamental necessity. Hand tools have been relegated to the small advertisement section or antique dealers, as though they were relics of the past whose use went out with grandfather.

SAVE MATERIALS, AND STAY COMFORTABLE

The price of timber once seemed of little consequence. Now, with rainforest problems and a general scarcity, this has become a very expensive raw material. A return to the use of hand tools, apart from being less wasteful, would add more value to this precious material. I fully appreciate that the average woodworker cannot render tree trunks into planks. Handsawing huge bulk is pure sweat, so the use of a power saw is necessary. That is all that is required to lead a full and satisfying woodworking life.

Power machines are unfriendly, for they are very noisy and make a lot of unpleasant dust. Craft woodworking should be a creative activity, with the practitioners as artists. Surrounded by ugly, noisy, dusty machines, the woodworker does not have the environment in which to do good work.

There are two main health hazards from frequent use of machinery, apart from cutting off the fingers: dust and noise. Neither is instantly apparent, as is an amputation, but nevertheless they are just as dangerous. The most frightening is nasal cancer, which is closely associated with wood dust. And constant exposure to high levels of noise can damage the ears and lead to deafness.

Of course you can wear protective clothing and apparatus against these ills. But to mummify yourself in this way can only be to the detriment of careful work. Picture, if you will, a cabinetmaker working on a fine piece of oak furniture clad in a hard hat. I am sure the sense of control of the operator is impaired by wearing all this safety equipment.

QUALITY OR QUANTITY

The reason for the introduction of machinery in the 19th century was to speed up the production in the factories. Water, then steam and finally electricity provided ample power, and in that great age of innovation, machines were invented to cope with more and more process. The owners cared not a jot for design or quality unless it affected sales. Quality was the main criterion. "How can we make more profit?" they asked. Unskilled people could be trained to work a single-operation machine in days. The fact that these operators had no interest in their work and did the job for what money they could get interested no one, except people like John Ruskin, C. R. Ashbee and William Morris.

Since the great war, it seems that these same principles have been adopted by modern woodworkers. Yet the motivation is entirely different. I have never known a craft woodworker who does the job only for money, or at least admits to this. Woodworkers pursue the craft because they love it. They enjoy working with wood, and they get great satisfaction from seeing a well-finished piece. They try their hardest to do fine work and to produce an artifact of delight. I don't suppose there has ever been a time when so much effort has gone into producing good work.

Unfortunately, a large part of the works on show are made by machines. And at what cost! Many thousands of pounds are spent on these machines, saws and re-saws, lathes, planers, thicknessers, spindle moulders, mortising machines, doweling machines and biscuit joiners, dovetail attachments, belt sanders and portable machines of all kinds. New ones every week. Apart from the initial expense of this armoury, there are attachments to buy, numerous cutters for different profiles and sawblades to be bought. Few of these things can be satisfactorily sharpened by the user. They have to be sent away. The operator becomes a mechanic producing precision engineered works. This has little to do with woodworking.

What about the extra time it takes to do a piece by hand? It can take a little longer, that's true. You need to be well organized, the workshop needs to be laid out properly and, above all, you must have a first-class bench. You must know your tools. Everything must be clean and sharp. Tools talk to the craftsman. You will know when they are right. What the machine does by noisy, brute force you will be able to do with quiet cunning.

I doubt there's much of a saving in machine work over hand work for the small, one-off maker. If you're an amateur, it doesn't matter, and the quality will be so much better. A professional will have to charge a little more. People will pay it. With the saving in capital cost, bank interest and the time-consuming business of setting up machines, you could be better off anyway.

It is difficult to know whether machine-mania was led by the woodworking press or the craftsman. I am inclined to the former opinion. It looks as though the machinery manufacturers have the technical press in a vice-like grip, leaving the humble hobbyist to believe that unless he buys the machines, he will be a second-class woodworking citizen. I was always led to understand that machines were there to do the tedious work and that the craftsman's skills should actually do the making. Gradually, the idea of what is tedious has been updated, for it is now possible to make complicated pieces entirely with machinery. The only handwork left to be done is to lift the wood to the machine. I am sure the manufacturers will cope with this in time!

APPRENTICESHIPS

It's a pity the apprenticeship system has gone, when young people were exposed for five years to good practices, working alongside skilled men. Pride in work, pride in a fine set of tools, I know this is now unfashionable, but there is nothing wrong with being proud of one's achievements. It is between a man and his God whether that pride is false or not. Some woodwork is quite tricky and needs a lot of practice. The wonder and joy as each hurdle is leaped has to be experienced to be believed. The material you work with is not uniform. It is moody, it can be deceptive, sometimes hiding faults until the very last moment of finishing, and you have to start all over again. Handwork breeds patience.

The kind of accuracy you can achieve cannot be measured in 'thous'. It's not necessary. I have heard of micrometers being used on tenons. Frankly, I find this ridiculous. Author Norman Potter tells the story of a visit to his workshop by a Gimson-trained cabinetmaker named Rex. Rex recalled how the famed English Arts-and-Crafts furniture maker would run his finger along the under edges of a newly finished piece, saying, "Kindly, Rex, keep your edges kindly." You will find no specification called kindly edges in the standard woodworking textbooks.

I would not go so far as to say that there are no skills necessary to working machines. It is important to be able to read and interpret complicated instructions. What you end up with is engineering skills – precision engineering in wood. As a substitute for apprenticeship these days, we have training colleges. These young people, having been taught design and machine skills, feel they should come out of college and jump straight into the first division. One or two cheekier ones do just this. The main skill required is in hiding machine marks. I suspect these young people never feel that wonderful, solid confidence of the apprentice who has just finished his five years, and with his beautiful handmade toolbox full of fine tools is about to set out in the world to do good work.

MADE BY HAND

Handmade work has soul, it has verve, a sparkle that a machine cannot reproduce. The apparent 'perfection' of some machined operations has trapped the craftsman into feeling that this is the way it should be. There is no excuse for lazy or shoddy work, by hand or machine, but it is nice to

Welsh stick chair and miniature, by John Brown. Photograph by the author.

think that this table or this chair was made by a human being.

You often see people inspecting furniture minutely to see if all the joints are tight or if there is any slackness in the dovetails. Perhaps they are looking for graving pieces that cover a mistake. This annoys me. Do these people do the same to a painting in an art gallery? A firm I know makes one-off pieces, things like Welsh dressers and furniture in the Georgian style. The joinery is impeccable. This company has the latest in machines. Yet the furniture is so ugly it is possible to detect their work from a good distance.

When they first started, organic farmers were ridiculed by the establishment as 'mud and muck', freaks. Now demand for their product far outstrips supply, and with farming problems as they are, I think they will have the last laugh. No one has grasped this particular nettle when it comes to woodworking. I often feel that the craftsman of today is recreating in his little heaven the very hell that the industrialists of the last century were so soundly drubbed for. Woodworkers should look anew at their hand tools. Take the meanest, rustiest

plane you have. Clean it, grind and sharpen the blade like a razor, and then set it up. Now, with the plane set very fine, run it over a scrap of oak. Hear the sound it makes, and feel the perfect finish. What a thrill!

I have worked with machines in other people's employ. I have owned some machines myself. Years ago I examined what I was doing and went organic. I haven't regretted it once. It was a renewal of my love affair with wood. We must do our best to turn things round. We must educate ourselves and our customers to realize what quality really means, quality in making, quality in design and, finally, quality in life.

Craftsmen who agree with these sentiments should, at a certain date, give up their machines. Then they should tell everyone what they are doing, broadcast the message, print it on their note paper, make a statement. But what I have said is about as fashionable as advising people to sell their cars and take a bus or even walk. Real progress can only be spiritual progress. The calm and unhurried atmosphere in my workshop makes enough to pay the bills for a simple life, no more. ●

147

WITH THE GRAIN

The revival of apprenticeship is essential for the future of crafts.

BARRIE THOMPSON
in conversation with Sophie Poklewski Koziell

ONE OF MY favourite quotes, from a sage of ancient Greece, is that: "Craftsmen in their intent, concentration and focus can contribute to the stability of the world." I believe that there is such a thing as the atmosphere from the workshop drifting out into the community. Thus, the effect of the place of work upon a craftsperson, and ultimately the wider community, is great. Until quite recently most craft workshops were based in villages and small towns. They had good light from windows that also gave views out to the surrounding countryside, or into the village to the theatre of life. These workshops gave a closeness and communality with other craftspeople and a constant exchange with the public, resulting in an open and creative work environment.

Unfortunately, workshops today are far removed from this ideal. They are usually on trading estates and are built for security and cheapness of construction. The result is huge machine shops of asbestos or tin. There is constant noise from machines or radios. There is little harmony. Craftspeople are isolated from each other. Worst of all, natural light and views are scarce. The drive behind these inhuman designs is to stop people 'wasting time' by talking to each other, or looking out of the windows. But the significance of daydreaming, human exchange or the inspiration of a view is enormous, and in turn becomes a part of the object you are making. In the end it is very difficult to make something beautiful in these surroundings. There is nothing of nature to inspire you; only brick walls. Today, in general, there is less time for the romantic element – for nourishing the soul. Only by surrounding oneself with beautiful things and ultimately by nature, can we feed our soul and our imagination.

THE TRAINING OF A craftsperson, I believe, should give respect to and knowledge of every aspect of the craft: from the characteristics of each tool, to the workings of machines. It is only by learning the whole art that students can become true craftspeople. There is no substitute for a proper apprenticeship. When I started, the first three months were spent sweeping up, the next six, sharpening. I learnt how to sharpen all the different tools, even pinchers, and the right way to sharpen screwdrivers to fit the exact screw you were using.

It was that slow learning, over years, that gave me respect for the tools. Unfortunately, there has been a twenty- to thirty-year gap in this country of young people not having apprenticeships and in many cases the hereditary continuity has been broken. Worst of all, during this time many of the basics have been brushed aside as the teachers weren't from a crafts tradition, but learnt from textbooks. This may give a few bones, but it certainly doesn't put the muscles and flesh on the whole subject.

Before people started travelling, furniture was made by the village carpenter, or handed down from previous generations. Today, the trend is more for people to buy cheaper furniture that lasts a decade, rather than buying something that costs three times as much, but that lasts three generations. In some ways furniture has become a 'product' that is more to do with a fashion statement, a form of lifestyle identification label, rather than a deeper personal choice. Moreover, a lot of the design is about being clever, being different, over-embellishing. The emphasis is on individualism, the importance of making a mark and impressing. This seems to count more than the quality of what is produced. As a result, the item created loses its integrity and simple beauty. Very often you find that the shapes that don't flow aren't organic. In some cases they are quite disturbing. Shapes come from nature, and we are part of nature. This vital fact is often overlooked in today's designs.

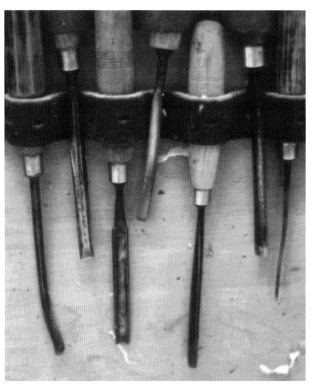

*Some of Barrie Thompson's chisels. Photograph
by Sophie Poklewski Koziell.*

RELYING TOO MUCH on a quick design on paper or computer is another fault line that has appeared in crafts. Properly trained craftspeople actually have special mental skills with respect to the language of shape, scale and proportion. Not so long ago, I came across a good example of this at a sawmill where, in 1973, the last barge in Britain was made. The design specification given to the craftspeople contained few instructions. There were just some notes describing what wood should be used, the weight the barge was to carry, and the length and width at the beam. There was no design, because the people that were building it knew, from practical reasons and from experience, what shape it should be. And of course it was beautiful, because usually practical shapes are beautiful. Today, however, if you ask a woodworker to make a window, even the glazing bars are badly designed, because that knowledge of the language of shapes isn't learnt any more. Instead people rely too heavily on designing on paper and on computers.

This is all linked to the attitude that one can design something on the drawing-board and go straight into making the final product. The ideal process is through making and experimenting with full-scale mock-ups. Ron Arad, the furniture designer, creates some very modern beds and chairs in stainless steel. However, they are very comfortable to sit on although they may look cold and uninviting. This is because he makes many mock-ups. Chippendale and most of the famous furniture designers did the same, and then gradually refined them, tweaking them until they got the famous pieces that we know today. The use of mock-ups is essential to the craft.

Another inherent problem with designing furniture today is that the timber sizes seem to dictate, and therefore limit, the design. Previously, the craftspeople would have been in touch with the timber yards that would have tipped them off about, for instance, a wonderful big piece of burr oak or ripple ash. Then they'd go along and see the wood, and the size, shape and feel of it would inspire in them a particular use for it – a bookcase or a table, for example. Today, that relationship between many furniture makers and timber yards is divorced since the wood is imported, and in uniform sizes.

Apart from the revival of properly structured apprenticeships, with a livable wage and good conditions, I'd like to see more experimentation in merchandising to allow for the production of things of beauty and quality. At the moment, manufacturers are constrained too much by economy and efficiency – producing things that are unadventurous and cheap. These things will sell but they lack any real integrity or longevity. It is the arrogance of companies who think that they are giving the people what they want, when in fact people have much better taste than they are given credit for. I wouldn't mind betting that if you put ten coffee mugs in front of the general public, and one or two of them were hand-made, but cost a little bit more, more people would choose the nicer ones. Once people start buying mass-market items, in shops with limited diversity, they forget that there are things being made individually. It would help a lot if company showrooms put on display other designs and types of furniture, adjacent to the mass-made items, so that people could have a choice.

Saying all this though, I am more optimistic about the future. There has been a 'dimming of the lights' over the past thirty years, when the status of crafts went through a low point in Britain. The fact was that my uncle, and many of his generation, wanted to 'get away from the bench'. The idea grew amongst craftspeople that working with their hands was somehow lowly, and that their life, and perhaps more importantly their status, might be improved by a dressed-up job. This kind of attitude is thankfully no longer so prevalent, and there are once more young people interested in the crafts. The important thing now is to show them the way and give them our support. Not only for making new things but also we should support the crafts of repairing, restoring and mending. Although it might be going against the grain of our time-poor, fast-rewards society to spend the time to make something of beauty, it may just contribute to the stability of the world as that Greek sage said so long ago. ●

ON THE MEND

Why live in a throw-away world when things are too precious to be cast aside?

BY ROGER SCRUTON

W HILE THE GRASS grows and the soil is pliable, our thoughts turn to mending. Time was when everything usable was also repairable: chairs, sofas, hats, accordions, wheelbarrows, carpets – all were in a state of flux, as new defects were discovered and new patches stuck over them.

Repair was a need, a habit and an honoured custom, with its times, its rituals, and its moments of celebration. People respected the past of damaged things, restored them as though healing a child and looked on their handiwork with satisfaction. In the act of repair the object was made anew, to occupy the social position of the broken one. Worn shoes went to the anvil, holed socks and unravelled sleeves to the darning last – that peculiar mushroom-shaped object that stood always ready on my mother's mantelpiece.

The custom of repair was not confined to the home. Every town, every village, had its cobbler, its carpenter, its wheelwright and its smith. In each community people supported repairers, who in turn supported things. And our surnames testify to the honour in which their occupations were held. But now we live in a throw-away culture: goods are cheap but shoddy, and it is no longer economical to repair them. For a decade or two – until the world clogs up with plastic – we shall go on treating objects as dispensable, without claims on our goodwill and without durable personalities.

In repairing an object you endow it with character; and when repair is the normal response to breakages, the final discarding is like a funeral. We still feel this about shoes, since they are shaped by our use of them, become friendlier with the years and are never seen as quite replaceable. Hence we still have cobblers – a few at least. Ours, in Malmesbury, is a lover of shoes, who sees the soul in the sole, and the wearer in the worn.

Shoes, for Mustafa, are the middle terms in human relations, objects of respect and signs of his own social value. He takes them from you with an intent, preoccupied smile, examines them and then lovingly describes first their defects, then the very great virtues – apparent to his expert eye – which justify the cost of mending them. And because he can live from his skills, and at the same time express himself through them, Mustafa is happy, as comfortable in an English farming community as he was in his Turkish village.

Repair, as a custom and a way of life, survives on the farm. Now is the time to mend fences, clear ditches and reinforce walls. It is the time to re-hang gates and doors, to stitch the stable rugs, to patch the roofs and sheds. Farmers, like sailors, spend half their day repairing things and, like sailors, they have a life-and-death relationship with the things they mend. Each year requires you to heal the wounds of the last one, and this year things are particularly bad, the incessant winter rain having made the fields impassable to tractors. Only now can we embark upon the fencing that should have been completed before the cows came out; only now have we been able to dig out the field drain that has been leaking slurry for weeks.

The thing about mending, said our neighbour Harry, who was busy repairing his trailer, is it's no good being in a hurry. Trailers, like tractors, are survivors from the world before plastic. They are designed to last and to shape themselves over time to the lives that are wrapped in them. Harry's trailer is a case in point. "He's in better shape now nor he was when he come," is Harry's verdict. The trailer has acquired alloy edging along the walls and tailgate, a new axle behind, deep-cut tyres that can get through all but the worst of the mud, and assorted hardwood slats in place of its splintered boards of pine. Each spring the trailer is repainted, its moving parts greased, and its bottom inspected for cracks or loose fixings.

Of course, repairs don't always work: it was a faulty coupling that led to disaster when the trailer

The Thatcher by Charles Tunnicliffe.

crushed Harry's foot. But Harry puts this down to temperament on the trailer's part, and in no way revised his obdurate attachment to a vehicle to which he is wedded till death them do part. The only question is, whose death? The trailer's, or Harry's?

It is one of the joys of country life that you are immersed in a culture of mending and bending. There is something ungrateful in the habit of throwing things away. You also feel more at home when you support the world that supports you and tend to the needs of the things that you need. This friendly relation with things underlies the appeal of Thomas the Tank Engine and Bob the Builder. Little boys identify with the heroic achievements of

steam engines, cement-mixers, diggers and trailers. They recognize these tools as comrades, bound to them in a reciprocity of need. Story-book characters like Thomas and Bob invoke a primordial experience of bonding, and one which is being driven from the adult culture to our cost.

As Harry says, however, mending cannot be hurried and farmers, like the rest of us, are swept along on winds of change. In place of the post and rail comes the electric fence with plastic stakes; in place of the laid hedge come the barbed-wire strings from stump to stump, and in place of the roof comes the ubiquitous plastic sheeting. We leave larger and larger footprints on the earth; and soon even our shoes will cease to be mended. ●

151

SEEKERS
OF MEANING

At the still point of the turning world
Neither flesh nor fleshless
Neither from nor towards;
at the still point, there the dance is
But neither arrest nor movement.
And do not call it fixity,
Where past and future are gathered.
Neither movement from nor towards
Neither ascent nor decline.
Except for the point, the still point
There would be no dance,
and there is only the dance.

T. S. Eliot The Four Quartets

Tie dyeing hands.
Photograph by Sue Carpenter.

CONTINUAL RENEWAL

In Indian culture, beauty is divine.

BY KAMALADEVI CHATTOPADHYAY

THE WORD TRADITION is still pronounced in a hushed tone which quivers like a delicate glass when filled with perfume. It can mean a million things to a million people. For it escapes a set format, and any attempt at a clear definition usually fails to project it in all its fullness. It is the essence of our being, *Rasa*, as it is named in our Indian language. It can also be described as *quality*, excellence. Tradition is all-pervasive and touches human life at every phase; it can never be broken.

As we view our world we tend to break it into unreal divisions – the developed and the undeveloped – as if the history of the earth began at one fixed point, then slid along on a straight line, as though there was nothing there. This appears to be particularly so where vast expanses of water continue to hold the land in their grip or mighty ranges of mountains stand as in eternal vigilance. But in reality none of these are permanent. Let us for instance take the Gulf area in West Asia, where big chunks of land have been rendered dry and infertile, turned into sand dunes. Not so long ago, the whole of it was a vast prosperous region, with big trade deals transacted.

As communities and nations keep moving away from tradition and adherence to settled patterns they invariably decline, but the essence persists and continues to flower. Every item that survives finally comes alive and a fresh life bubbles into play. Nothing *really* perishes fully. It is perpetually renewing itself. What survives as essence is tradition. It is the essence of the millennia since life came to be. It has attributes that clothe it with multifarious forms, shapes, colours, sounds. Tradition is the seed from which life always blossoms.

Here I am attempting to take one definite attribute of the Traditional, and the most distinguishing: beauty. Beauty not merely in form, shape, design and colour, but beauty in Concept, an element that pervades our entire life and our being.

IN INDIA BEAUTY is elevated into godhead, interchangeable with divinity, in fact worshipped as Beauty. There are rich incantations and devotional lyrics addressed to Beauty, the source of life. It is therefore inevitable that this reaching out to beauty and its manifold manifestations has been a constant factor in the life of the people, in rituals and ceremonial, festivals and celebrations.

All over the world as human beings evolved, this gem which lay in their inmost being had to find unfoldment. They were not content to fulfil themselves by merely satisfying their creature comforts. They had to adorn themselves, first drawing on nature, then inventing and contriving decorative objects. Their abode of dwelling had to be something more than merely four walls and a ceiling. Every article used had to be elegant; lovely to look at, elevating to live with. Beauty in this concept is, therefore, not divorced from life as lived every day. The commonest object is endowed with grace and colour. Every act and function human beings perform must be touched by this magic wand. Beginning with the harsh, severe walls of the primitive dwellings to baskets and pottery, from clothes to objects of worship, all was involved with this grand spirit.

Thus Beauty is not confined to hanging a frame on a wall, an image in a niche. The objects are not meant to be kept in glass cases as status symbols. For anything superfluous in the traditional world would be an object without a significance, regarded more as a sign of human vanity, not creativity.

Handicraft has always been a basic activity in human society; in fact it is more cohesive and permeating in human relationships than even language, for it can penetrate the normal barriers to communication.

THE GROWTH OF CRAFTS in society was the sign of the cultivation of sensitivity. It brought elegance and grace into an otherwise harsh and drab human

Photograph by Sue Carpenter.

Metal worker in India. Photograph by Mark Edwards/Still Pictures.

existence. In fact, our elevation from gross existence is marked by our yearning for something beyond the satisfaction of mere creature comforts and needs, which found natural expression in crafts.

The most primitive people began to ornament their articles of everyday use: their weapons, their garments, and their own person and surroundings. The walls of their huts became canvasses on which blossomed pictures. A death-dealing but very strategic item like the bow and arrow became embellished with decorations, water pots took pleasing shapes, and alluring designs were invented for mundane kitchen pans, coverings and trappings for animals, and even ordinary carts were ornamented.

Here we see the transformation of the merely functional into works of aesthetic value, the common becoming the cherished, the joy giving. Utility is a necessary part in the completeness of life. Through aesthetics in utility, beauty is brought into our intimate life.

Obviously craft skills emerged and unfolded in the peace and refulgence of the countryside, where the community lived in close intimacy with nature, with its many-splendoured mien, and in tune with its changing rhythms of the day, of the night, the varying seasons and the life cycles. A culture evolved that was in harmony with the environment. The seasonal observances through festivals were a sign of awareness of the wonder of nature's transformation, and the desire to transcend the routines of everyday life. Its social content was a fabric woven out of the million tinted strands of local romances and heroic tales, from the core and substance of everyday life mingled with vibrant memories transformed into myths and fables, songs and verses, and not the least out of nature's own rich storehouse.

Each community lived an integrated pattern that responded to the joys and burdens of life, taking them in its flow. There was a natural acceptance of the human cycle like embracing the air and the sunlight, with no resort to escapism. Craft skills were conceived and nurtured in an embryo of fullness generated by an unhurried rhythm of life. Such products naturally had vitality and character, for they were the direct expression of human creativity, but with a purposeful emphasis on the functional, on endowing it with beauty. Handicraft was an indigenous creation of the ordinary people to meet their direct human

A weaver in Bangladesh. Photograph by Mark Edwards/Still Pictures.

needs. Satisfaction in eating calls as much for the right kind of spoon as the food to be consumed. This genesis accepted intimate kinship with and understanding of the human urges that create the needs. It also proved an intuitive sense of going with, rather than against, the grain of daily existence. Handicraft became an activity that involved the entire person, closely relating the mind and the material to a certain function for a specific purpose. There was no professional caste or class of craftsmen or women. Each was a maker and creator.

IT IS OBVIOUS that human beings developed a sense of aesthetics from the pleasure they derived from a job well done. They must have imbibed a deep sense of fulfilment when they looked on their handiwork. They satisfied, maybe unconsciously, but with the right instinct, all the conditions demanded later through learned treatises on what constituted superb handiwork. This was not determined merely by the outer appearance of an object. It had to be a human activity that fulfilled a definite function, had a place in the social pattern, for each human being is part of a social milieu. Therefore the tangible forms they shaped were meaningful and led to the makers transcending themselves and

being transformed into artists, that is, creators. This accounts for the superb handiwork of the tribals, the result of an unobscured imagination, extreme concern for details, sincere devotion to objectives, all of which generates powerful inspiration and endows the object with quality. But this was not the offspring of a philosophy, nor lessons learnt from learned treatises, guidebooks or texts.

Here one needs to define quality in this context, for it would go beyond the normal dictionary meaning.

One gazes with wonder on the objects the tribals turn out. The textile designs range from the most delicate and suggestive to the most elaborate manifestation of complex techniques. The basketry is most exquisite, with incredibly refined weave and in a wealth of beautiful shapes and designs. The wood carvings are startlingly alive.

Tribals decorate themselves and almost everything about them. The boards in the frontage of their houses have carved human heads in high relief. Similarly doors, eaves in the roof, drums and musical instruments, the couch on which the dead are laid out (in fact this has some of the most elaborate carving), graves of famous warriors; items of household use like mugs, plates, pipes for smoking,

A craftswoman sewing sequins onto gold motifs. Photograph by Sue Carpenter.

combs, etc.

In fact their products vibrate with life, as though the makers infused some of their own selves into their creations. Each has to be a craftsperson to be a creator, for when we shape an object, we are in a way shaping our own personality. Here there is no duality of the subjective and the objective. Creation is a self-involved experience, of basic oneness of the personality which later came to be described as *sadhana*, a cultivated state of being. The tribals did not probe or delve into themselves to build up the complex analytical philosophy that others were later to contrive. The tribals' intuitive mode was primarily inspirational, and they seem to have been guided by an aesthetic conscience. For their mental exercises were simple and direct. Being intimate children of nature they were conditioned to following certain natural laws, which taught techniques and guided processes, sensitivity to the right proportions and balances which nature so exuberantly portrays, and sharpens sensibilities that make for economy in material and operational time.

ANCIENT PEOPLE MUST have learned in the infancy of their evolution that what their aesthetic conscience prompted – *quality* – lay in the *seed*, for nature proved it, an experience that later became one of the basic tenets of Indian philosophy. Just as human beings learnt that health can be maintained only by respecting the laws of nature, they also learnt that where their handiwork failed to acquire the excellence which was yearned for and the eye sought, they knew there was a lack of co-ordination between their concept, the material they used and the method they employed. This fusion was the fundamental pre-condition for quality – the mastercraftsmanship. This was also the beginning of the laws of discipline. Their hearts must have surged up in joy at their successful handiwork, the satisfaction which comes from creating and giving tangible shape to a mental concept or image. We must remember that every object that a tribal made was for himself or herself, for their daily use and therefore an intimate part of themselves, things they lived with. The value of the object was not in terms of what it would fetch but rather how well it would serve the social purpose, above all provide the inner sense of satisfaction. In the early days of striving and straining, the result of each movement must have seemed magical, each achievement a miracle. This is how the great tradition must have been moulded and history made, for their every act contained all the past, bringing to birth again old memories transformed into fresh inspiration, and as they put together parts out of the infinite possibilities before them, they worked out the future. Thereby emerged mastercraftsmanship with all the requisite qualities of excellence, a dynamic embryo emerging from the womb of timelessness. For creativity in our philosophy is an eternally moving current like a cycle. Culture has therefore always been defined as dynamic. The basic idea behind the tradition is that every human being is endowed with creative talent and can find appropriate expression through stimulation and disciplined guidance. Because, while self-expression is a new and fresh expression each time, tradition does not take the risk of leaving it to chance and the exigencies of the moment. There are stern standards to be maintained to prevent deflection from the concept of Beauty which, however conventionalized, carried in it inspiration and attraction to respond both to the head and the heart.

Notwithstanding the fact that traditional crafts are handed down from generation to generation in pupillary succession, the tradition could never get fossilized into rigidity for the crafts have to reflect the common experiences of the community. Changes there have to be, not for the sake of novelty but in order to reflect the flow and movements in the way of changes in psychology and taste. When something new shoots up, it is to reflect an immediate experience. Tradition, to be meaningful, has to be a live force, unlike the copying of styles which has now come to replace it.

TRADITIONAL CRAFTS reflect the landscape around, the seasons, the moods of the day. Into the crafts are woven the epics, the legends, the romantic heroic tales of the countryside. They heighten the big events in human life: the wonder of birth, the joy of marriage, the mystery of death. In each event the crafts play a special role, for they live and grow and have their being in everyday life.

Where we wander away from creation and fill it with sheer mechanics, we get out of our depth. We are lost in a vague, nebulous, colossal mass. We want to recover our identity and set out on a great search to find ourselves. For so much in our life becomes 'other-directed'. We see symptoms of this vigorous search for self-identity, for us to feel self-directed; not a tiny nut in a vast monstrous mechanism, as life threatens to become.

The answer is creativity, not in the isolation of the poet in the ivory tower, but as part of a living community with a dynamic tradition that continues to infect love and compassion, grandeur and humility, as the traditional crafts represent and bring home to us.

We stand now at the beginning of a new age. Let me narrate the eternal creative credo. Our old history has ended, and our new history has begun. We stand as one within the black starlit womb of creation. As one, we face this new unknown, this greater reality, this universe. The tradition continues. At all times and ages human beings are part of one body. We know we no longer live in fragmented, isolated cultures divided and alone. We know we no longer live separated from one another by space, time, ignorance and intention.

Humankind is a union of almost infinite diversity. Each person is different and makes a difference on each individual, equally on the population. Each receives some gift from the past and has a gift of new hope to give to the future. The act of each affects the destiny of the whole.

The challenge of our time is to offer each other the opportunity to give our best to the future; to hold our beliefs inviolate; to develop a faith that we can control our own destiny through our creative powers whatever they may be; to give ourselves the opportunity to do so in independence and without fear.

We call on all creative people everywhere to join with us in affirming our credo of our power to control our own destiny, of our power to build new citadels, to form new concepts of living in harmony with one another, to prepare a new life for all within an ever-expanding universe. ●

KEITH CRITCHLOW

Inspired buildings embody the language of arithmetic,
geometry, harmony and astronomy.

INTERVIEW BY SATISH KUMAR

**IN WHAT WAY is your practice of architecture
different from from other architects?**
Probably our practice is different because we
deliberately choose to embrace a deeper perspective, what you might call a metaphysical dimension; things other architectural practices either feel
unnecessary or haven't the time to research. We are
particularly fortunate in having spent so much of
our lives investigating the more subtle effects of
architecture; I mean the sacred traditions which
have left both documentary evidence and the magnificent forms behind . . . . These are the crystallized wisdom of past ages.

Surely there are profound differences, say,
between the Temple of Heaven in Peking, Khajura-
ho in India and Salisbury Cathedral, yet the evidence is there that there are four universal
languages which all three of them were concerned
with. These are the languages that all people can
agree upon – the objective basis of experience one
might say: arithmetic or pure number is the first,
followed by geometry or the direct relationships of
order in space, followed by the principles of music
or harmony, and fourthly, the objective evidence of
the night sky and the rhythms of sun and moon we
call cosmology or astronomy. Once you take all
these into design account, your architecture
becomes different – you are dealing with more than
mechanical or 'functional' criteria.

I believe that architecture can be designed and
built with a sense of caring and sacredness rather
than being ruled by economic force or any other
abstract element. The return to an awareness of
sacredness will come through people being aware
of their own sacredness and their interdependence
on all aspects of the planetary environment – the
body of the world, one's community and one's own
body. One Chinese philosopher said "Whether you
concern yourself with the big or the small, you start
with your own body." Architecture is the next bodily envelope after one's clothes.

How did you get interested in Islamic design?
Some time ago I was invited to Iran by Seyyed Hos-
sein Nasr, who is a pre-eminent Islamic scholar, and
he asked me if I would write a book about Islamic
Art? I said "Why? I'm not a Muslim." He said,
"Well, the point is that the only way we are going to
regain the dignity of our own art is through the
young people. But they only look towards West. We
need somebody in the West to tell them to to look to
their own roots." I said, "Very well, but I'll only do
it if you will write the foreword to the book!" So I
wrote the book and it has done very well. I am very
pleased when I go to Saudi Arabia or to Kuwait; the
book is well known there and people immediately
have a relationship with me. I am very happy to see
that the young Muslim architects are very interested
to try to regain their cultural forms. These patterns
have many layers of symbolism, and most significant-
ly it is an expression of unity where science and art
are inseparable. We have always treated Islamic Art
as decorative and decorative meaning it is inferior to
'fine' art, like Rembrandt and so on. Well, to my
mind it is in no way inferior to Rembrandt. The reason that they are in small pieces is often extremely
practical. They did not have large trees. Most often
they had small, very twisted little trees, so they had
only little bits of wood. So to make a door you have
lots of little bits of wood and you put those together
as cleverly as you could. It was very good because
the joints were never glued so they were able to
breathe with the change of temperature. So there is
an immensely practical thing about Islamic design,
as well as the symbolic allusions to the cycles of the
sun and the planets, which is a way of chronological
teaching just purely by the eye picking it up. There
is no lecture given. The eye is attracted to beauty
and the beauty speaks for itself – through symmetry
and light.

So the building is a message.
That's right. And the body of the building is a

reflection of a healthy body. Similarly, if the body of the building stands out and is well poised, that helps you the user to be healthy. If you go into a beautiful building, the first thing it does is that it draws you up, and as you look it opens your chest, you breathe better. If it is a Gothic cathedral you look up at the vaults and you get in a lovely deep breath: that's the secret of a sacred building. It makes you realize your own ability, it puts you in touch. The ancient Greek name for Spirit was *pneuma* – breath.

What was the process of losing this sacredness? How come that we are surrounded with these monstrous structures?

Well, it is an interesting question. I would like to answer this with a story. Before this interview I just opened one of my books. I have a lovely book here; I'm going to mention it because it is very rare and if anybody has a chance to track it down it is an absolutely staggering book; it is called *The Bread of God*. And it is even written anonymously, which is quite rare these days. It was written by a hermit and a monk who prayed. I opened this book, and in it there is a commentary on the man who sows the seeds in the Bible story. The metaphor in that is that there are four kinds of soil. The soil which is too rocky for a seed to get in, is too hard and won't let anything in. Then the soil which is too sandy, too insecure (a mind like a butterfly) so the seed can't take root. Then there is the ground which will take any seed, which is the wilderness, which is very profound and important, but in terms of human mentality it is the mind full of confusion. Then there is the soil which is perfect for a seed and will grow with roots. Likewise there are four worlds, the fifth world is the world of unity. There is only one world in the end. But there are four grades of world. At the top grade there is the divine world which is the world of light and symbolizing the experience of light as we receive it through the eye.

The next level down is often called the world of intellect. Our intellect is functioning at its best when it is engaging itself in the universal intellect. In other words there is order. Order is evidence of intellect. It is also called symbolically the world of air. The next level down is the world of the psyche which is traditionally much more than the modern world of psychology. Psychology often abandons the upper two worlds. But the world of the soul and psyche has access to the upper worlds and to the lower worlds. It is like a bridge. Now, modern psychology tends to deal with the problems of the lower world, the conditions of our particular incarnation, hence its limitations. Then below that you have the physical world, the world of natural resources and the world of material economics.

Now what has happened is that modern archi-

tecture has slowly but surely abandoned the three upper worlds and is now primarily determined by the physical, material and mechanical world. The basis of a lot of the buildings designed and built today is purely physical calculation and monetary considerations and concerns. The only acknowledgement of the psychic world is the minimum amount of space somebody is allowed to be in, so we have rules about that. But whether it is *worth* being in, in any particular building, is never asked. So the spaces don't even allow the psychic question, let alone the intellectual principle of universal order. This is something quite real which can actually reveal through the metaphor of form to the person in that room, where they came from and where they are going and what it is all about. Let alone the final level. Is there a chance that a light might come in – not physical light through the window – but some sort of light which will make you realize that everything is as it should be, which is the hardest realization? This is the experience of unity itself.

There was a particular theologian, I can't even remember his name now, in the 17th century he and Descartes together had a lot to do with the abandoning of the three subtle worlds. Descartes put it in writing: he said that psyche is not something that we can investigate logically, therefore he said he would put it to one side. Now once that became a practice it meant that those who accepted Descartes' logic were allowing their psyche to wither. If you leave something to one side and don't nourish it, what can it do but wither? It is pointless to throw mud at people, but Descartes crystallized this European attitude which was utterly dangerous. And he was only saying we can't deal with the psyche, let alone whether we can deal with universal laws or with divinity itself! So once the divisions were made then we got into the mess. William Blake said, if you want to bring a civilization down, bring its art down. Now what was fascinating was that around this same period there began a steady perversion of language. The Age of Enlightenment they called it, which was absolutely the opposite. Descartes decided to carry out some experiments on animals, alive and without any anaesthetic. The screams and howling that came out of his house caused an uproar in the local village, and the police came asking, what the hell are you doing to these dogs and animals? Descartes appeared in court and he defended himself by saying: animals don't have souls. The noise that you are hearing is the grindings of a machine not working properly. And he was allowed to get away with it. He actually got away with it. Now that decision released something; which has been a tragedy ever since. We can allow things like battery hens and factory farming and all these awful ways of producing food and processing,

The Super Speciality Hospital at Puttaparthi, inspired by Sai Baba, designed by Keith Critchlow and colleagues.

because unconsciously, we are saying, oh these animals don't have souls. Well, of course a lot of people believe that certain human beings don't have souls! But once you allow that you sink to the lowest level and then the architecture will express that level.

As architects, what can you do?
Architects have to act on their conviction by putting a building up. I have been working in Colorado for Lindisfarne Chapel which we call the Grail. We have been working on that for four years. We decided that the people who build it, the way it is built and the building itself are all of equal importance. Therefore the example that one sets is not that one is designing and telling everybody, that's how to do it, but you design by sacred principles. There are laws of beauty and harmony, and those laws must also point to the ultimate goal of humankind. The making of the building is done with people who understand that the act of building is the act of building oneself. The Grail is a universal chapel. Anybody can go there and sit and be quiet or meditate or pray towards Mecca, or hold a Mass: whatever is appropriate. It's a circular building with 72 seats in it. It has a millstone in the middle which is a symbol of the turning of the universe. As I say, it is really evidence of an approach, an attitude.

In India, the people in the villages didn't build permanent structures. They built mud structures with thatch roofs and they built more permanent structures either for their kings or for the temples.

Building in organic materials, such as mud and thatch, is absolutely correct and is a reminder that this building that we are carrying, called the body, is also impermanent. I can't get hold of anything in my body which is more than 18 months old, even if I get hold of my head it is only 18 months old! The whole body changes every seven years. So, in a way, the Indian wisdom of building domestic houses of organic material and not too solid or permanent a structure was a spiritual reminder that we are transitory beings and the only permanence should be in the temple, or possibly the palace which is really the permanence of governing the physical plane by the mandate of heaven. Any good ruler can rule only because they are ruling by the great principles. So the palace and the temple surely can be permanent because they are representing permanent principles. The Lindisfarne Chapel is itself made of woven beams of timber with a more permanent outer skin of copper tiles, a way of indicating both levels of permanence and impermanence.

Also, the Indian village houses did not need specialist builders or architects.
That's right. It is part of the technology of modern days that the citizen himself can't build his own house. Why? Because we don't teach building at school. But some very good experiments have been taking place in the west where a group of people together who pool their financial resources, include an architect in a community of maybe ten or twenty families and then build a little set of houses using the skill of the architect, who is building for him-

self, which is a completely different attitude than building for other people. All sorts of different skills within that group get together. That, to me, is a very good collective way of trying to break down the barrier between specializations. You make a small selection of people who can actually get together and build their own houses. The bricklayers can teach the other people a certain amount of bricklaying, and the architect can show everybody where the decisions come which are not specialist.

When we come into this world we know everything we need for life in the physical plane, but then as Plato says, we drink the waters of forgetfulness. So the business of being reminded is to remember that we do know everything. But our misguided modern education says to a children, you are an empty milk bottle, until you have been filled up with the knowledge that I am going to give you, you are nothing, just an empty bottle. So the West has tended to coerce so many of its young people by saying you know nothing until I tell you. Whereas, in the Platonic doctrine the opposite is true. You know everything, but you need me or others to help you to remember it. So there is a difference. You have everything, every person is able to be their own architect, but of course you need to go through learning in order to remember your own knowledge. It is useful to have specialization but only as long as everybody acknowledges the fact that they have chosen to specialize that piece of their knowledge but everybody else inherently has that knowledge.

In modern education we are told by everybody that specialization is the most important thing yet this is just the opposite of developing a *whole* view, and the biggest threat is the specialization of computers because it not only isolates by subject but also from human contact and interaction. It is *the a*moral tool. In other words, we are all made to feel impotent unless we can speak a computer language which, of course, is a tragedy.

I would never be against having good tools, but tools for what? In other words, unless we develop a psyche and a relationship to the nature of unity the tools will always lead us to more confusion. Tools are absolutely valuable to live a physical life and nourish the planet as best as we can. If we need computers, that's fine, as long as we know what we need them for. If it is just to direct more and more atomic warheads, forget it. Tools are tools, and it doesn't matter how sophisticated they are, it is the motivation behind using them which is so important.

Architecture is also a tool, but far more than merely a mechanical tool. Le Corbusier did an immense bad service by saying the house was a machine for living in – because it became just a machine and we all forgot what *living* was. Now the task is to acknowledge the miraculousness of life, the preciousness of life, and the vast beauty of what we do not know about life and the living.

To treat life, ourselves, our neighbours, our land, our green life, our architecture, as sacred at least teaches us to be careful, appreciative and sensitive – from here on it is up to each one of us how we build. ●

163

BOBBIE COX

Weaving is functional as well as symbolic.

INTERVIEW BY SATISH KUMAR

LET US START by talking about your own story.

I was trained to be an artist and a teacher at the same time. On my course they said that very few people can make a living as an artist, but there are many artists who have a wonderful contribution to make. So I was trained to be a teacher-artist and I moved into part-time teaching, always keeping two days a week to paint.

Then how did you take up weaving?

I felt that some kind of first-hand experience would very much help my teaching. I decided to go to Greece to study Byzantine mosaics. And that involved walking across rural Greece from monastery to monastery, over the hills and down the dales. I found that all the valleys were laid out with wonderful tapestries and carpets. They were being washed in the spring rivers. Up on the hills I found people spinning. I became fascinated and thought that perhaps the children at my school could do something like this and make tapestries from their paintings. I went back to school with this new input, tried it out myself, became hooked, and moved from painting to weaving.

Did you find a difference between the medium of painting and weaving?

I thought that we would take a painting, set up a warp and weave it. But very quickly I discovered that things you can do in paint you can't do in weaving. In paint, for instance, you can start anywhere on your rectangular canvas. In weaving you have to start at the beginning and it has to go line by line, horizontally laid in against the vertical structure of the warp. It's a very strong discipline. As an artist, I was trying to stretch this medium unnecessarily to make it behave like paint. Then I learned to design paintings which were weavable and responded to the horizontal/vertical construction; the unique language of weaving. When you've got a few inches or feet up in a tapestry you think

that the bit you put in the bottom could have been a wider blue. Now in paint, you simply go back and paint over. Well, you can't do that in weaving, which does mean fairly careful working out at an initial stage. So, there is an enormous difference in that kind of way.

Did you do any particular training for weaving?

No. None at all. If I wanted to be a weaver I would have gone to a weaving school and I would have learned to use a loom and make yards of cloth. Very few people were making tapestries in England; it was considered an antique trade. I could have gone to France and learned how to make huge, antique tapestries, implanting a painterly image into weaving and getting it as near the painting as you could.

Teaching yourself, did you not find it a bit daunting, going in the deep end like that?

No, because my weaving is very simple: you go in and out of one string and on the way back you go out and under the other – what's called straight tabby weave. The difficulty was in choosing the material to use, because when I went to the wool shops to buy wool, I found it awfully boring. It was flat colour and flat texture. As a painter I wanted my colours to shift more slowly. There simply was not the vocabulary in the wool shops or wool agents that gave me what I wanted. I had to teach myself the processing of the material. I started with wool and I have stuck with it and never got bored since.

How did you develop the texture and colour for your needs?

Through starting with the raw fleece. I discovered that the raw fleece, if you look at it in the warehouse, has far more textures than is ever evident in the end result in a wool shop. It's over-processed, over-mechanized, over-smooth in order to work on modern machines. And I'm not a machine so I didn't want that. I started spinning it in different ways.

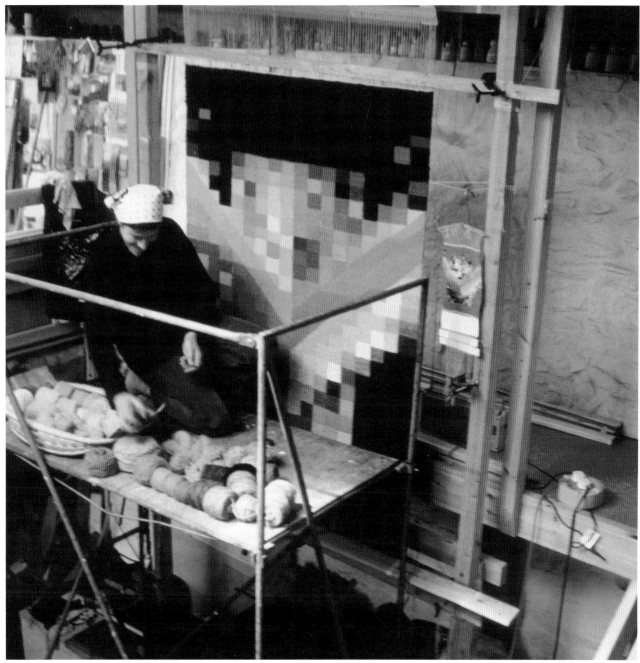

Bobbie Cox working in her studio.

Then I found that the traditional spinning wheel is fine up to a point, but when you start looking at really fat stuff, there was nothing. It's really taken me half a lifetime to arrive at the right sort of equipment which can handle many different sizes and scales and do what I want. This meant designing my own equipment.

You seem to take much inspiration from India. What did you discover there? As a weaver and a painter yourself, did you discover the art and craft of India?
Well, on our first day we drove along a single-track highway. The sides, washed away by the monsoons to mud holes, were being filled up by women with little stones. Now, these women were dressed in the most beautiful tribal saris of exquisite weave. They were crouched on the ground in these gold brocaded saris, wearing all the silver jewellery that they owned – in their hair, their hands, their noses, their feet, their ears and their toes – and they were absolutely exotic. Not only that, but these women were laying walnut-sized stones piece by piece along the side of the road to make the road. The road was being hand-made. A great backup for these women was a huge team of people who were breaking up

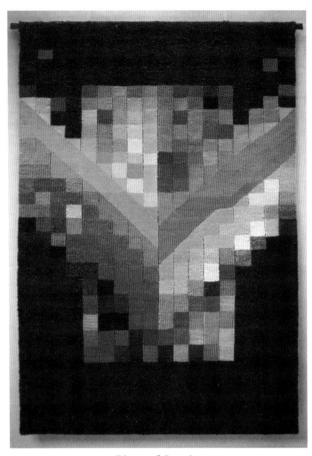

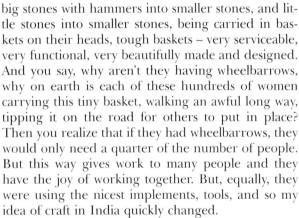

Pieces of Sunrise.

Nasik.

big stones with hammers into smaller stones, and little stones into smaller stones, being carried in baskets on their heads, tough baskets – very serviceable, very functional, very beautifully made and designed. And you say, why aren't they having wheelbarrows, why on earth is each of these hundreds of women carrying this tiny basket, walking an awful long way, tipping it on the road for others to put in place? Then you realize that if they had wheelbarrows, they would only need a quarter of the number of people. But this way gives work to many people and they have the joy of working together. But, equally, they were using the nicest implements, tools, and so my idea of craft in India quickly changed.

We saw a marvellous water tower being built near the airport in Delhi, all encased in a wonderful scaffold as it was being made – made of lashed bamboo, like a great basket thirty feet high with beautifully lashed, wonderful knots. So I found that craft and textile and art was a part of daily living. That was my initial response. But as travellers with limited language, we could not understand everything we saw. It has taken years to understand what it was we were seeing and how it pieces together. After four visits, and having talked to a lot of people and read so much, I realize that it's part of a much bigger philosophy of life.

We drove 15,000 miles and we were able to move in rural India, which I loved and valued most of all. People are so ingenuous. There was a lovely basket which was made from one palm leaf. One leaf! A man was sitting at a gate of a market with a whole pile of these leaves and with just a knife, he was slicing the stalk, bending it into a handle, curving the folds of the leaf up under it, and handing them out for a pittance for us to take our shopping in. I think it's one of my most precious possessions. It must have cost half a farthing. That you can make such a beautiful, useful object from simply what's around you with a simple tool like a knife and imagination. I was much inspired by such simple examples.

Is that why you called your exhibition *Indian Journey*?
Yes, the exhibition started after my first journey in 1974. Something about the colours in India, something about my appreciation of the texture, something of India which I can't even explain started creeping into my work. It was somehow leading me in some new directions. The exhibition has been put together as nine groups of work. The first subject, which is *Rising and Falling* patchworks, is my response to the plasticity of textile that everybody

166

in the streets is wearing; an uncut length of cloth – no shaped garments as we have. The versatility to which that length of cloth is put, the way men and women handle it every day and have an unsaid understanding of it, is beyond words. The use of a border which accentuates contours of form, the way different weights of cloth fall and have their own shape; it began to emerge in me that I might move my flat tapestries into something more of a relief, more of a sculptural form.

The Sufis used the patch as an outward symbol of their inward giving up of material things of the world. And the Buddhists also have it. The itinerant musicians of Bengal always wear patched garments, symbolic of a frugality of materialism but an inner richness of spiritualism. And the idea of pieces of a whole lit up my imagination in weaving – putting pieces of experience together into a whole.

Then there's another group which is called *Woven World*, because weave in India goes beyond the functional to the symbolic. The creation in the *Rig Veda* is described as the world having been woven – the ancient elders threw out the warp and weft upon the dome of the sky. Over and over I found references to how the "water was woven on the atmosphere", "the atmosphere was woven on the worlds of wisdom". And this triggered off my imagination that the actual act of weaving, the integration of the vertical and the horizontal, is again symbolic of the creation of the universe. And so this *Woven World* group has titles taken from the *Upanishads*, which relates the weaving of the water on the winds. I have used a quotation from Kalyan Kumar Ganguli: "Threads are also regarded as a means of communication". Now that gets perhaps the very nearest to my role as a weaver-artist. The medium of weaving is my language of communication. And it's that language that I've always explored.

My excitement about India is simply that it is a country where this language of weaving has been symbolic as well as functional as long as time goes back. The clothes that people wear, the saris, the colour, will tell you where they are from, maybe what village, maybe what their beliefs are. Gandhi cloth's texture will tell you the philosophy of the wearer. You don't have to say, "Do you follow Gandhi?". It fascinates me, this language of textile which is used as a matter of course. Indians are not only bilingual in the many languages of tongue, but they're bilingual in reading the visuals of their weaving.

The last section in the exhibition is called *Pieces of Daytime*. The daytime is something of great importance in India. Firstly, you may be walking along the street, and at the moment when the sun rises, you'll see people stop and give thanks. And you realize, my goodness, a new day is never taken for granted. It's something to give thanks for. And that each time of day has its moments of recognition. Inspired by this experience I began to evolve a series of tapestries in my mind. I completed the series very recently and put four large tapestries in the exhibition, each commemorating a time of day in India – pieces of first light, before the sun comes up; pieces of sunrise; pieces of midday, pieces of afternoon, twilight and darkness are all represented in this. This is the biggest section of the exhibition. To start with it was a problem to find a form which would embrace the total experiences of the day. But then I likened my experience to the musical form of *raga*, where there's a basic format which is improvised differently to convey, in speed, time and rhythm, the characteristics of a particular time of the day. Thinking about the series in India two things affected me. One was flying into Delhi from Jodhpur. I saw the whole of India spread out as *little fields* below, and I began to think of little pieces: a little bit of the first sunrise hits something and makes a shadow; the soft quality of twilight colour could be compiled over several hundred little squares. And also by a woman in a village in West Bengal who showed me her embroidery. When I asked her about it and why it was all made in little pieces she said, "Well, you see, I do it bit by bit at the end of the day when I've finished my work in the fields. You could say it's my life all stitched up there."And I thought, what a wonderful idea – little bit by little bit each day you add some new experience and you may not finish it for a year, but there is a year's work. That's why I chose that format for that group. All the colours are dyed especially for each. I dye them here.

You've been working on this for twelve years.
Yes, it's taken me a very, very long time to digest the experience. It would be easy to come back from India and churn out work that was literally lifted from India and had an Indian look. That's not what I wanted to do at all, nor to adopt the Indian techniques. They're so perfect. I've really wanted the Indian experience and the Indian thinking to direct me in new directions. Although there is a problem in this country, the integration of aesthetics and art and craft in daily life is impossible. Our industrial and commercial civilization makes it so. It's far too divided, particularly in the world of tapestry weaving. I'm afraid I have to say that the tapestries I make are not used as mats for people to sit on every day. There's a gulf there. I have to admit that I am working in the world where you need money to buy things. I'm sorry that has to be so.

I am trying to say to people, look again at what's around you; ideas aren't inspiration that float from heaven, they're to do with your your eyes and how you interpret what's around you. ●

KAFFE FASSETT

Knitting is the most therapeutic thing in the world.
INTERVIEW BY SUE LAWLEY

Kaffe surrounded by some of his patchwork quilts. Photograph by Anne James.

IF YOU HAD BEEN told as a young man that you would make your reputation knitting and stitching, I wonder how you would have reacted?
I think I would've fallen down laughing! I couldn't have imagined it. My mother and my sister were incredible knitters. I loved the fact that they were making garments from one piece of yarn that was being fed into these loops, but it never occurred to me that I was going to do it.'

Of course it is a craft, isn't it? But you considered yourself an artist.
That's right; we were above crafts! You didn't dabble in the crafts if you were going to be a serious painter. But now I think that if you pour your heart and soul into some colours in any form, then that is art. If you arrange pebbles at a beach or put together a stunning building or an incredible tapestry; why isn't that as important as a painting? What makes a painting important is that somebody is trying to reveal an impression they have of the world and to share that with other people in a very intense way. Certainly, I try to do that with my knitting: pouring hundreds of colours into my fabric so that people can really get a bounce out of looking at a piece of knitting. I am painting with wool.

Are there any famous knitters in history?
Well, Albert Einstein is the one name that comes to my mind. When I was growing up in the fifties I was always hearing about Einstein knitting between projects to calm his mind down and to clear his thinking. Certainly, I find knitting the most therapeutic thing in the world. When I go to paint in my studio, I get terribly lonely and want to do anything but be in that studio. When I am knitting, the hours, the weeks fly by and I have no sense of time, I am so happy. It is the most enjoyable pastime I have ever had in my life.

Are you a fast knitter?
Very fast! After twenty-three years, I'd better be fast, but I do look at what I am doing. That is why I don't watch television while I am knitting. I am concentrating very much and looking at the colours, building tip little patches of intense colour. One has to look and see if it is working, if it is exciting and what it is producing. I keep putting the work up on the wall and standing back and looking at it like a painter, even though it may be the sleeve of a sweater.

How do you work out all your measurements? Are your designs created mathematically?
No. I just look at someone and think, 'She's about one hundred and fifty stitches on number nine needles,' so I cast on and get rolling! If it turns out

that she can't fit into it at the end, I will make her another based on that experience and sell the original to someone else. I have also worked with an incredible genius called Zöe Hunt for years and years. She will take my rough swatches of knitting home and make them into garments for me and then work out the patterns for them. I have a team of knitters, and each knitter will knit one garment, taking my work and developing it from the swatch.

Your childhood by all accounts was rather unconventional.
Yes, very! First of all the town had a population of about 300, situated by a wild piece of coastline which was absolutely stunning. It was like a Japanese print, with great redwood trees growing down to the ocean and mist coming in fingers up the canyon. We built a restaurant on a piece of land that was on a mountain which stuck out over the ocean. We had forty miles of coastline view from the terrace of this restaurant. The restaurant was very glamorous. It was designed by a Frank Lloyd-Wright student and had huge terraces where you could sit out in front of a great big fire, and look at this incredible view of the mountains and coastline and the ocean. People came from all over the world: there were writers, artists, painters and musicians coming, so we were constantly talking to people who were realizing their fantasies and visions in the world. The seeds of what I am doing in my life now, started there.

It must've been difficult as a child at school if that was the sort of home life you led.
Yes, it was terribly difficult. I wore my hair like the Beatles and this was years before the Beatles turned up. I also wore colour, and remember, these were the days of beige and black and grey. I would go to school in tangerine trousers, I would dye my tennis shoes bright pink – it is nothing now! You go to any high school nowadays and the kids are all dressed in these colours but in those days, I was like an incredible, wild freak!

I changed my name. I found it in an Egyptian book about a little boy called Kaffe and I just loved the sound of that name. I grabbed it and became that person. It was a romantic whim.

The way people remember it in America is that there is this little Jewish woman selling my knitwear. She goes into the shops and says, "Look, let's get it straight! You've got a safe asset with Kaffe Fassett!"

But when you talk to art students these days, how do you explain it to them?
You can imagine what a rebel they think I am. When I go into the schools I say to them, "Well, what are you kids doing here?" And they say, "Well,

we've been here four years and we want to go on for another five years . . ." I say, "Listen, you are not brain surgeons. Get out of this class and get into life! That will teach you more than anything."

Who did you find who told you about England?
I met Christopher Isherwood at a dinner party, and he was the most extraordinary man. He must have been seventy and yet he had the most alert and curious mind; he was like a teenager, fascinated about everything and absolutely turned on to the world. So I rushed out and bought every book that Christopher Isherwood ever wrote and that gave me such a taste for England. The feeling of, 'I want to know where he comes from to make him the man he is.'

So I came here in the mid-sixties and made a living by drawing. I drew and met extraordinary people. I was shown around some incredible English country houses, which I took to like a duck to water. The frowsy old over-stuffed furniture and the vines growing in through the windows and the wind blowing through the house. The casualness, the elegance, the warmth and the wit – all of it – just lapped it up. I liked the style; it wasn't pretentious, and I have loved it ever since.

Tell me about your trip in the late sixties when you went up to Scotland with Bill Gibb, the dress designer who wanted you to look at a woollen mill in Inverness, and in you went and it all happened.
That's right. We went buying the old ancient tartan which was something gorgeous to me because it was beautiful: soft, old, vegetable-dyed colours, which were so marvellous. I wanted to know how they got these colours, who invented them? I then heard of this extraordinary man who worked in the mill who put together these beautiful tartans from the landscape colours. I went to the back of the mill and here was this shop filled with these gorgeous yarns. I took the yarns in my hands and thought to myself, has the world gone mad? There is not one single memorable piece of knitting in this entire country, and here is a palette that Rembrandt would have been thrilled with. They were just so subtle, so beautiful. I took twenty colours and got on the train and on the way back to London I asked Billy if he knew how to knit: "I've bought some knitting needles and some yarn, and I've got to learn right now!" He taught me how to knit and that is how it all got started.

And it's stocking stitch you do; you don't do fancy stitching, do you?
No. It is only mixing the colours that really thrills me. When I finally have done every colour in the entire universe, maybe I'll start playing with fancy stitches, but it doesn't interest me that much. What interests me is putting those colours together in a

Zig Zag jacket. Photograph by Tony Boase.

very simple way so that I can pass it on to other people as well.

So there you were, knit a row, purl a row. What was the first article you knitted?
Well, it was a rough old cardigan which ended up looking like a piece of sandstone. It had about twenty colours in it which were changing constantly. Of course I didn't know how to knit my ends in, in those days, so I had these great shag-rugs under my arms!

Now, the second article you knitted was a three-quarter-length multicoloured jacket on which you put a price tag of £100. It was featured in Vogue, and really that was your departure point, wasn't it?
Yes it was, because that garment caught the eye of the Missonis, who were the greatest knitwear designers in the world. They flew over on the next plane and hired me to design for them.

What is funny is that I only had a little shoe-box full of gnarled up pieces of knitting; they asked to see my next collection and that was it! I hadn't done anything, but it didn't seem to matter.

You find inspiration in art treasures like Roman glass. How does that work?

170

What I'd do is take a source that is very rich in colour, so that it would make me reach for dozens and dozens of colours, rather than just a few. And it is not just knitwear. I got into needlepoint very quickly after the knitting, and that became a parallel career where one can be very figurative with wool by stitching it on to canvas with very simple stitches, but creating anything you want – from great faces to shells, fruit and vegetables.

There is a certain irony you must have thought about, that you, a colourful Californian from the colourful part of the world comes to drab old England and finds this kind of inspiration through all this vibrant colour.
But there is a subtlety of colour here. Anyone who thinks that England is drab only has to go along to gardens. Gardens are the jewel of inspiration. The silver and bronze, the lichen-covered stones and subtlety of lavender in gardens is so wonderful and has been a source of tremendous inspiration to me. That quality of creating something that is so subtle and so rich, beautiful and timeless, that smearing with history, it is something that constantly attracts me.

Would you go so far as to say that you might never have found inspiration if you hadn't come to Britain?
Well, I think that people wouldn't have listened to me in the same way in America. I met this extraordinary man called Stephen Sheard who had the Rowan Yarn Company, and he develops yarns to my specifications. Now no one (even here) listened to me, except this man with a little tiny mill in Yorkshire amongst the rolling hills. He started turning out yarns that were so subtle and beautiful.

Unlike a lot of experts, you are not at all dismissive about the amateur. You want people to create for themselves, don't you?
Absolutely. The Craft Council here were just brilliant in putting a slide show together for me and sending me all around the country to talk to people. I began to realize that there was such a response: things I took as normal, were totally astounding to other people. Also they were saying that they couldn't possibly do what I did, and that was curious to me because all I was doing was the most basic knitting that anyone can learn how to do. The only thing that I do is to use lots of colour. What is extraordinary is that now, when I go and give lectures, half the audience is dripping in the most incredible flights of fancy using wonderful colours!

You were given an exhibition at the Victoria & Albert Museum. How did that come about?

Well, Princess Michael came across my work at my parents' shop in California. She got very excited about the knitting and asked where I could be found. She came to see me when she got back to London and told me she would like to buy a jacket. Then she asked if there was anything she could do for me. I asked, "What is on offer?" The princess mentioned that she was a trustee of the V & A and asked if I would like an exhibition!

It was unashamedly commercial though, wasn't it?
Yes, and I don't apologize for that at all. It's educational. People buy a box full of yarn and go home and begin to knit: they might do their first one from my design and then realize that it is not so difficult.

I starved for years. The first four years I made about one hundred pounds. I was certainly living on brown rice and my friends' generosity. It is nice now, to be able to travel where I want to and to have the things that I want, but that is not why I knit. I would be a billionaire if I worked that way. I could develop mass-market designs. But no, we give people incredibly complicated designs to work with that take a long time to develop.

Now your exhibition is on its way around the world, and you, a knitter, have full recognition as an artist. Is there still an element of surprise in you at that?
Well, yes. I used to sit on my bed knitting away, for twenty years. I used to think that it was the most magical, thrilling, soothing and inspiring thing in the world. Why wasn't everyone catching on to it? The magic of it is that it is basically so simple and yet you can pour your heart and soul into every piece. So in a way I saw that it could go to great heights and reach many people, but I began to despair. I felt it would never reach anybody! Until *Glorious Knitting* came out, the message reached very few. What is exciting now is that it goes from one museum to another across the world and packs people in. In Sweden 107,000 people queued to see it. People were saying, "What is in that museum that is making people crowd there?" I just think that there is an incredible hunger for things that you can make with your hands. Things that anyone can do. The simplicity of it and yet the ability to reveal one's inner self. It is not like poetry or music where one has to have a certain talent to reveal it.

But don't you fear that you'll run out of inspiration?
Oh no, not at all! Every design you do gives birth to a dozen more. You sit there not knowing which one to do first. It is a total turn on from beginning to end and I feel I will never lose inspiration in knitting. ●

CERAMICS

SPONTANEOUS POTTING

Making pots is full of creative expression.

BY SANDY BROWN

Slab plate.

IF YOU ASKED ME, am I a potter, a craftsperson, a sculptor, an artist, a painter, I would say yes, I am all of these. I make life-sized figures, large abstract colourful paintings, and big fecund sculptures. Yet the origin of my work is in making pots we can use. I may spend months working on large-scale sculptures, but I always come back sooner or later to making functional pots. It is grounding, rooted in everyday life, and gives me a way of developing my love of ritual.

This all began in Japan. My early life was not creative, artistic, nor cultural. I was restless, looking for something; and when I was nineteen I answered an ad in *The Times* from someone wanting co-drivers to go overland to Australia. To cut a long story short, I ended up in Japan instead, and have often thought back and wondered how that happened. I remember being in a café in Singapore, talking with some people who had just come back from Japan, and they were very enthusiastic about it, and I am pretty certain they were using the word culture, saying that Japan had a rich culture. If you'd asked me at the time I would not have known what culture was, but my unconscious must have done, and I found myself booking a ticket on a boat to Japan.

I arrived with five dollars and the address of a youth hostel in Tokyo.

Throughout the next few months I was gradually drawn into Japanese language and life, and met a lot of potters. You do there. I met a lot of other people who love pots too, as many Japanese people do. Pots are their thing.

I was invited to a tea ceremony. Its importance in Japanese culture is huge: it is as significant, for example, as mass is to Roman Catholics. The tea ceremony is a model for every occasion involving food and drink. It is a slow, highly stylized ritual to prepare tea, and effectively it is a meditation about appreciating a tea bowl. And the tea bowl we were invited to appreciate that day was a crude, irregular bowl. I thought it must have been someone's first pot. I loved it for its freshness and its awkwardness. The bowl was imperfect, I am imperfect. I identified with it absolutely. My admiration for it was heightened when I was told by my host that she had paid nearly a quarter of a million pounds for it. From a living potter. This was an astounding new sense of values and aesthetics. To appreciate objects not for their perfection or their superb technique or their fineness; but for their imperfections, their warmth and their humanity. A culture which valued spontaneity and awkwardness to that degree was a culture I wanted to stay in.

THEN LATER, visiting Mashiko, village of a thousand potters, someone offered me some clay and a wheel and said, have a go, and off I went. Subse-

quently, I started working in a traditional folk pottery. They made lively pots arising out of a local vernacular and even now these pots look very modern: vibrant, expressionistic.

I returned to England after five years in Japan with my then partner, a wonderful potter and great companion, Takeshi Yasuda. He was a marvellous inspiration and guide, and gave me confidence in my intuition and the courage to work spontaneously.

I AM QUITE RITUALISTIC before I start making pots on the wheel. It is definitely the Japanese influence, as I am not by nature tidy. But in the studio, before starting creative work, I spend time cleaning the wheel, washing the boards around it, and the tools. It slows me down, warms me up, brings me into the making process. I have a special cloth I always sit on, a special pot I use to hold the thick slip, and I clean the cherrywood tools I made sitting in the sun by the kiln in Mashiko.

Then I prepare the clay, kneading it gently, rhythmically, in a spiral form.

I believe that throwing pots is a medium with a rich potential of creative expression, just as drawing is. I like to use soft clay, and to have the wheel turning very slowly. I like there to be sensual irregularities in the clay, for the pot to be off-centre, asymmetrical, and still moving. Warped, even. Then the clay looks soft and the pot has a vulnerable malleability.

My use of clay is robust, direct. I like to see fingermarks and thumbprints, and I look out for interesting accidents. I don't plan, I don't sketch in advance, I respond in the here and now and do something immediate.

That sense of the immediacy shows in the colour too. I love colour, and have developed a free painterly use of glazes on my ceramics. Over the years I have made and painted thousands of plates, each one different. So I say I am an abstract painter, with a language of painting which has evolved over time. There is a balance and structure in the language; with large masses of colour being counterpointed with squiggles, splashes, swishes, squidges and dots. If I am painting, say, 50 plates in one day, then to start with I will refer to my favourite one from the last series, and use that as a jumping off point. Then I go off from there, sometimes thinking of things to do with the colours, sometimes not thinking just doing. The key is to be relaxed, meditative, laid back. Like a jazz riff. I spend time getting myself into this relaxed state by preparing in the same way as I do for throwing on the wheel; by cleaning all the brushes, washing the tables, tidying away everything surplus to the job in hand. It is another ritual, this pre-painting preparation. I do tend to hurry, to move too fast when I do things, but my creativity works best when I am

173

Standing form.

Textured slab platter with handles.

slow, steady, rhythmic, in touch with my heartbeat, with time to become more aware of every movement, every nuance of every movement, and every nuance of every colour that I apply.

With glaze painting there is the additional suspense factor of not knowing how it will look until you open the kiln. Glaze colours are very different in their raw state. The copper green glaze for example is grey when raw, as is the cobalt blue. It is quite easy to mix them up. It is also difficult to gauge the intensity of the colours when painting with glazes; is this cobalt quite strong or weakish? I have to wait until the kiln cools to find out.

In 2003 I was invited to Bandol in the south of France by the French potters association to demonstrate and exhibit. I did not know until I arrived that the demonstration, rather than lasting the one day I normally do, was in fact to go on for three days! This meant that I would be working in front of a seated audience of potters and ceramic artists from all over Europe for three whole days. I decided to conquer fear and anxiety by doing what works best for me, which is to do my Spontaneity Performance, in which I do not know what I am going to do. It means starting with two things; a big pile of clay, and an empty mind; being open, responsive, childlike, playful.

I love using my pots, and I love visiting other potters' homes too, because they know how to live with and use pots. Functional work has been undervalued in our culture, even derided, and this saddens me. A functional pot can be equal to a Picasso, a Mark Rothko, a Matisse, a Brancusi.

It is simply a medium. We often limit ourselves

175

as to what we are willing to think of as a functional object; even some potters are guilty of this. I consider myself very fortunate to have lived in Japan and to have seen how outrageous and adventurous they are about what they will consider as a functional piece. It has allowed me too to be adventurous, to challenge our perceptions about what dining ware is.

I HAVE MADE a bowl which I use and love. I made it on the wheel with soft clay. Using soft clay means that the marks of the potter's hands will be softly there, so that you can see the way it is made, see the immediacy of the moment. It means that the form itself will be soft, the profile gentle, the rim undulating quietly. The rhythm of the potter's hands will show. The pot will breathe.

My wheel is made of a beautiful Japanese hardwood, keyaki, a kind of elm. It is very simple, about the most simple potter's wheel it is possible to have. It turns very slowly, and is powered by my foot. When I work with it I feel as the wheel and I are one, as if it is an extension of me. I can stop it, slow it down, speed it up, all by stroking the small lower wheel with my bare foot. It is very sensitive, responding immediately. It is quiet.

So, my hands are on the clay, using thick soft slip as a lubricant, and as the wheel turns slowly I can allow myself to make full earthy contact, pushing juicily into the clay. It feels fluid, easy almost, and I need to pay full attention as the form changes so quickly, and I do not want to overwork it. I want the bowl to look unfinished, unformed, with potential. Then I let a wire pass through the clay under the bowl, allowing enough clay to form a chunky foot.

The next day I turn the bowl upside down, on a smaller hand-turned wheel, and form the foot. This is a process called 'turning' and is as important a part of the spirit of the bowl as is throwing on the wheel. Turning is a way of removing some of the excess clay to leave a pleasing foot. I like my turning to have the same character as the throwing; in other words I like it to be bold, obvious, earthy, not refined. So I do it while the clay is still soft, and I do not use a sharp tool, but prefer a spoon. I hold the bowl in my hands occasionally as I go to see how it feels.

Then I leave it to dry to a leather-hard state until it is ready for the thick white slip. The slip, which I pour all over the clay, is very thick when I do it, thicker than double cream. It gives to the bowl a lovely fat buttery quality. This also makes it feel delicious in the hands.

Now I leave it to dry out completely, to 'bone dry', when it's ready for the first firing, a biscuit firing. This is to 1000^0C, and means that it is not clay any more, but now is fired ceramic, like a biscuit. It is still porous, which is what I want, so that it will absorb the glaze. I use a transparent glaze, made of feldspar, whiting, quartz and china clay. Many potters create their own glazes; we are alchemists. A little bit of this, a little bit of that.

Before it is glazed, I paint it with my coloured glazes, which have been coloured with more elements of alchemy. Copper oxide for example, which is made from copper rust which is green, makes a lovely deep deep diffuse green, as deep as the deepest ocean. And cobalt oxide: inky inky blue. I like to take tea from this favourite bowl because I love the way I have painted it. I used cobalt oxide, first a thin wash with water, lightly brushed over the bowl, so lightly that it looks almost invisible in the raw state. Its strength is what makes it so rewarding to use. It has a range from barely perceptible to wow! that is the blackest of black holes. And in between are the most wonderful blues. Inky, wet, sea, sky, water, translucent, deep.

After I had painted the thin wash of cobalt oxide, I used a much stronger mix, and brushed some wavy lines on one side and a circle on the other. The bowl is then dipped into the bucket of glaze to be thinly covered and goes into the kiln to be fired a second time, this time much hotter, to 1280^0C. This means that it is fired high, to white heat, it is stoneware, so it is hard, durable, and has a rich quality in which glaze, slip and clay all fuse. When the kiln cools – a frustrating 24 hours as the waiting is hard – I must resist the temptation to open the kiln too early. I have to wait until the temperature is around 100^0C. When I pull the bowl out of the kiln it is still hot, too hot to hold. It looks good, the form is great, the cobalt shows every nuance of its colour; the strength was just right. I use it every day and my life is enriched because of it. I am calmed and uplifted at the same time.

Often what I wish to use in my kitchen is the inspiration for what I make in the studio; serving platters, fish dishes, toast racks, cookie jars, tea bowls. When I was growing up I was aware of the immense power of the everyday objects we live with when I visited my grandma's house; I loved her and the things in her house as being part of her. Now I find that power in my own pots, my kitchen is full of them, they go in the oven, they are washed up and placed and used every day. So actually, although I exhibit and sell my pots, I am of course really making them for myself. I like living with them. It is a way of having art actually central to my life, to live with ceramics. And I encourage you to live likewise, to live with art as part of your lives. Living with art, using it everyday, is the difference between touching and holding your lover and putting him on a plinth and just looking. Art is not something to be distant from, but rather something to celebrate the everyday, to enrich the ordinary, and elevate it into something spiritual. ●

SPIRIT IN THE WOOD

I have learnt as much from my students as they have learnt from me.

BY DAVID CHARLESWORTH

A Japanese Inro box in African Blackwood by David Charlesworth, with silver beads by Charmian Harris.

I HAD ALWAYS LOVED making things by hand, and working with wood came very naturally to me. I met Ted Baly who had worked for thirty years just outside Dartington. He was a delightful man who taught cabinet-making to two students a year.

When I went to start my year with him, I did not really know what to expect, but he got us into quite big and difficult jobs straight away. He just showed us what to do and we did it to the best of our ability.

One day he said to me, "I've got a job especially for you. I've had this design for at least fifteen years though I've never felt I've had a student who could make it, but I think you would enjoy making it." The job was a very complicated circular mirror done with yew oysters, an oyster being a cross-section of a branch. It was very fiddly and complex work with inlay, but I really enjoyed this great challenge, and I think Ted was pleased with the result.

After this year with Ted, I decided to start my own workshop in the Lake District; an extremely beautiful place. I rented a dry stone barn for very

A meditation stool in English yew made by Gustav Lünning, a student of David Charlesworth from Stockholm.

little money and bought some tools, and got started. I was twenty-four then. It was quite easy to get some work. People were very interested in what I was doing. There were very few cabinet-makers in the country at that time. I joined the Lakeland Guild of Craftsmen and produced some good pieces. However, working on my own in a rural workshop with no company made me feel isolated.

I had always wanted to be by the seaside. I loved the sea and I wanted to be somewhere where I could go surfing and walk on the cliffs. I came to Hartland one January purely by chance – I was looking for a small cottage with a nice barn, but, of course, small cottages do not have nice barns! But eventually I found the Manor in Hartland, which was completely ruined. It had stood empty for four years and the roof was falling in, but it was very cheap. It was within my budget and it was marvellous, but what really attracted me was the workshop. Although it was a ruin, it had a wonderful feeling about it.

Once in Hartland, I soon realized that I was going to struggle to make a living as a craftsman. By chance at this time there was a knock on the workshop door, and a young man appeared and asked me to teach him furniture-making. At first I was very reluctant as I felt 1 hadn't enough experience, but the young man was adamant that he wanted me to teach him, and eventually I decided to give it a go.

THIS WAS A REALLY important decision in my life – he was my first student and it was a very exciting year we spent together. He was terribly keen and I was still learning to perfect my techniques. I discovered my teaching skills. I also realized that having company in the workshop is very important, and the feeling of isolation vanished.

I get tremendous satisfaction from watching the students doing good work. They bring interest into my life. The students enrich the teacher's life as much as the teacher enriches the student's skills and understanding.

A great deal of pleasure is also derived from the process of working with my hands, using the beautiful material of wood. There is a relationship between who we are and what we are doing – to make a right decision, to make a cut in the right place, to create a beautiful piece. As long as you have eyes to see, you know whether you have done a good job. You don't need to be dependent on outside approval. Making things by hand does give one

A round dining table in English oak, with tapered laminated legs and sycamore inlay, made by David Charlesworth.

tremendous satisfaction – something which is lacking in a lot of other areas of modern life.

Ted Baly was keen on the concept of art therapy. He had taught many students who had problems of various sorts. One was a young man who did not get on with his father and had a very bad stammer, and after he had been with Ted for two years doing good work which he was pleased with, his stammer went away. Ted felt that if one could do good work, then it was going to have a healing effect. I believe that to be the case through my own experience.

The work of a craftsman or craftswoman in whatever field is very slow and ordered. You can't do good work if you rush. I think this slowness helps to bring order into one's mind. Without that slow, ordered approach, one can't do the work. Working with one's hands is like a meditation. Satisfaction comes from the work itself rather than from making money. You have made a beautiful thing, and that in itself is good enough.

A lot of art colleges seem to encourage the self-conscious pursuit of originality, which only hides the true beauty of the wood. Simple design is the key. Wood does have challenges. Wood is constantly moving. It is often full of stored tension from when it was growing in the tree, and it isn't a simple material to use, but if we obey the rules and use it correctly, it will be structurally sound for many lifetimes. Working with wood is a communion: one does have a relationship with the piece one is working with.

Since I have been teaching – over twenty years now – there has been a terrific resurgence of interest in these crafts. There are more and more people with small furniture workshops all over the country and I hope that it will continue in this direction. A lot of people are consciously trying to find themselves a more satisfying way of life. Modern working practices create great stress and unease for people and, wherever possible, they seem to be turning to the natural speed of handicrafts – and there we see the healing dimension at work.

I do not think I am being idealistic in hoping that this revival continues. I do not see why in every house there should not be one or two things made by your favourite local craftsman or craftswoman, which are a bit special, of high quality, and of which no one else will own an exact copy. As William Morris said, "Have nothing in your house that is not beautiful and useful." ●

TOBIAS KAYE

Finding the voice of wood is fundamentally important.

INTERVIEW BY SATISH KUMAR

WHY DID YOU WANT to become a craftsman rather than a businessman?
I was very rebellious as a teenager, and I found it very difficult to understand why the world was as it was, why people did what they did, how I was supposed to do anything in a world like this. After various short careers in cars, coffins and computers, and various excursions around Europe and the USA, I found myself working with my aunt and uncle at Wynstone's school in Gloucestershire. At this school there was a recreational woodwork shop. One day I popped down to the workshop to make a little birthday present for my sister who was a student there. My uncle said "Well, if you enjoy doing woodwork, would you like to do it with the kids?" I said, 'Yes, I'll have a go." It was just a matter of having fun.

I ran that workshop for three-and-a-half years and I realized that I was really enjoying turning wood. I began to take on little jobs, little commissions here and there.

You learned as you went along . . .
Yes, with the children, to start with. And then, once I set up my own workshop I quickly discovered that I wasn't as good as I thought I was, and when it comes to making a living from things, you have to get better and better. So I had already learned to listen to the wood and listen to the tools, and see how they liked to work together, and it was through doing that that I became better – and I'm still learning.

When you say, 'listening to the wood', what do you mean? How do you listen to the wood?
During the cutting process, wood does make a noise and it's quite audibly perceptible that this noise is either pleasant or unpleasant. At the worst extreme, the tool is chattering and squealing so much that it's deafening, and it actually becomes difficult to hold it. And at the best the tool moves through the wood so smoothly that it feels almost as if it's greased. One of my students called it "the but-ter cut". When the tool is cutting in such sympathy with the wood it just hisses through it, just moves with great ease through the timber.

Then the shape. You see, at the one end is craftsmanship, which comes from listening to tools and the wood, and at the other end is art. And in between these there is a meeting-point where things of beauty are created. Bernard Leach in his *Potter's Handbook* said, "It's no accident that a jug is described as having a foot, a belly, a neck, a lip, a mouth. . . . Everything we make is an image of the body." Now for me, the body is a work of art, the artist of which is the individual soul. So I took Leach's doctrine a step further and concluded that everything we make is a reflection of the soul. In the soul realm there are archetypes, there are images, and there are forms which can be brought into the material world.

And so, on the one hand there's the struggle to find the right relationship with the material and on the other hand there's the struggle to bring the perfect form into the material. And the relationship between the tools and the wood serves the relationship between form and matter. Within the wood there is a penchant, an inherent liking or disliking for this form or that. If you take a wood like box-wood, it wants to be treated delicately. If you make a fairly clumpy form out of it, it feels wasted; whereas, if you take pine and you make a very delicate form out of it, it feels fragile, it doesn't feel right. If you make a good solid form out of it, it feels satisfying, it feels warm. So each wood, each tree and each part of each tree has its own penchant towards a particular type of form. Therefore, listening to the wood and knowing the wood and finding the voice of the wood are fundamentally important.

Sometimes, you even use the phrase "God in metal". What do you mean by that?
We are all created beings. Some people believe we are created by accident and some people believe

we're created by consciousness, but one way or another, we are all created beings. Trees are also created beings. So within me there is something which is also in the tree. As we are created, we are also creators. The creative act is important to the human being. I feel as if wood is satisfied to have something created out of it.

Someone in Australia wrote a book about wood-turning called *Wood Dreaming*. He said, "When the craftsman or woman takes the wood and makes something out of it, it's the wood 'dreaming'." There is something in the wood which dreams about having a new form. Trees are beings too. They are well rooted in service, their whole being is an act of service. It is the creative in me who meets the Creator in the tree. 'God' in the soul meets 'God' in matter.

You make a distinction between perfection on the one hand, and harmony on the other.
Within each soul there is a capacity to think, to feel,

and to do, or act. Each has its own patterns, its own mysteries. But the mystery of action is perhaps the most difficult to penetrate. It's important that, when we act, we have the courage to act – not just to think or feel that we ought to act, but to act, to actually Do it. To act out of ourselves, not out of habit or convention but out of an inner perception of beauty or truth. To seek the truth is a task for our thinking. Within our thinking there's an element of perfection. Things are either right or wrong. If you look at technology which has been designed through human thinking, things are generally either right or wrong. But in human life things aren't like that. In human life we are all a mixture of wrong and right. Those things which we think are wrong may be of most value. In my work I have discovered that if I want to make things perfect they don't serve the world in the same way as if I try to make things harmonious. It's important that I am able to look at something I am making and know at what point it's important to say, 'Well,

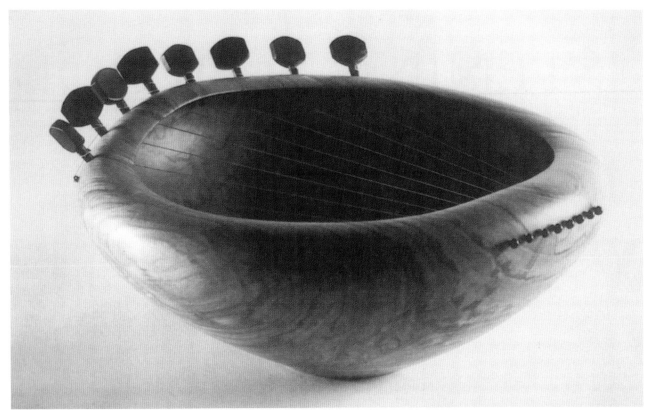

Sounding bowl.

that was a mistake but I'm leaving it there.' So that step beyond perfection into harmony and into the acceptance of the rightful place of imperfection has been a good discovery for me.

You also talk about the hand and the machine.
If human beings don't make, then where is the Creator alive in us? If everything we are surrounded with is made by a machine, then the Creator in us begins to die. If we don't exercise 'God' in us, the creative self, it will weaken and die. 'God' is dying out of our society because we are not making things by hand.

But the problem is that in our modern society where most things are made by machine. Hand-made things have become a luxury.
Wood-turning is coming back. By the 1970s you could count the creative wood-turners on the fingers. Now, there are thousands of them. The hobby has just mushroomed in recent years.

A group of five of us creative wood-turners got together. It was Ray Key who called us together – and he said to us, "Look, it is in our craft, as it has been in most crafts, that we don't share our secrets with each other for fear that the other person will take our livelihood. But it doesn't have to be like that. If we all agreed to share everything, then nobody would be poorer; we would all be richer." And he said, "I know this can work because they've

done it in Ireland. And now they're doing it in America, and wood-turning has taken off there."

So we agreed that we would all share everything we knew with any other wood-turner who was interested. We held a seminar, to which a hundred-odd wood-turners came. We said. "This is our idea. Who would like to join?" Within a year we had nearly a thousand members, and wood-turning has just grown and grown since then. In Devon there are now five wood-turning clubs, and most of them have about eighty members, and they have a waiting list to join. And then there are many more who aren't members of these clubs. There is a resurgence of skills.

Do they make things for daily use, or are they making ornamental objects?
I would say most of these amateur wood-turners are making decorative items to begin with. Quite a few of them do go down the road of marrying mass-produced items with handmade items. So they'll make a lovely frame for a mass-produced clock. Another example is the pepper mill, where there is a mass-produced mechanism inside, but the outside is still handmade. As these people get deeper into the craft they begin to leave the crutch of mass-produced bolt-on's behind and make more simple and even more practical things. Bowls, spoons, containers etc. There's no right or wrong in it. There's just this seeking for handmade items and

through that a seeking for a contact with nature. Then also, in seeking to express the creative within, these people begin to ask themselves how simpler forms can become art, and then all kinds of development begins. The more people have been excluded from handmade items, the more desperate their need for nature has become. It gets to the point where the buyer at the crafts market prefers something which is badly made because it doesn't have that gloss of mechanized perfection on it. If it has got bits of bark still on it, they think, 'Wow! Look! That's a part of a tree!', and they'll buy it. So both needs are in there: the need for the handmade item and the need for the contact with nature.

In your own work you are doing musical wood-turning.
Yes, I started off making craft-market items, decorative and functional. For me, every bowl I made was a sculpture. A gallery owner said to me once, "What are you making: is it art or is it craft?", and I said, "Well, the process is art; but the result is craft." "Funny," he said, "because I asked Richard Raffan (a leading bowl turner in the 70s and 80s) the same question last week and he said, 'The process is craft and the result is art.'"

Looking at the way we work, I can see that. For Richard it was craft. He was making maybe twenty bowls a day, and sometimes he would say, "Oh, that one's particularly beautiful; I'll put it on one side." The rest of them would go to the kitchen shop, and the particularly beautiful one would go to the gallery.

Whereas I was making four bowls a day. I would struggle over every bowl to get the shape right, and I was seeking for a form on the outside which was harmonious, a form on the inside which was harmonious, that the relationship between the inside form and the outside form should be harmonious, that the relationship between the chosen form and the timber should be harmonious. And I'd look at the final item and I'd say, "Nice, but it's not art," try again, try again. That pursuit of ridiculous perfection in art caused me such inner pain that I couldn't carry on. At that point somebody came to my workshop and said, "I need feet for my sofas. The sofas I'm making cost a lot of money and I want really well-made feet. Would you like to make them?" I said, "Yeah, you bet." And I got into making sofa feet, and he paid me well enough for those that I could go through the bad times, and I learned a lot more craftsmanship there, just making sofa feet. It's a great satisfaction to me that I have tried my hands at almost every aspect of wood-turning. And yet that intense struggle bore the most wonderful fruits. I began to notice that the bowls I was making had a rich acoustic response from the interior. Hold it to your ear and it sounded like a shell. Speak towards it and your voice was gathered up and returned to your ears in a rich way. Not just one bowl; many were like this. The pursuit of visual harmony had created forms that embodied an audible harmony. Exciting. But the question then raised its head: 'What to do with this acoustic so that others could find it too?' I could find no answer that pleased me till one night, sitting down meditating, the image of a bowl with a string across it popped into my head. From there the sounding bowls developed.

Now at this point in my work there are three strings to my bowl and each of them is equally important. One is the teaching: I do three day-courses twice a month and people come from all over the world. Most of them are retired or approaching retirement, and they similarly seek to find the creative in themselves. It's a great joy to me to help them kindle that creativity and to help them find a relationship with 'God' in the timber.

Secondly, there's making the musical instruments, the bowls with strings on them, and these go out to music therapists mostly, and they're using them to heal all kinds of people. Hospitals in Japan, Canada, Australia, Sweden, and all over the UK are using these Sounding Bowls. That is satisfying for me. Making the musical bowls is also very satisfying. When a form takes music it begins to breathe.

And then there's the third string, what I call the poetry bowls. I'm struggling to bring the word, the sound, as well as visual forms, into harmony with each other.

Do you have some kind of vision for Britain where craft, not only in wood but in other spheres as well, will become more mainstream, rather than just a luxury?
I don't know what's going to happen to our society. If we are to find a living relationship with handmade objects again we are going to have to want less. So long as we continue to want a plethora of personal possessions, there is little room for craft. I do have a vision for humanity, one which I hope to be playing a small part in, to be a small part of a re-touching between 'God' in nature and 'God' in us. So long as we continue to pursue our future through the machine, the path of nature and the path of humanity will continue to diverge. This can only lead to death: death of nature and death of humanity. So if, through the tuition I offer, the instruments and sculpture I make (and the way in which I relate to my fellow human beings), people can see that two poles, nature and humanity, are striving to find harmony, that they themselves are part of this attempt at a cosmic marriage, then we have come a little bit closer to my vision of a happier future. ●

LET THE INGREDIENTS SING

Preparation of food means handling each ingredient with gratitude, with appreciation, with respect.

BY ED BROWN

ENTERING THE CRAFT of cooking, you let go of thought-patterns and physical habits of a lifetime. Thoughts and habits which involve manipulating people and things to make them perform the way you want. Cooking in the usual sense is to put foods together to make a meal, and the accompanying thought is that we really have something better to be doing. 'Isn't this a waste of time?' And then – is it any surprise? – sure enough, cooking is a waste of time. You have not given your heart. You have not let things come home to your heart.

My Zen teacher, Shunryu Suzuki Roshi, mentioned that, "When you are cooking, you are not just working on food. You are working on yourself, you are working on other people." You are working on giving yourself to what you are doing, giving your heart, giving your hands, arms, eyes, ears, your body to the endeavour. You work to make cooking a craft rather than a chore. You 'throw yourself' into it. You work to become absorbed.

Absorption does not come easily or cheaply. The price is a full measure of devotion, devotion to seeing beets and fresh greens and wilted ones; devotion to sorting the dirt from the leaves of lettuce, the stone from the black beans. Devotion to standing at the counter-top trimming and peeling, dicing and mincing, stirring and folding; to leaning over the sink washing and scrubbing; to stooping to pick up the spills, to plug in the mixer, to fetch the pan. Each activity is the centre of the universe where things 'stand still', where things are no longer 'things' – those material elements to be manipulated – but have become heart flowers in the spring breeze.

You taste what you put into your mouth. This is not about 'getting it right' or 'making it taste the way it should'. This is to discover the woodiness of mushrooms, the vibrancy of lemon – to discover and know for yourself. With this devotion to experiencing your experience intimately, you are no longer cooking by rote or by measurement, which maintains boundaries. You are moving inward and flowing outward – things are flowing inward and moving outward. Your action accords because you taste the true spirit of the grain, the true spirit of each ingredient. Everything is 'real-izing' itself in your presence, with your devotion.

Devotion means ongoing study, a study of the whole process: the space, the equipment, the tools, the ingredients, time, occasion. Which differences make a difference? Eventually you know what is 'yours', yours so intimately that you have disappeared. Food appears. I know what makes my cooking mine: a really sharp knife, distinct assembly, fresh herbs, the element of tartness, a variety of garnishes. I have few students because few choose to study in this way, and if they do, their cooking will be theirs.

This absorption, this devotion can also be called trance. Things are not just things. Things become animate. Alive. Friends. Companions. The world is no longer inanimate. You are working with mind, various aspects of mind, transforming appearances into food. People do not understand this. They think you learn to manipulate things to make them taste pleasurable. To create a good impression. To please others. That you manipulate food to manipulate others.

Letting go, stepping back, work to bring out the

Aubergines, chilli peppers and tomatoes. Photograph by Rick Lawrence.

best, to let the ingredients sing. This is not complicated. Crepes with goat cheese, oregano, and sundried tomatoes over black beans with garlic and cumin, a side of spinach goes bananas with sesame seeds. A beet soup with potato, onion, celery, and carrot – a garnish of orange slices with fresh mint. Or maybe a carrot yam soup with a radish garnish, oh, and some stewed leeks. A radicchio salad with green onions, roasted walnuts, avocado, and grated asiago. Perhaps some rhubarb tart cake.

Craft – you take up, handle each ingredient with gratitude, with appreciation, with respect. Allow awe. Experience these things closely enough that they become pieces in the imagination. Enough intimacy with the ingredients that they populate the imagination. They begin to speak, to call out, to you certainly, but more importantly to one another. They begin to congregate and co-mingle. It is no longer something the cook does – no, the cook stands back and the ingredients come forward.

For each cook the ingredients will congregate differently. Each cook will have different tendencies, ways of creating the environment where particular congregations flourish and others are unlikely. Beets, beets and walnuts, beets and watercress, beets and sour cream, beets and orange, beets and apple, beets sweet and sour, sweet and pungent, beets with cucumber? Arranged? Tossed? Designed? The ingredients begin whispering, hobnobbing: How have you been? Long time no see. What have you been up to? We should get together more often.

The ingredients congregate, the cook creates space and assists the ingredients, facilitates the meetings. The cook enters trance: we are no longer in ordinary reality, everything matters, matter responds, and we are all children of the Infinite.

Yes, there is work. Work is necessary to enter trance, to enter non-ordinary reality where vitality flourishes, life after life, life beyond life. You gather your mind by cleaning, by cutting, bowing, clearing, you attend. You show up. You attend by attending to, by tending to the details, by thorough endeavour. When you cut the carrots, you cut the carrots. You don't waste a gram.

You see with your eyes. Work with your hands. Not even. You invite your hands to realize themselves through the work at hand. You invite apples and peaches to appear to your eyes; you invite earth, stem, leaf, flower, and fruit to inspire the nose. As 'you' recede into the background, food comes forward. ●

WABI-SABI

Japanese culture of simplicity

BY LEONARD KOREN

● WABI-SABI IS a beauty of things imperfect, impermanent and incomplete.

● It is a beauty of things modest and humble.

● It is a beauty of things unconventional.

● Wabi-sabi is a nature-based aesthetic paradigm that restores a measure of sanity and proportion to the art of living.

● Wabi-sabi – deep, multi-dimensional, elusive – is the perfect antidote to the pervasively slick, saccharine, corporate style of beauty.

● Get rid of all that is unnecessary. Wabi-sabi means treading lightly on the planet and knowing how to appreciate whatever is encountered, no matter how trifling, whenever it is encountered. 'Material poverty, spiritual richness' are wabi-sabi bywords. In other words, wabi-sabi tells us to stop our preoccupation with success – wealth, status, power and luxury – and enjoy the unencumbered life.

● Obviously, leading the simple wabi-sabi life requires some effort and will and also some tough decisions. Wabi-sabi acknowledges that just as it is important to know when to make choices, it is also important to know when *not* to make choices: to let things be. Even at the most austere level of material existence, we still live in a world of things. Wabi-sabi is exactly about the delicate balance between the pleasure we get from things and the pleasure we get from freedom from things.

● Mud, paper and bamboo have more intrinsic wabi-sabi qualities than do gold, silver and diamonds.

● 'Greatness' exists in the inconspicuous and overlooked details. Wabi-sabi represents the exact opposite of the Western ideal of great beauty as something monumental, spectacular and enduring. Wabi-sabi is about the minor and the hidden, the tentative and the ephemeral: things so subtle and evanescent they are invisible to vulgar eyes.

● Like homoeopathic medicine, the essence of wabi-sabi is apportioned in small doses. As the dose decreases, the effect becomes more potent, more profound. The closer things get to nonexistence, the more exquisite and evocative they become. Consequently, to experience wabi-sabi means you have to slow down, be patient and look very closely.

● Things wabi-sabi are unpretentious, unstudied and inevitable looking. They do not blare out 'I am important' or demand to be the centre of attention. They are understated and unassuming, yet not without presence or quiet authority. Things wabi-sabi easily coexist with the rest of their environment.

● Things wabi-sabi are appreciated only during direct contact and use; they are never locked away in a museum. Things wabi-sabi have no need for the reassurance of status or the validation of market culture. They have no need for documentation of provenance.

● Things wabi-sabi can appear coarse and unrefined. They are usually made from materials not far removed from their original condition within, or upon, the Earth and are rich in raw texture and rough tactile sensation. Their craftsmanship may be impossible to discern.

● Simplicity is at the core of things wabi-sabi. The essence of wabi-sabi, as expressed in tea, is simplicity itself: fetch water, gather firewood, boil the water, prepare tea, and serve it to others.

● The simplicity of wabi-sabi is best described as the state of grace arrived at by a sober, modest, heartfelt intelligence. The main strategy of this intelligence is economy of means. Pare down to the essence, but don't remove the poetry. Keep things clean and unencumbered, but don't sterilize. (Things wabi-sabi are emotionally warm, never cold.) Usually this implies a limited palette of materials. It also means keeping conspicuous features to a minimum. But it doesn't mean removing the invisible connective tissue that somehow binds the elements into a meaningful whole. It also doesn't mean in any way diminishing something's 'interestingness', the quality that compels us to look at that something over, and over, and over again. ●

Kizaemon Ido teabowl. Korea, Yi dynasty.

A COMPARISON BETWEEN MODERNISM AND WABI-SABI

Modernism	Wabi-Sabi
A logical, rational world-view	An intuitive world-view
Absolute	Relative
Looks for universal, prototypical solutions	Looks for personal, idiosyncratic solutions
Mass-produced/modular	One-of-a-kind/variable
Expresses faith in progress	There is no progress
Future-oriented	Present-oriented
Believes in the control of nature	Believes in the fundamental uncontrollability of nature
Romanticizes technology	Romanticizes nature
People adapting to machines	People adapting to nature
Geometric organization of form (sharp, precise, and edges)	Organic organization of form (soft, vague shapes and edges)
The box as metaphor (rectilinear, precise, contained)	The bowl as metaphor (free shape, open at top)
Artificial materials	Natural materials
Ostensibly slick	Ostensibly crude
Needs to be well-maintained	Accommodates to degradation and attrition
Is intolerant of ambiguity and contradiction	Is comfortable with ambiguity and contradiction
Everlasting	To every thing there is a season

Details of craftspeople and contributors

If you wish to contact any of the craftspeople featured in this book and his or her address is not included in the list below, please write c/o *Resurgence*, Ford House, Hartland, Bideford, Devon EX39 6EE.

Jackie Abey and Jill Smallcombe can be contacted at: Abey Smallcombe, Burrow Farm, Drewsteignton, Exeter EX6 6PT. Tel: 01647 281282. www.abeysmallcombe.com.

Philip Baldwin is an American artist based in Paris, where he works in collaboration with his partner Monica Guggisberg. bgnonfoux@bluewin.ch.

Richard Batterham is at 8 Durweston, Blandford, Dorset DT11 0QB.

Mary Barratt is the author of *Oak Swill Basket Making in the Lake District*, and lives at Red Bank Farm, Skelmergh, Kendal, Cumbria.

Richard Boston is a writer and journalist.

Clive Bowen lives and works at the Shebbear Pottery, Shebbear, Beaworthy, Devon EX21 5QZ. Tel: 01409 281271.

Ed Brown was ordained a Zen priest. He is also a chef and the author of several cookbooks, the latest of which is *Tomato Blessings and Radish Teachings: Recipes and Reflections*. He can be contacted through www.yogazen.com or at PO Box 631, Inverness, CA94937, USA.

John Brown is at Y Garreg Filltir, Priory Close, Carmarthen SA31 2EJ. Tel: 07870 813435.

Sandy Brown, the co-editor of this book, is a ceramicist who lives in north Devon. She has recently published *Sandy Brown: A Monograph*, about her work. sandy@sandybrown.freeserve.co.uk.

Peter Bunyard is an ecological campaigner and writer. He is the author of *The Breakdown of Climate*, published by Floris Books at £9.99.

Anna Champeney now combines creating handwoven textiles and Spanish folkcraft research with running Casa Dos Artesans, a holiday cottage with optional craft courses in rural Spain. Tel: +34 988 20 74 04. www.casa-dos-artesans.com.

David Charlesworth teaches cabinet-making in Hartland, north Devon. He also writes regularly for *Furniture & Cabinet Making* and other magazines, and is making a series of instructional videos. Tel: 01237 441288.

Kamaladevi Chattopdhyaya (1903–1989) was a visionary Indian political activist, campaigner for women's rights, and champion of the crafts.

Margot Coatts is a craft historian who also works as a writer, lecturer and exhibition curator. She is a tutor in the Department of Goldsmithing, Silversmithing, Metalwork and Jewellery at the Royal College of Art.

Kitty Corrigan is Deputy Editor of *Country Living* Magazine.

Louise Allison Cort is an art curator. Her book *A Basketmaker in Rural Japan*, is published by the Sackler Gallery.

Bobbie Cox is at Higher Manor, Cudliptown, Peter Tavy, Tavistock, Devon PL19 9LZ. Tel/fax: 01822 810305. bobbie@bobbiecox.net.

Keith Critchlow can be contacted through Kairso at 4 Abbey Cottages, Cornworthy, Devon TQ9 7ET. Tel & Fax: 01803 732996.

Roger Deakin is a writer and broadcaster with a special interest in nature and the environment. He is the author of *Waterlog* (Vintage Books), and is working on *Touching Wood* (Hamish Hamilton), a new book in search of what lies beneath our kinship with wood and with trees.

Marta Donaghey can be contacted on Tel: 0208 965 4385.

David Drew can be contacted c/o The Crafts Council, 44a Pentonville Road, London N1 9BY.

Maureen Duke, Fernbank, Trotton, Petersfield, Hampshire. GU31 5ER. Tel: 01730 812432. For further information about bookbinding, consult the Society of Bookbinders, www.societyofbookbinders.com.

Ianto Evans teaches construction of permacultural buildings. He is a founder/director of the Cob Cottage Company. Box 123, Cottage Grove, Oregon 97424, USA.

Kaffe Fassett is the author of numerous books, including *Glorious Knitting* and *Glorious Needlepoint*, published by Century. He is at 62 Fordwych Road, London NW3 3TH.

Shoji Hamada, one of the twentieth century's most important ceramicists, died in 1978.

Tanya Harrod is a design historian. She is the author of *The Crafts in Britain in the Twentieth Century* (Yale, 1999).

Gwen Heeney can be contacted on 01938 536557.

Kazuo Hiroshima can be contacted through the M. Sackler Gallery, Smithsonian Institute, Washington DC 20560, USA.

Lorna Howarth is co-editor of *Resurgence* and a keen gardener.

Sara Hudston is a writer specialising in the arts and cultural criticism. She can be contacted at admin@agrebooks.co.uk or Groom's Cottage, Nettlecombe, Bridport, Dorset DT6 3SS.

Details of craftspeople and contributors

Edward Hughes is a potter whose work has been widely exhibited in the Japan and England. His studio is at The Stables, Isel Hall, Cockermouth, Cumbria CA13 0QG. Tel: 01900 825557.

Robert Hughes is a noted Australian art critic, author and journalist.

Tobias Kaye is at Hazel-Ash, 39 Gipsy Lane, Buckfastleigh, Devon TQ11 0DL. Tel: 01364 642837. www.TobiasKaye.co.uk. Tobias@TobiasKaye.co.uk.

Leonard Koren was trained as an artist and architect, and has produced several books about design and aesthetics. He lives in San Francisco and Tokyo. leonard@leonardkoren.co.uk.

Satish Kumar is the Editor of *Resurgence* and the author of *No Destination*, *You Are Therefore I Am*, and *The Buddha and the Terrorist* (all published by Green Books).

John Lane is a painter, and the Art Editor of *Resurgence*. His books include *The Living Tree: Art and the Sacred*, *Timeless Beauty* and *Timeless Simplicity*, all published by Green Books. He lives at Kiverleigh Manor, Beaford, Winkleigh, Devon EX19 8NP.

Sue Lawley is a BBC presenter.

Oliver Lowenstein is Editor of *Fourth Door Review*. fourthdoor@pavilion.co.uk.

Kate Lynch is the author of *Willow, a book of paintings and drawings*, published by Furlong Fields Publishing, £12.95. For further information, or to order, contact Kate Lynch: Tel: 01458 250367. kate@lynch-mail.fsnet.co.uk, www.katelynch.co.uk.

William McDonough is an architect, and is the co-author with Michael Braungart of *Cradle to Cradle: Remaking the Way we Make Things*, published in 2002 by North Point Press.

John Makepeace is an internationally renowned designer and furniture maker. He can be contacted at Farrs, Whitcombe Road, Beaminster, Dorset DT3 3NB or www.johnmakepeacefurniture.com.

Guy Martin can be contacted c/o The Crafts Council, 44a Pentonville Road, London N1 9BY.

Clio Mitchell, formerly art and architecture editor of *The European*, is writing a book about the Wissa Wassef Art School.

John Moat is the author of 14 novels, plays and short stories. He has been contributing to *Resurgence* for 25 years. www.johnmoat.co.uk.

Alexander Murdin is Director of The Devon Guild of Craftsmen in Bovey Tracey, Devon.

Brigitte Norland writes regularly in *Resurgence* about gardens. Her garden surrounds The School of Homeopathy in Uffculme, East Devon. www.homeopathyschool.com.

Geraldine Norman is an art critic and journalist.

Breon O'Casey is a jeweller and painter and lives in Cornwall. He can be contacted at Trungle Farmhouse, Paul, Penzance, Cornwall TR19 6UG.

Victor Papanek (1927–1999) was author of *Design for the Real World* and *Design for Human Scale*.

Julia Ponsonby is on the staff at Schumacher College and is the author of *Gaia's Kitchen*, published by Green Books.

William Phipps is at 31 Chepstow Villas, London W11 3DR. Tel: 020 7229 1460. w.h.phipps@clara.co.uk.

Brian Richardson is a self-builder and retired local government architect. He is co-author of *The Self-Build Book* with Jon Broome.

Professor Roger Scruton is a writer, philosopher, and publisher; also a journalist, composer, editor, businessman and broadcaster.

John Seymour was a broadcaster, farmer and green campaigner, and the author of over forty books, including *The Complete Book of Self-Sufficiency* and *The Forgotten Arts*. He died in 2004.

Haku Shah can be contacted at 16 Nemnath Society, Narayan Nagar Road, Paladi, Ahmedabad 380007, India. Tel: 6636741. hakushah@jindalonline.net.

Jill Smallcombe and **Jackie Abey** can be contacted at: Abey Smallcombe, Burrow Farm, Drewsteignton, Exeter EX6 6PT. Tel: 01647 281282. www.abeysmallcombe.com.

Ken Sprague (1927–2004) was a craftsman, artist and designer.

Tim Stead (1952–2000) was an English-born sculptor and furniture maker.

Barrie Thompson can be contacted at The Ark, Gores Lane, Bottlesford, Nr Pewsey, Wiltshire SN9 6LL.

Edmund de Waal is a ceramicist and author of many books, including *Bernard Leach (St Ives Artists series)* published by Tate Publishing. He can be contacted at Unit 7, Vanguard Court, R/00 36–38 Peckham Road, London SE5 8QT.

Jon Warnes is at Braehead, Holm, Orkney KW17 2SD. jon@fxferry.demon.co.uk.

David Whiting is a critic and writer in the applied arts and a regular contributor to *Crafts Magazine*.

Acknowledgements

The publishers gratefully acknowledge the financial assistance of the Tedworth Charitable Trust towards the costs of producing this book. They are also grateful for permission to reproduce the articles listed below:

'All Hands to Work' by Satish Kumar is extracted from an essay in *The Case Against The Global Economy*, published by Sierra Club Books, San Francisco.

'Amish Quilting' is an extract from Robert Hughes' book *Amish: The Art of the Quilt*, published by Alfred A Knopf, Callaway, New York, 1990.

'William Phipps, Silversmith' by Margot Coatts was first published in *Crafts*, May/June 2002.

'Breon O'Casey, Hand Skills' by Kitty Corrigan was previously published in *Country Living* magazine, January 2002. To subscribe, tel 01858 438844 or visit www.countryliving.co.uk.

'Buildings Like Trees', William McDonough's interview with Tim Stead, originally appeared in *Orion Afield*.

Kaffe Fassett's interview by Sue Lawley was made for Desert Island Discs on BBC Radio 4, and the article is an edited version of the conversation.

'Kingdom of Beauty' by Breon O'Casey 'Kingdom of Beauty' is a slightly shortened version of his original letter to Bernard Leach, reprinted from *Ceramic Review*.

'Shoji Hamada' by Edward Hughes is reprinted from *Ceramic Review*.

'The New Alchemists' by Anna Champeney is adapted from *Reclaimed: Contemporary British Craft and Design*, published by The British Council, 10 Spring Gardens, London, SW1A 2BN, price £9.95.

'On the Mend' by Roger Scruton was first published in *The Financial Times*.

'Poetry of Practice' is an edited extract from John Moat's Introduction to *The Way to Write* by John Fairfax and John Moat, Penguin Books, 1981.

'Wabi-Sabi' comprises edited extracts from *Wabi-Sabi: for Artists, Designers, Poets and Philosophers* by Leonard Koren.

'The Wonder of Work' is taken from John Seymour's book *The Forgotten Arts*, published by Dorling Kindersley in association with the National Trust.

Credits for the photographs on the Contents Pages (6 & 7) are as follows:

Bowl by Shoji Hamada.

Biscuits from *Gaia's Kitchen: Vegetarian Recipes for Family and Community from Schumacher College* by Julia Ponsonby.

Blue bowl from *Reclaimed: Contemporary British Craft and Design*, published by The British Council, 10 Spring Gardens, London, SW1A 2BN, price £9.95.

Chair by John Makepeace.

David Drew making a basket.

Banjara woman from *Painted Prayers* by Stephen Hyler, published by Thames & Hudson.

Cob interior from the *Hand-Sculpted House* by Ianto Evans, Michael Smith and Linda Smiley, published by Chelsea Green Publishing Company.

Available from Green Books & *Resurgence*, in the same series:

Images of Earth & Spirit

A RESURGENCE ART ANTHOLOGY

Edited by John Lane and Satish Kumar

"*Resurgence has been a longtime friend to artists looking to forge a meaningful relationship between art and soul. Readers who treasure this rich and varied artistic lineage may now enjoy its startlingly sensuous images within the pages of a single, elegantly designed book.*"
—Suzi Gablik, author of *The Re-enchantment of Art*

Images of Earth & Spirit features the work of over fifty artists, with over 140 sumptuous illustrations accompanied by interviews and insights into their work. Artists featured include Robin Baring, Cecil Collins, Alan Davie, Morris Graves, Andy Goldsworthy, Andrzej Jackowski, Richard Long, John Meirion Morris, David Nash, Margaret Neve, Peter Randall-Page, Haku Shah, Jane Siegle, Evelyn Williams and Christopher Wood.

All the artists have been featured in the pages of *Resurgence* magazine, an international forum for ecological and spiritual thinking. Besides challenging much of the conventional wisdom of our times (including the dream of unending material progress), Resurgence stresses the wisdom of beauty and, above all else, the holistic view – the relevance of interconnectedness. The work of these artists speaks of a new sense of the universe, a new sense of spirituality, holism and interconnectedness, openness and non-determinism. It gives hope for the renewal of life in the future.

192pp with 147 full colour illustrations 290 x 215mm ISBN 1 903998 29 8

Published October 2003 £20.00 hardback

Resurgence

"Resurgence illuminates some of the most profound questions of our age; thoughtful, passionate, never shrill, always challenging."—Jonathan Dimbleby

"The spiritual and artistic flagship of the green movement."—The Guardian

Resurgence magazine connects you to the heart of the environmental movement. Since 1966 it has been one of the pillars of environmental thinking, and has generated an ecological awareness essential for human well-being and survival. It draws wisdom from the world of nature, traditional cultures, and people at the forefront of ecological thinking.

If you would like a sample copy of a recent issue, please contact:

Jeanette Gill, Rocksea Farmhouse, St Mabyn, Bodmin, Cornwall PL30 3BR
Telephone & Fax 01208 841824 www.resurgence.org

In the USA:

Walt Blackford, Resurgence, PO Box 404, Freeland, WA 98249